Daily Life in Ancient Egypt: Recreating Lahun

This book is dedicated to my One

*I am now your slave, and no one will henceforth be able to take me from you, nor shall I be able to assign myself to another, but I shall remain in your service . . . I shall not be free in your precinct for eternity. You will look after me, keep me, safeguard me, keep me healthy, protect me from all male and female spirits, from every man in trance, from every epileptic, from every drowned man, from every drunkard, from every nightmare, from every dead man, from every man of the river, from every madman, from every foe, from every red thing, from every misadventure, from every plague.* (British Museum Papyrus, 10622, 7–14; after Loprieno 1997)

# Daily Life in Ancient Egypt

## Recreating Lahun

Kasia Szpakowska

**Blackwell**
Publishing

© 2008 by Kasia Szpakowska

BLACKWELL PUBLISHING
350 Main Street, Malden, MA 02148-5020, USA
9600 Garsington Road, Oxford OX4 2DQ, UK
550 Swanston Street, Carlton, Victoria 3053, Australia

The right of Kasia Szpakowska to be identified as the author of this work has been asserted in accordance with the UK Copyright, Designs, and Patents Act 1988.

First published 2008 by Blackwell Publishing Ltd

3   2010

*Library of Congress Cataloging-in-Publication Data*

Szpakowska, Kasia Maria.
   Daily life in ancient Egypt : recreating Lahun / Kasia Szpakowska.
      p.   cm.
   Includes bibliographical references and index.
   ISBN 978-1-4051-1855-2 (hardcover : alk. paper) – ISBN 978-1-4051-1856-9 (pbk. : alk. paper)   1. Egypt–Social life and customs–To 332 B.C.   2. Egypt–Antiquities.   3. Kahun (Extinct city)   I. Title.

   DT61.S96 2008
   932′.014–dc22

                                                                                            2007022247

A catalogue record for this title is available from the British Library.

Set in 10.5 on 12.5 pt Galliard
by SNP Best-set Typesetter Ltd., Hong Kong
Printed and bound in Singapore
by Fabulous Printers Pte Ltd

The publisher's policy is to use permanent paper from mills that operate a sustainable forestry policy, and which has been manufactured from pulp processed using acid-free and elementary chlorine-free practices. Furthermore, the publisher ensures that the text paper and cover board used have met acceptable environmental accreditation standards.

For further information on
Blackwell Publishing, visit our website at
www.blackwellpublishing.com

# Contents

# Illustrations

# Preface

This book presents a reconstruction of the daily life of middle-class townspeople living in the Ancient Egyptian town of Lahun during Ancient Egypt's Late Middle Kingdom. As it is geared toward the wider audience of university students and the general public as well as scholars, a few notes regarding the presentation of texts and images are in order.

In order to convert a textual document from Ancient Egyptian signs into a modern language, Egyptologists first "transliterate" the text; that is, write it in another alphabet. An alphabet is used that best corresponds to the sound of the Egyptian signs as the Egyptologist understands them. Because the Egyptians did not write vowels, the words can sometimes look strange and unpronounceable. To help the general reader I forego the use of transliteration here, and transcribe the words instead. This format is friendlier to read, and the underlying transliteration will be familiar to the Egyptologist anyway.

For many of the texts, there are numerous translations available – I have selected those that I feel best capture the flavor of the text, and that will be easily understood by the reader. In some cases, I have felt the need to adapt the translation and will note this in the reference. If a translation has no acknowledgment, then it should be assumed to be my own.

Much of this book is based on artifacts from the settlement of Lahun. Wherever possible, I have included a reference so that the interested reader can easily find an image. Many of the excavated finds are now at the Petrie Museum of Egyptian Archaeology or the Manchester Museum, University of Manchester, and are readily available online at www.kahun.ucl.ac.uk/main.html. For ease of reference, the ones from the Manchester Museum are identified by their EGY number, and the ones from the Petrie Museum with their UC number. A virtual reconstruction can also be found on www.kahun.man.ac.uk.

# Preface

To animate what could easily become a dry academic exercise, names have been given to the characters whose lives are interwoven throughout this study. All the names (with the exception of that of the dog) are attested in the surviving texts of Lahun. The name of the main character, the young girl, is *Hedjerit*, her older brother is *Senbubu*, their mother is *Dedet*, their father is *Sasopedu*, and their dog is *Kemy-shery*. The short introductions to each chapter are written as if from the memory of Hedjerit, and are based on the style of actual Egyptian texts.

# Acknowledgments

This book would never have been finished without the help of many individuals and institutions. The University of Wales Swansea School of Humanities allowed me a sabbatical to conduct my research, and I have learned much through the questions asked by my students, in particular the 2005–6 class on "Problems and practice in material culture."

I am deeply grateful to Stephen Quirke for numerous helpful insights and discussions, and I am indebted to Ellen Morris for her gracious and extensive feedback (especially at the last minute). I also thank Anthony Spalinger, Deborah Sweeney, and Terence Duquesne for their comments and support; Ken Griffin, who generously provided photographs; Sam Channer, who contributed many of the illustrations; the Manchester Museum, University of Manchester, and the Petrie Museum of Egyptian Archaeology for permission to use line drawings of artifacts in their collections; and Jan Picton of the Petrie Museum, who supplied me with photographs of artifacts. The Egypt Exploration Society's library was an important resource, and I would like to thank the EES for permission to use an illustration from one of their publications. Thomas Schneider, David Gill, Greg Mumford, and Sarah Parcak helped keep me on track, while JJ Shirley not only created maps and illustrations, but encouraged me with good cheer.

My family's support and comments were invaluable in so many ways: Jean-Luc, Sophie, and Ania soothed my nerves with their honest opinions, while my mother's support never wavers. I am grateful to Kiera and Reece, who taught me so much about children, and to their father Jon for generously providing me not only with art, but also with a firm guiding hand when I needed it most. Finally, I offer never-ending recitations of all things good and tasty to the *ka* of my little Vladdie, who stayed with me as long as he could.

All of these individuals did their best to help, and any errors and inconsistencies are entirely my own.

# Chronology

# 1

# The Setting

This book is about daily life in Ancient Egypt, at a specific representative time in its long history. It reconstructs everyday life in Egypt as experienced by a young girl of the middle class. Focusing on a young girl rather than a male and on someone from the lower middle class rather than from the elite makes the task doubly difficult, as the textual evidence was written by the male scribes and reflects life from their point of view. The words of women, children, and the bulk of the population that was illiterate have not been recorded. Nevertheless, material evidence has survived that can be combined with a judicious reading of the texts to formulate a sketch of daily life.

The town of Lahun was selected rather than the better-known settlement of Deir el-Medina (Fig. 1.1) in part to take advantage of newly published textual data from the settlement of Lahun and to re-examine the archaeological finds. But it was also selected as representative of the Middle Kingdom – a time period that in many ways can be considered as the Classical Age of Ancient Egypt. As far as possible, evidence from Lahun and other contemporary settlement and mortuary sites is used as the main data to address issues related to everyday life.

Throughout the book, the sources for our knowledge are stressed, so when we have physical artifacts available from that specific time, they are discussed, as is the way the artifacts might have been produced and used. This book thus attempts to provide an authentic representation of daily life in Egypt's Classical Age as experienced by an individual of a certain status, without creating the false impression that the realities of life were the same for individuals from all levels of society or from different times or locations. It is hoped that by applying a gendered approach, this reconstruction will locate within the context of Egyptian society representatives of the lower middle class, including women, children, and infants, who usually remain invisible in discussion.

1

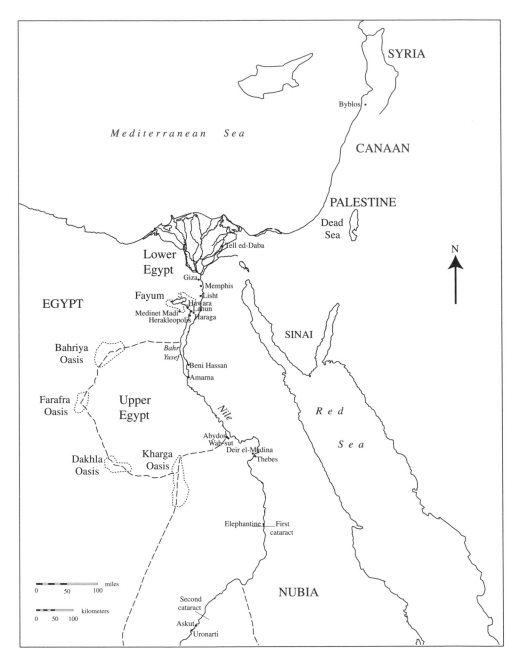

**Figure 1.1** Map of Egypt (courtesy of JJ Shirley).

## Historical Context

This book is set relatively early in Ancient Egypt's long history. Because time periods are often referred to in this book, it will be useful to begin with a brief historical overview up through the Late Middle Kingdom, the time in which this book is set.[1] Egypt's history begins with the Predynastic Period, a time before the culture was formally unified and ruled by a single pharaoh. Culturally distinct groups lived in settlements near the Nile under the protection of local rulers or chiefs, and unified slowly over time. The material evidence on which we must rely (this was a time before the development of writing) indicates that cultural unification was a slow process that eventually resulted in a single ruler laying claim to the dominion of all of Egypt in about 3000 BC. This series of events was symbolized in the famous commemorative palette of the ruler Narmer,[2] which encompassed many of the ideals and symbols that were to be a part of the Egyptian worldview for its entire history.

The binary topography of Egypt, with its northern agricultural landscape of the Delta region (Lower Egypt) versus the more arid southern region (Upper Egypt), was complemented by the visible differentiation of agricultural land versus desert. This duality became a fundamental concept in the ideology of the culture as reflected in the victory of order in its struggle versus chaos – themes that were reflected in the development of series of paired symbols. Upper Egypt was represented by a white crown, a lily, and a vulture goddess, while Lower Egypt was represented by a red crown, a papyrus, and a snake goddess. The ideal state, that of a unified Egypt, was represented by combinations of these icons – for example, the double crown combined the white and the red and was worn by the pharaoh in his capacity as ruler of all of Egypt. While Egypt was unified, it was always in danger of splitting back into the two culturally distinct areas. Recognizing this, historians have divided Egyptian history into a series of "kingdoms," which are epitomized by the country being governed by a single pharaoh, and "intermediate periods," characterized by the country's separation into two or more territories with their own rulers. These historical divisions are further subdivided into dynasties, which are composed of sequences of pharaohs who were often, but not necessarily, related. Our understanding of the historical time periods relies on a combination of native Egyptian king lists, copies of texts based on those of Greek historians, and archaeological evidence.

Recent archaeological work, particularly in the Upper Egyptian area known as Abydos, has revealed that there were also kings prior to Narmer, who ruled Upper Egypt. The term "Dynasty 0" has been coined for these rulers, but it is not until Egypt was unified under a single pharaoh that the historical period begins. The Early Dynastic Period (beginning c.3000 BC[3] and encompassing Dynasties 1–2) featured the establishment of the basic administrative and political structure, the foundation of religious and funerary beliefs and practices, the encoding of symbols, and the development of writing. Most of the characteristic features of Ancient

3

Egyptian culture were ingrained by the end of the Early Dynastic Period, although subject to changes and modifications over time.

The Old Kingdom (Dynasties 3–6) begins about 2800 BC. The time period is one of the most familiar to the general public today, in large part due to the development of massive pyramid complexes as tombs and cult centers for the pharaohs. This time is also called "the Pyramid Age" for this reason, and is characterized by a strong central government with the divine pharaoh as supreme ruler. The world's earliest religious texts can be found in this time period, as well as biographies providing deeper insights into the careers and public lives of the people themselves. The social and class structure develops with a marked rise in power of the upper classes, particularly toward the end of the Old Kingdom. At the end of Dynasty 6, in tandem with the steady rise of the upper classes, there are clear signs of a decline in the power of the king and royalty. Indeed, the First Intermediate Period (c.2200–2025 BC) is ushered in with no central authority, but rather a number of local governors who act as kings over their territories.

The complexity is apparent, as there are concurrent and overlapping rulers and the country is divided, with independent rulers in the north centered on Herakleopolis (Dynasties 9 and 10) and in the south centered on Thebes (Dynasty 11). In funerary autobiographies, the local rulers stress how well they take care of the people living within their jurisdictions in troubled times. That there was a lack of centralized control is apparent in the material culture, which shows wide regional differentiation. The art shows a range of styles, individuality, and experimentation that was expressed by artists and workshops that had less contact with each other. Even the pottery shows a marked distinction in shape and material reflecting the opposition between northern and southern traditions. Although there were no more giant royal funerary complexes, the burial assemblages of many men and women of the upper classes show an increase in wealth.

To judge from later king lists as well as contemporary sources, the Eleventh Dynasty seems to have begun with a series of three rulers laying claim to the kingship and dominion over Upper Egypt.[4] These individuals, all bearing the name of "Intef," took as their power base the strategically located city of Thebes, and from there attempted to extend their rule. But it was not until the middle of the Eleventh Dynasty, in approximately 2025, that the next Theban ruler, Mentuhotep II, succeeded in reunifying Upper and Lower Egypt into a consolidated state, and ushered in what we call the Middle Kingdom (Dynasties 11–13). To clarify the extent of his dominion, he even changed his throne name (kings had multiple names) from "he who causes the heart of the two lands to live" to "unifier of the two lands." This ruler and his immediate successors made Thebes the capital of Egypt and ruled from the south.

The first ruler of Dynasty 12, Amenemhat I, was not related by blood to the previous rulers and it is unclear how he came to the throne. Perhaps to emphasize his legitimate right to rule and to emulate the divine rulers of the Old

Kingdom, he moved the capital north to a new capital, just at the boundary between Lower and Upper Egypt. This town was called "seizer of the two lands" *Itchy-tawy* (probably around the area of modern-day Lisht). Whereas the kings of the Eleventh Dynasty built tombs underground separate from their mortuary temples, Amenemhat I and his Twelfth Dynasty successors returned to the practice of building pyramids as their tombs. In the thirtieth year of his reign, Amenemhat I was assassinated – an event that was mentioned in two major literary texts. He was succeeded by his son Senusret I, who may have reigned jointly with his father for a few years prior. During his long reign, like his father before him Senusret I focused on rebuilding temples around Egypt and keeping the country stable. He campaigned in Nubia and began a program of building forts to control trade and imports. His successor, Amenemhat II, is less well known, though inscriptions reveal that he sent expeditions to the Sinai to mine precious stones such as turquoise. After a brief co-regency, his son Senusret II took the throne.

Senusret II is perhaps best known for beginning a major reclamation project in the region of the Fayum to increase its agricultural potential. Dykes and canals were built to extend the links of the lake that already existed there with the Bahr Yusef, a major tributary of the Nile. He also chose that region to build his pyramid. Lahun, the town upon which this study is based, was built nearby to house the workers who would build this complex. When Senusret III succeeded his father, he greatly expanded Egypt's borders deep into Nubia, increasing Egypt's wealth and control through a complex network of fortresses strategically placed along the Nile in Upper Nubia. His successor, Amenemhat III, is most famous for his immense building campaign throughout Egypt, and for building "the labyrinth," a massive pyramid located in the Fayum. The reign of Amenemhat IV was short, and he was succeeded by his sister, SobekNoferu, who ruled not as queen but as the last pharaoh of Dynasty 12. Like her probable father Amenemhat III, SobekNoferu concentrated her efforts on the region of the Fayum, though unlike her more powerful ancestor, she left little to indicate her activities outside of this region. Following the reign of this female pharaoh, the rule of a single family ended. Early Dynasty 13 featured rulers that are poorly attested in both the archaeological and textual sources, and who probably came from the most prominent administrative families of Egypt. The middle of the dynasty seems to have stabilized with rulers well attested throughout Egypt, though again not necessarily related by kinship. Eventually, however, their dominion seems to have weakened until they could lay claim to the southern region alone, and the Middle Kingdom was clearly over.

After the political turmoil of the preceding First Intermediate Period, the Middle Kingdom in general was characterized by an increase in controlled bureaucracy and centralized education. Literature and the arts flourished, and this is often regarded as the Classical Age of Ancient Egypt. The powerful pharaohs expanded Egypt's territory particularly in the south, into Nubia, and the army correspondingly rose in prominence. Peaceful trade and contact with foreign cultures such as those based to the east in the Levant and those to the north in the Mediterranean (such as Crete) increased.

In the Late Middle Kingdom, the setting for this book, there was a marked increase in foreigners migrating into Egypt, particularly within northern settlements such as Lahun. Some of the settlers in the Delta, whose origins were in the Levant, eventually took advantage of the weak rulers at the end of Dynasty 13, and proclaimed themselves rulers of the north. In Egyptian these were known as "rulers of the foreign lands" *heqaw khasut*, a word that is retained today as Hyksos. Once again, Egypt was split into two, with the Hyksos ruling in the north, and native Egyptians in the south. This time period, known as the Second Intermediate Period (Dynasties 14–17), was rich in change and innovation. It left an indelible impression on the Egyptians of that time and on future generations, for this was the first time that Egypt had been ruled by foreigners. The southern rulers who eventually ousted the Hyksos from power and reunified Egypt were determined it would not happen again.

## Illahun

This book focuses on life in Egypt from mid Dynasty 12 to Dynasty 13. The scene is set when, at the height of Egypt's Middle Kingdom, the reigning pharaoh, Senusret II, chose to build his pyramid complex at the entrance to the large fertile depression of the Fayum (Fig. 1.2). His complex included a smaller pyramid for his queen, shaft tombs for the royal family, and *mastabas*[5] for his courtiers. On the eastern side of the pyramid he had his mortuary temple built, and in a direct line approximately 1.2 km to the east, he had his valley temple where the cult of the king could be maintained. This was no small matter, for the king was the living embodiment of Horus, the falcon god who represented kingship on earth. When he died, the king was identified with Osiris, the god of the dead, and he continued to be worshiped for up to two centuries. Part of the king's role was to guard and maintain *maat* (a fundamental Ancient Egyptian concept that embodies the concepts of justice, truth, right, and order on both a cosmic and a social scale) in the world, and to act as the intermediary between mankind and the gods. During the Middle Kingdom, the deities most closely connected to the pharaoh were actively worshiped with him. Indeed, in the early Middle Kingdom, the mortuary temples of the Eleventh Dynasty rulers focused primarily on the gods (specifically Amun-Ra, whose name reflects the hidden nature of the sun god). Perhaps the decision of the rulers of the Twelfth Dynasty to return to the Old Kingdom custom of building pyramids for their tombs was in part inspired by the desire to emulate the royal cult of that earlier time that was focused first and foremost on the king. Thus the entire complex that Senusret II had built at Lahun was dedicated to venerating his memory and divinity, perpetuated by a religious cult that was maintained by rotations of priests.

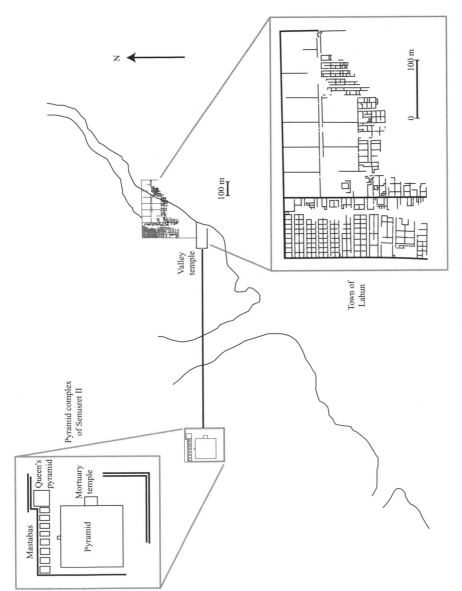

**Figure 1.2** Plan of Illahun region (courtesy of JJ Shirley).

Constructing the pyramid of a king, the royal tombs of his family and top officials, and the mortuary and valley temples was a vast undertaking, and resulted in an immense expenditure of resources in terms of materials, labor, and time. Settlements had to be planned and built nearby to house the labor force. Thus, just to the north of his valley, Senusret II had a town constructed to house not only the workmen and builders, but also the many different types of people one would expect to find worshiping the king and living in an active Ancient Egyptian town: priests, officials, craftsmen (and all the Middle Kingdom representational and textual evidence suggests that, with the exception of textile spinners and weavers, they were men, sometimes aided by children), weavers, cooks, and soldiers along with their families. The purpose of this book is to build up a picture of daily life in this town that the Egyptians called Hetep-Senusret "Senusret is satisfied," and that in modern times we call "Lahun".

Trying to describe daily life even in the modern world is not an easy task. Lifestyles vary tremendously depending on the individual's circumstances: the time period, location, class, wealth, gender, and age. Life in Ancient Egypt during the time of Cleopatra was certainly vastly different from life nearly 1800 years earlier, the time which is under consideration here. Unfortunately, it is often a temptation to see Ancient Egypt as a monolithic, static culture, and to assume that activities, rituals, practices, and beliefs can simply be transplanted backward by centuries. But because so much of our evidence, particularly textual, comes from the elite, it is their world, or that of the king and his retinue, that is most often presented in discussions on daily life. Compared to the cemeteries and tombs situated in the dry desert areas, few settlements have survived to offer us insights into how the Egyptians lived. The reasons for this are many. Buildings in towns tended to be made of more perishable material (such as mud-brick) than temples and tombs that were built of stone. Settlements were also often built close to the moist soil of the banks of the Nile, which hastens decomposition particularly of organic material, compared to the sealed tombs in the dry desert. In addition, good-quality locations were often reused, and many of Ancient Egypt's dwelling places lie below those of the modern Egyptians. Nevertheless, some of the ancient settlements, buildings, furnishings, and items that were used in life have survived the millennia, as well as documentary texts such as accounts, legal documents, and letters. By examining the evidence from one of these sites, and using contemporary data from other sites judiciously and with the understanding that it may reflect different lifestyles, a more accurate picture of life in a time period may be developed. This book will focus mainly on material from the settlement of Lahun itself, inhabited in Egypt's Late Middle Kingdom.

## Social Context

There are two basic approaches to understanding society in the ancient world. One is to try to discover the classification system used by the peoples themselves, and the other is to approach the culture with our own categories, and use our own criteria in order to make cross-culturally relevant comparisons. In terms of the former approach, we are to a certain extent lucky, for the Egyptians themselves have provided clues as to how they categorized their world and their peoples. A number of "onomastica," lists of the phenomena that made up their world, organized in categories have survived.[6] Most date from the New Kingdom but a fragment of one of these was found dating to the Middle Kingdom.[7] The Middle Kingdom papyrus fragment does not contain categories of people, but these can be found in the later versions. The most complete example is the New Kingdom "Onomasticon of Amenemipet," and his ambitious goal is clearly stated at the start:[8]

> Beginning of the teaching, explaining to the heart, instructing the ignorant, to know all that exists, created by Ptah, brought into being by Thoth, the sky with its features, the earth and what is in it, the bend of the mountain, what is washed by the waters, consisting of all this is useful, illumined by Ra, all that is made to grow upon earth, reported by the writer of god's books in the House of Life Amenemipet son of Amenemipet.[9]

Not surprisingly, the categories do not always reflect those that are prevalent in the modern west. For example, bats appear under the category of birds, and crocodiles with fish. In this composition, there are hierarchical groups of beings. The first of these lists the god (*netjer*) and goddess (*netjeret*); male transfigured dead (*akh*) and female transfigured dead (*akh*); the king (*nesut*) and the goddess of kingship (*nesyt*); the king's wife (*hemet nesut*); king's mother (*mut nesut*); king's child (*mes nesut*); the leader of the nobles (*iry pat*); vizier (*tjaty*); sole companion (*semer waty*); and eldest son (*sa nesut semsu*). To a large extent, this category reflects our understanding of the highest echelon of Egyptian society. Later in the text categories of people are listed. These reflect Egyptian categories that do not correspond directly to ours and are still poorly understood. These include the people (*remetj*), nobles (*pat*), the populace in their function as worshipers of the king (*rekhyt*), the populace in their function as worshipers of the sun king (*henmemet*), followed by military personnel that reflect a New Kingdom hierarchy rather than that of the Middle Kingdom, groups of foreigners and foreign lands, and finally people grouped by age or life-stage. Because the terms themselves are problematic, and the classifications do not correspond to those of our own culture, it is useful to approach the question from the outside.

As with other aspects of life in Ancient Egypt, to do this we base our understanding of the social structure of Ancient Egypt on archaeological evidence. Cemeteries are useful in our reconstructions as individuals are rarely buried randomly, but are carefully placed in groups.[10] These patterns often reflect kinship ties, and on a broader scale, the spatial stratification reflects class and status.[11] Unfortunately Middle Kingdom cemeteries are rare, and most of the ones that have survived were hastily excavated decades ago and were poorly recorded. Recent re-examinations reveal no clear interpretations, even with careful analysis. For example, wealth could have been displayed by the size of the tomb, by the materials used for burial goods, by diversity of types of goods, or by a combination of these.[12] Housing patterns within settlements can also reflect stratification, but without certain clues as to who inhabited the apparently different quarters, details are again obscured. Textual evidence in the form of titles is illuminating, but mostly in terms of the elite and literate ranks. Each of these sources in isolation is insufficient, but together they allow scholars to formulate a basic picture of Late Middle Kingdom society. One of the scholars who has extensively studied this aspect of the Middle Kingdom is Wolfram Grajetzki, and the following summary is based on his reconstruction.[13]

In the Late Middle Kingdom, the pinnacle of mankind was the pharaoh, who was also considered divine – the living manifestation of the god Horus. His role was to act as an interface between the people and the gods, to maintain *maat*, to protect Egypt, and to watch its people. The royal family, while enjoying many special privileges such as the honor of being buried closest to the pharaoh, played no obvious role in terms of administration or politics. The sons are rarely mentioned, and few are even known by name. Judging from the lack of references to husbands and the fact that they were buried close to their father, the daughters of the king seem to have played some role in the palace, probably a religious one. There is also no reference to their being married to officials. The king's wives are barely known either, and from the slim evidence it seems as though they were not necessarily of royal birth, although it is likely that they were members of the higher classes.

Second in power only to the king was a small group of ministers who came from elite families throughout Egypt, though their offices were not hereditary. Based in the royal residence, they were loyal to the king, and privileged to be his closest counselors. This group included not only the vizier (or prime minister), the treasurer, and the high steward, who between them constituted the chief authorities in terms of the administration of justice, the main economic institutions, and the agricultural lands, but also all the other state administrators. The latter consisted mainly of state bureaucrats whose titles can be divided into five basic groups associated with the administration, military, priesthood, organization of labor, and certain non-specific classifications. These offices could apparently sometimes be inherited and links were formed between particular powerful families. While there was social mobility within this level, the likelihood of an Egyptian from a poor lower-class family rising to this rank was virtually nil. There is some evidence, however, for outsiders such as foreigners being able to attain a high level, even if their own background was poor, by virtue of their close association with a master of high rank. A lower stratum of bureaucrats modeled their local administration upon that of the state level. Many of the titles attested at the royal level were used by these officials, whose authority was more localized and limited to the town or at best the nome that they governed.[14] Nevertheless, they were also members of the elite, and were part of those upper classes who constituted a minority of the population and who left behind the most evidence.

The preponderance of the population was illiterate and has left behind little textual evidence. For them we must rely on other types of archaeological evidence. These included marginalized groups – those such as "marshland dwellers" and beggars, who lived literally on the fringes of society, and who are but rarely referred to in texts and representations. The working classes made up the largest group, and these included the peasants and farmers, herdsman and fishermen, laborers and builders, craftsmen and entertainers. At this level we can also place the many servants who seemed to have been dependent either on a private individual or on an institution. These subordinates could be either native Egyptians or foreigners, in particular foreigners that had been captured and brought back to Egypt during military campaigns.

There was no Middle Kingdom term for a class of "slaves" such as existed in the Roman Empire, though there were two terms for "servants."[15] One of the terms, *bak*, reflected the status of one subordinate to another, and was used with pride by individuals to emphasize their loyalty, especially in relation to the king. The other term, *hem*, referred to individuals who served a household and were economically dependent upon it. They were connected to that specific area, and could not randomly disconnect their service to it without negative repercussions. It has been noted that this does not constitute slavery, for even in the modern workplace one cannot simply leave one's place of employment without consequences.[16] The work of the *hem* was tied to a household or to land, but because these dependents did seem to have some sort of social mobility and rights (although the rights to their labor could be transferred along with the land or the household with which they were linked), they should not be considered as slaves.

Between the bulk of these lower classes and the elite minority lay a level of untitled yet wealthy individuals that we call the middle class. As Grajetzki argues, the question of the possible existence of this middle class, defined by him as "a significant social stratum of people not belonging to the administrative class but with a certain level of wealth," is exceedingly complex, and certainly debatable.[17] A level of independence may have been achieved by this class as well. In her recent work on her investigation of socio-economic differences revealed by mortuary patterns in the Middle Kingdom, Richards suggest that bureaucratic control seems to have been rigidly enforced

on matters directly related to government trade, building, and finances and on the members of social and economic groups in society most closely connected with those government concerns: the wealthy, the titled, specialist workers such as royal craftsmen, and conscripted laborers. However, the combined evidence from cemeteries and other avenues of archaeological, textual, and pictorial data seems to indicate the existence of several social and economic groups in society whom the

11

government may not have chosen to control, or could not control, for ideological or logistical reasons. There existed a flexible private system, and a widely differentiated society, functioning at least partially outside a regimented government rubric.[18]

These individuals were able to attain their own wealth, although it is unclear through what professions. Within this class, there was also a range of levels that are manifest in the mortuary data, as will be discussed later. The focus in this book is on reconstructing the life of a family belonging to this middle class.

If the outline of this social structure were sketched, it might resemble a somewhat bulbous pear, with certain professions such as the military, priesthood, and scribes running vertically through all but the lowest horizontal strata. The social structure of Ancient Egypt in the Late Middle Kingdom was hierarchical, but not inflexible. There do not seem to have been any prohibitions against marriage between individuals of different social classes, and an individual could (at least theoretically) move up in rank, even if in practice it was only minimally, regardless of parentage. Positions were not generally inherited, but a good family could certainly help.

## Settlement Context

Geography, environment, and landscape play important roles in the development of the cultural identity of people, but so do the settlements themselves. Egypt's dependency on the Nile for food, water, and transportation was reflected in its religion and in lifestyles. One of the unique features of Egypt is the 3,000-mile-long river Nile, which flows from its southern origins deep in central Africa northwards to empty out into the Mediterranean. Lower Egypt consisted of the area in the Delta to the north and Upper Egypt consisted of the southern regions. Boats could easily travel north by gliding with the flow of the river, while because the prevailing winds blow from north to south, sails were used for travel upriver to the south. In the region of Middle Egypt, one branch of the Nile led westwards until it reached a natural depression called the Fayum. A deeper section filled with water, creating a vast lake, now known as Lake Moeris. Even in Predynastic times this was recognized as an ideal location for a settlement, with plenty of fishing and hunting (though the latter should not be considered a primary method for acquiring food), and of course it was a rich agricultural region. However, after this time it was largely uninhabited by the living, but was used as a burial ground right through the Middle Kingdom. Late Middle Kingdom pharaohs initiated intense reclamation projects in the region to increase its agricultural use, which included irrigation canals as well as the building of a large earthwork dyke at the mouth of the Fayum. It also was the site chosen by Senusret II to build his pyramid tomb and complex, leading to the development of the town of Lahun.

This area as a whole is often called Illahun, on the basis of the nearby modern Arabic town of el-Lahun. The town is sometimes called Kahun, because this was the name that Petrie, its first excavator, heard used for it in 1887. Apparently, he misheard the name, but today it is still referred to as Kahun, as well as the more precise Lahun, or sometimes as Illahun. To the Egyptians it was probably Hetep-Senusret, but for the sake of consistency, in this book it will be referred to as Lahun.

It is difficult to say whether Lahun should be considered a typical town for Middle Kingdom Ancient Egypt. So few settlements have survived the millennia, and each of them has unique features. Probably the best known and the one about which the most is written is the New Kingdom town of Deir el-Medina. Located on the west bank near Thebes, this settlement was built to house the workers who constructed, carved, and decorated the tombs of the pharaohs in the Valley of the Kings. Both textual and non-textual remains have survived from Deir-el-Medina, but because it was a planned community of elite workmen, it is debatable whether or not it represents a typical town. The settlement of Amarna, built at the end of the Eighteenth Dynasty to provide a new capital for the pharaoh Akhenaten and his unique religious practices, may be a unique example as well. The recent excavations at the workers' village that was inhabited by the builders of the pyramids at Giza also offers insights into the life of a planned community.

Turning to other Middle Kingdom towns, Elephantine was located far to the south on a rocky island in the region of the first cataract, the traditional southern boundary of Ancient Egypt (near modern Aswan). This settlement was founded in the Predynastic Period and was inhabited continuously through the Roman Period. Its strategic location made it ideal for the control of trade and peoples moving in and out of Egypt from the south. But the immediate environment was a dramatic contrast to that of Lahun, and although there are certain similarities, especially in terms of practices that seem to be common in settlements throughout Egypt, the dissimilarities are equally obvious. The structure and layout of the town itself were different, as were individual homes, reflecting the limited space on the island, the rocky environment, and the town's different function. At the other extreme, the recently excavated eastern Delta town of Avaris (modern Tell ed-Daba), while certainly more similar to that of Lahun (especially in terms of domestic architecture), was a melding of native Egyptian traditions with those of the Asiatics who had settled there. These foreigners probably intermarried with the local population, and the merging of the two distinct cultures is manifest archaeologically, particularly in the burial practices, which are unlike those found anywhere else.

To the south of Lahun, but also on the west bank of the Nile, a Middle Kingdom town called "Wah-sut" is being excavated at Abydos. In some respects this town is the closest parallel to that of Lahun, at least in terms of elite homes, but Middle Kingdom Abydos also served a very different purpose than Lahun. As a religious center dedicated to the cult of Osiris, Abydos was an important destination for pilgrimages by people from various parts of Egypt. An annual festival was held there, re-enacting the mysteries of the god of the dead, in which the public could participate. During the Twelfth Dynasty the town also maintained a permanent population associated with the mortuary complex of Sensuret III, which included workers, but also administrators, officials, and a mayor. In this respect, it perhaps most closely parallels the social structure of the town of Lahun. Continuing excavations here will eventually reveal much more of life in the Late Middle Kingdom.

Lahun, on the other hand, began as a town built to house the workers who built the pyramid of Senusret II and the tombs of his family and top officials, the priests who worked to maintain his cult for decades, and the administrators who managed the entire complex. Even after the construction was finished the town continued to be inhabited, though its character seemed to change. Some of the smaller homes were expanded to house the growing families of the laborers, but so were the homes of middle-class families who inhabited medium-sized residences, while royal officials, including the mayor, lived in larger mansions. Both the material and textual evidence testifies to the existence of a productive, complex society living here, and yet after a relatively short period of 100 years, the town seems to have been suddenly abandoned. The cause of this evacuation remains a mystery, but from an archaeological standpoint it is a convenient happenstance. For whatever reason the inhabitants vacated their town, they left within it many of their household goods, the tools of their trades, their personal possessions, and caches of documents. From these, we can attempt to reconstruct a picture of what their daily life might have been like.

## Homes

The townspeople of Lahun also left behind the remains of the physical structures that made up their home. Built of bricks made of local mud, these have been much weathered and eroded over the millennia. In addition, the entire south-east section of the town lies today under the modern agricultural region, and will remain unreachable and unexcavated. Nevertheless, enough remains for us to have a good picture of its general plan in terms of the town as a whole, and of individual homes. Certain features are comparable to ones seen in the later New Kingdom planned communities of Deir el-Medina and the workmen's village of Amarna – settlements which were also developed by the state to fulfill a particular function. The town itself was rectangular in shape, measuring approximately 350 meters north to south by 400 meters east to west.[19] A mud-brick wall, approximately 3 meters thick and perhaps originally 6 meters high, surrounded the settlement on the west, the north, and most of the east. Because so much of the east and the south has been lost, we cannot be certain that the wall enclosed the entire town, but on the basis of other settlements this is certainly a strong

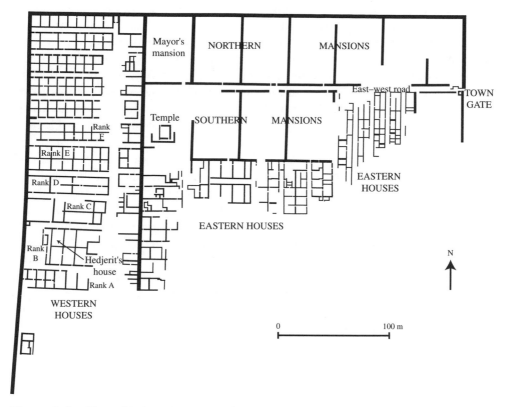

**Figure 1.3**   Plan of Lahun (courtesy of JJ Shirley).

possibility. Because the structure of the town has been discussed in numerous other works[20] only a general overview will be presented here.

As is readily apparent from the plan (Fig. 1.3), the town was laid out in an orderly fashion, with a wall dividing the rectangular western quarter from the square eastern quarter. The western quarter was bisected by a broad avenue (9 m across) running north and south, which had a drainage system in the center of bricks slanted downward from the road into the central trough. The homes were arranged in blocks of up to six connected small houses facing eleven streets running east and west, which at 4 m were also relatively broad. This section consisted of homes that were mainly small (50 m² and consisting of only three rooms) to medium (100 m² and double the number of rooms). To the north of the eastern quarter a series of palatial estates were built (2,700 m²) along a broad avenue running from the west to a gateway in the enclosure wall to the east. Three of the estates were built south of the avenue, with six to the north. Because the wind in Egypt blows from north to south, the ideal location to live would be in the northern section of the town. Those homes with porticoes and vents facing north would be able to take the best advantage of the fresh cool breezes.

15

These mansions incorporated reception halls, granaries, administrative offices, kitchens, a pool, possibly stalls for animals, servants' quarters, and of course private living quarters, including dressing rooms and bathrooms for their owner, his family, and guests. In the north-west corner of the eastern quarter, an even larger mansion was built on higher ground. Its size and location suggest that this was the residence of the mayor of the city. Indeed, its size is comparable to the palaces found in the Delta site of Tell ed-Daba and at Dashur.[21] Directly to the south is an open area, which contains the remains of a columned area. This may have been a further administrative area or a temple. The rest of the eastern quarter consisted of a mix of very small to medium homes, at least as far as we can tell bearing in mind that nearly half has been lost. Indeed, although the small size of many of the houses has been emphasized, the majority fall into the realm of medium-sized homes ($31$–$84\,m^2$) compared to the settlements of Amarna, Deir el-Medina, and Lisht, which featured a greater proportion of smaller homes.[22]

As was the case with most domestic dwellings in Ancient Egypt, the homes of Lahun were built of dried mud-brick. They would have been roofed with wooden beams and poles, and straw or reed tied to the poles. Plastered with mud on the inside and outside, and sometimes supported by a column, the flat roofs may have been used as an extension of the living space. They may have been used for storage, but there are signs in other settlements that they could also be used as a place for cooking or other activities in the hot weather. Some reconstructions feature vents on the roofs that would have caught the cool breezes from the north, but as these are based on models of buildings that were placed in tombs (sometimes called "soul houses") they may not reflect architectural features in the houses of the living.[23] More reliable evidence stems from New Kingdom drawings of residential housing, which feature vents as well as latticed windows that would let in light and air,[24] as well as a drawing from Lahun possibly depicting the front of the elite homes there.

Other models show details such as gardens and pools – features that are confirmed by the archaeological remains of elite homes, but may not have been part of dwellings of those lower in rank or wealth. However, many of the other main features of the actual living quarters were the same for homes whether they were palatial estates or small workmen's houses.[25] Because little is left of the buildings in Lahun, comparable houses in other settlements, particularly those at Lisht, Deir el-Medina, and Amarna, provide us with clues as to the layout and function of rooms. Settlements contemporary to that of Lahun, such as Elephantine and Tell ed-Daba, also provide some guidance, but some of these dwellings in the Middle Kingdom levels of those sites seem to follow a different plan, perhaps betraying their disparate functions or geographical locations. In general, however, the space in both Middle and New Kingdom homes can be divided into three zones: the one closest to the entrance was the most public and contained a reception area; the second was a columned hall or open courtyard that functioned as a communal area for the family, with stairs leading to the roof; while the private living quarters were at the back.[26]

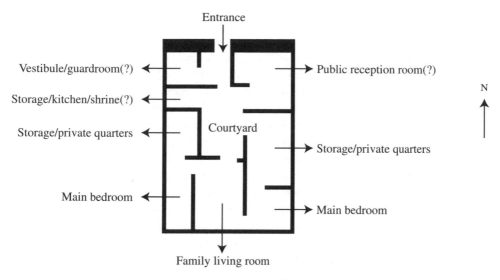

**Figure 1.4** Plan of Hedjerit's house in rank B (courtesy of JJ Shirley).

The houses in the western quarter opened either to the north (thus taking full advantage of the cool north wind) or to the south. The plans for the north-facing ones were all of similar types, and while the ones to the south were based on a slightly different blueprint, the basic constituents were the same in either case. To set the stage, we shall use a medium-to-large residence (approximately 168 square meters) with a north-facing doorway in rank B of the western quarter[27] as an example of domestic quarters, and as the setting for this reconstruction of daily life (Fig. 1.4).

A single door made of wood (as were the door-bolts and the threshold itself), and possibly painted red to repel any hostile entities that might attempt to enter during the day or night, led from the street into the home. Most of the doorways were arched with two rows of bricks, proving that the Egyptians had already perfected this architectural technique. Because the homes were joined together on three sides, there would be no place for windows, except possibly in the front wall or in the form of skylights in the roof. The walls were smoothed with mud and whitewashed, and some retain traces of a painted dado. This was usually painted black or dark near the bottom, with red and black lines 1–1.5 m up, and a yellow wash above.[28] In many cases a corridor from the front door led to a central hall from which the other rooms could be reached. This hall was likely unroofed, thus creating an open courtyard in the center of the home that would also have allowed light and air in to reach the other rooms. Parts of the courtyard could have been shaded in order to protect the dwellers from the glare of the sun, perhaps with portable shades made of cloth on poles. It is in this room that stairs leading to the roof were usually found.

Rooms to the west of the entrance of this residence and ones like it could have housed a shrine, or have been reception rooms, or a combination of both. Our model home includes a small room just to the right of the door. Most of the medium-sized south-facing houses in rank B had such a room just off the entrance, and in palatial estates this compact room may have served as guardroom for a doorkeeper who would control access to the estate. In the smaller non-elite houses, it may have served as a storage area for water jars or other goods. Although no toilets have survived from Lahun, limestone and wooden seats with holes in the center under which pots would have been placed have been found at Amarna, testifying to their use in the New Kingdom. In the Middle Kingdom, simple pots could have been used by the less affluent, and perhaps the small room could have doubled as a lavatory, allowing for quick and easy disposal of the waste into the central gutter of the street. In the large estates of Lahun, adjoining the bedrooms are smaller rooms which are thought to have been bathrooms (sometimes with an adjoining area for a lavatory). Some of these have breaks in the wall that may have allowed drainage via a channel to the main gutter conduit running down the center of the street.[29]

Defining the specific function of rooms is difficult without clues and it is probable that, as is the case with modern urban and rural compact dwellings, most rooms were multi-functional. Although the homes were not cramped, maintaining versatility in each room would allow an efficient use of limited space for households that were continually expanding (through marriage, births, and even the moving in of dependants such as relatives or servants), or contracting (through deaths, marriage, or conscription). Indeed, there is evidence that the walls between houses were at times collapsed in order to expand the living space. Not only could walls be removed or modified, but the features within rooms could be as well. A bench could be used for sitting, conversing, and eating, but then could be converted into a bed by simply laying a sleeping mat and headrest on top of it. The most private areas were probably at the back, with the central room used as a main living room (on the basis of the occasional finds of columns in this room and the existence of wall decorations). The larger room on either side was probably used for sleeping, and the smaller for storage, as a bathroom or lavatory, or as an additional sleeping area. In general in the larger rooms, which contained a raised sleeping platform, that bed-niche was placed directly against the south wall of the room.[30] This area of the house was kept cool by the winds flowing in from the north (some houses may have had small vents in the roof to increase the airflow), by the layout of the walls and doors, and by the columns in the central areas, which would prevent the sun from shining in directly.

Furniture was fairly simple in form, and usually carved of wood or stone. Chairs, stools, small tables, pillows, and mats were the main pieces of furniture that might have been used in a middle-class home. Headrests were used by some for sleeping, and there is evidence that they could be padded as well for more comfort. Many examples are carved with apotropaic figures that would protect the vulnerable sleeper at night. When not in use portable goods, including clothing, dinnerware, pots, knives, jewelry, tools, and cosmetics, were stored in baskets and chests that were likely often nearly brimming, and could be stored under other furniture such as tables. To allow for ventilation, the cooking area could have been in an open section such as the central court, or in the case of our model house, in the corridor just before the court. Small granaries were found in many of the homes, and these would probably have been close to the kitchen area as well. In general, we can expect that the common areas and reception rooms were located at the front of the house.

## Village Animals

Domesticated animals were also an important part of life in an Ancient Egyptian town, and some may have been welcome members of the household. Dogs in particular were well loved and given names by the Egyptians, and probably shared the living quarters with their humans. Cats were also popular, though they were less likely to have been kept within the home as pets, but were admired for their usefulness in catching rats, mice, and other pests. In the Middle Kingdom cats are commonly depicted in the context of marshes, thickets, and fields, thus emphasizing their association with the outdoors. Textual and artistic representations of monkeys kept as pets abound in the Old and especially the New Kingdom, but are rare in the Middle Kingdom.[31]

Livestock also are found in many towns in Egypt today, but any possible areas designated for the housing of animals do not seem to have survived from within the town of Lahun. Neither did Petrie note any accumulations of dung that might have indicated a gathering of a particular species of animal, or of animal bones as evidence of slaughter. While there is evidence for pigs being farmed at Elephantine, Tell ed-Daba, Memphis, and Amarna, they have left no sign at Lahun.[32] Middle Kingdom depictions of swineherds usually show them as outside the town, but the possibility cannot be ruled out that families at Lahun kept pigs within the town. This has recently been discovered to be the case in the Middle Kingdom town of Wah-sut at Abydos, where evidence for pigs has been found in the larger homes. As has been noted there, pigs breed quickly, and "requiring very little care, pigs efficiently converted organic waste into protein."[33] At Lahun, if pigs were allowed to wander in the streets, they would have readily helped in the disposal of food waste, keeping the waste drains cleaner than might otherwise be the case.

Horses were not known in the Late Middle Kingdom, but donkeys would have formed an important part of the working life of many individuals in Lahun. Donkeys are depicted in Middle Kingdom decorated tombs, and are mentioned in texts such as those describing the expeditions to the great quarries of the Wadi Hammamat.[34] Most of the detailed testimony for their use derives from the textual evidence from the New Kingdom settlement of Deir el-Medina, but corroborating data from the Old to Middle Kingdoms indicates that donkeys would have played a similar role in Lahun. A recent study on donkeys by Janssen suggests that they were used for a wide variety of purposes.[35] Both male and female donkeys were critically important for the transportation of goods, especially heavy items. Water, wood, grain, hay, firewood, and dung would have been carried to the town by donkeys. Usually these goods would be loaded on the backs of donkeys, but there are rare references to donkeys pulling wagons as well. As well as using them for trampling and threshing grain, people could also profit both by selling and by renting out donkeys. While donkeys did not live pampered lives, they would have been valued and cared for – at least to some extent. There were cases of abuse, however, and Janssen's recent work on Deir el-Medina reveals one case where a donkey eventually died after being beaten with a stick, and notes a number of instances where donkeys died after having been rented out.

The documentation suggests that at night and when not working some donkeys were stabled. The structural remains of Lahun do not include any obvious zones for stables or pens within the town itself, but it has been suggested that some areas of the large estates would have been suitable for housing animals.[36] The dung of donkeys could have been collected for burning when dry from the unpaved streets or estate stables, and successfully used as a fuel.[37] Donkeys may also have been allowed to roam around outside the walls of the settlement near the floodplain, foraging on their own in the day, while for protection at night they would have been brought inside, perhaps into stables that were outside the town walls. Finally, the importance of donkeys in the daily lives of the Egyptians is highlighted by the fact that, at Deir el-Medina at any rate, they were given names.

Along with domesticated animals, Lahun would have had its share of wild visitors such as birds, butterflies, and bees, as well as less desirable creatures such as rats, mice, flies, ticks, fleas, spiders, scorpions, and the occasional snake. The walls that surrounded the town would have prevented any larger unwanted animals entering the town, leaving its inhabitants safe.

## Sources

Millennia after the human and animal inhabitants of Lahun had left, a relative abundance of evidence testifying to their presence has survived. The outlines of the town and foundations of homes provide information on living and working quarters, as well as social stratification. In Lahun a veritable trove of texts was also discovered, which further enrich our understanding. Many of these will be referred to throughout this book, and one particular genre deserves to be noted – the accountancy texts. Though these documents are not often emphasized in discussions of Ancient Egypt, their importance in animating day-to-day life in any culture cannot be overemphasized. Though perhaps lacking in glamour and grace, these are the texts that can reveal what lies beneath the idealized image projected in formal literary texts and political statements. Collecting and analyzing a shopping list will give a much more realistic insight into a lifestyle than will even a direct interview during which positive elements are highlighted while other aspects that might be deemed more boring or less respectable are concealed.[38]

While we do not have shopping lists from Lahun, more than half of the documents found there are hieratic papyri containing "administrative records, from commodity accounts to day-by-day copies of business letters and transactions ('journals')."[39] Their content reveals an administration concerned with registering what in Egypt were the main objects of control: people (as labor), grain, and livestock. Other staples of life such as tools, cloth, finer foods, and jewelry also appear.

The existence of many of the items documented in the textual evidence is corroborated by physical evidence. A wealth of objects remains, ranging from fragments of broken pottery vessels that were used repeatedly everyday to artifacts that are unique to this settlement and that raise more questions than they answer. Whenever possible, these objects will be used to illustrate life in that time and town. At times, however, examples must be drawn from other locations and times to present a fuller picture, and these will be duly noted. Interpretive problems will also be discussed, and indeed, this book begins with an aspect of life that is less readily visible than some of the others, and that is birth itself.

## Notes

1   For a more detailed understanding of Egyptian history, see Shaw 2000 and Morkot 2005. For the Middle Kingdom in detail, see Grajetzki 2005.
2   Kemp 2006, 84.
3   For the sake of convenience this book follows the chronology of Quirke 2006.
4   The following historical overview is based largely on Grajetzki 2005 and Morkot 2005.
5   *Mastaba* is the Arabic word for "bench" and refers to tombs that had a rectangular mud-brick superstructure over the shafts leading to the tomb proper. The *mastaba* often had a cult chapel that was accessible to the family and friends of the deceased.
6   Gardiner 1947.
7   This is known as the Ramesseum Onomasticon because it was found in a box, along with other texts, in a shaft under a storeroom at the Ramesseum on the west bank of Thebes.
8   Quirke 2004a, 3–4.
9   Ptah is a creator god; Thoth is the chief registrar and god responsible for recording judgments; the primeval waters from which the initial act of creation took place are also called Nun; Ra is the main sun god; the "god's books" are hieroglyphs; and the "House of Life" refers to the scriptoriums where sacred knowledge was stored.
10  Humans are not unique in this regard – even ants spatially organize piles of corpses in consistent patterns (Theraulaz et al. 2002).

11 This book largely follows the standard definitions of "class" (socio-economic level) and "status" (the social standing of an individual or group within a class) that are explained in Richards 2005, 16.

12 These issues will be discussed at a later point in this book.

13 For an accessible presentation see Grajetzki 2005, 139–65.

14 Egypt was divided into 42 regions called "nomes," and the governor of each was called a "nomarch."

15 See now Hofmann 2005.

16 Hofmann 2005, 257.

17 Grajetzki 2005, 149–51.

18 Richards 2005, 178.

19 The figures are based on those in Uphill 1988, 27–33.

20 See most recently Quirke 2006.

21 F. Arnold 1996, 13–14.

22 F. Arnold 1996, 13–14.

23 Quirke 2006, 54.

24 D. Arnold 2003, 110–12.

25 The following is based on Quirke 2006; Kemp 2005, 211–21; O'Connor 1997, 389–400; von Pilgrim 1996b; Bietak 1996; F. Arnold 1996; Uphill 1988; Petrie et al. 1890. Extensive research on Deir el-Medina has been published by Lynn Meskell (see for example Meskell 1999).

26 F. Arnold 1989.

27 Petrie labeled the rows of houses in the western quarter in alphabetical order from south to north and called them "ranks."

28 Petrie et al. 1890, 24.

29 F. Arnold 1989, 83–4.

30 F. Arnold 1989, 77–8.

31 R. Janssen and Janssen 1989.

32 For pig consumption at Giza see Redding and Hunt 2007.

33 Rossel 2006, 41.

34 Osborn and Osbornová 1998, 132–6.

35 See J. Janssen 2005. The following section is based on this work, particularly 69–74.

36 Quirke 2006, 67.

37 See Delwen Samuel's experiments with dung cakes for fuel and palm fronds for tinder in Samuel 1989. Donkey dung is a versatile ingredient and was used as temper in clay, and as an ingredient in a recipe to stop a woman from bleeding and seeing bad dreams.

38 Today, credit card companies and frequent buyer cards are well aware of this and use data on prior purchases to target consumers.

39 Collier and Quirke 2006, ii.

# 2

# Birth

*It was on the third day of the first month of the Coming Forth that I was born.[1] I emerged from between the thighs of my mother and lo, I beheld an ivory tusk carved with strange entities, some wielding knives, others brandishing snakes. My cry was as loud as the honk of the Great Cackler himself,[2] and my limbs twitched like those of a nervous jerboa,[3] and so my nickname thereafter was "Hedjerit."[4] I heard the sound of the hushed voices of the nurses and my aunts praying and reciting incantations to keep me safe, while my mother reached out her arms for me. It was later that I learnt that the first child my mother bore never took his first breath when he left her womb, while another child had just died just after reaching her fourth year.*

The preceding is one *possible* scenario for the beginning of life for a citizen of Lahun. It highlights one of the great problems in reconstructing daily life in Ancient Egypt in general – the lack of sources for so many aspects. Childbirth is a particularly traumatic and private experience for both the mother and the child (who, unlike the fictional child above, is unlikely to ever remember the event). Clues are few and far between, and their interpretation is based on a combination of factors including archaeological context, comparative items, and in rare instances, corroborating data in the form of images or text.

## Childbirth – the Process

The delivery process itself is an area of life that is generally not documented in detail by any culture, and Ancient Egypt is no exception. From the few material clues coupled with ethnographic evidence it is reasonable to suggest that women gave birth in the same manner as women around the world: squatting (or kneeling) over a hole, with their feet on two or four birth bricks.[5] The squatting position is the most natural both anatomically and in terms of gravity. This

23

position is carved in relief at the *mammisi* (birth house) at the Ptolemaic temple of Hathor at Dendera. There, the woman is being helped by two goddesses, a feature that is repeated in other representations as well, including on a birth brick (discussed below). The Middle Kingdom Papyrus Westcar includes a fictional tale of the birth of royal triplets, and goddesses once again are in attendance at that birth.[6]

It is likely that Hedjerit's mother, Dedet, would have had women attending her delivery as well. In many cultures two women attend the birth: one to hold and support the mother, the other to hold and support the child. The helpers would probably have been women experienced with childbirth, and perhaps they held the title of nurse. Midwives are surprisingly scarce in the material record, although one may be depicted in an Old Kingdom tomb relief with a title related to that of "nurse."[7]

Whoever they were in reality, symbolically, helpers would have represented the type of supernatural aid that can only be provided by the gods. Numerous spells function in part by re-enacting a myth. One of the most popular is the cycle of myths associated with the great magician and goddess Isis protecting and curing her child Horus from the many dangers facing him. The healer, or person reciting the spell, thus plays the role of Isis, while the patient plays the role of Horus (irrespective of the gender of the actual people involved). Likewise, it is probable that Dedet's birth attendants were imbued with the power of goddesses associated with birth (Hathor, Taweret, Heqat,[8] Meshkenet, Isis, and Nephthys[9]) in the same way as the general healer was imbued with the power of Isis. The mother as well may have embodied the sky goddess who successfully gives birth to the sun god each morning.[10] Divine forces were thus used to drive away malignant forces at all levels of society.

The goddess Meshkenet was specifically related to the two birth bricks that a woman would squat upon during delivery.[11] That these were actually created, and almost certainly used, has now been verified by the critically important finding of a surviving example in the Middle Kingdom town of Abydos (Fig. 2.1).[12] The analysis by the excavator clearly demonstrates the significance of this artifact in terms of our understanding the myths underlying childbirth, the location and process of delivery itself, and the function and meaning of other birth-related apotropaic devices such as birth tusks (discussed below).

The mud-brick was decorated with the image of a woman holding aloft a newborn boy (in typical Egyptian fashion he looks like a small naked adult, colored red to indicate his sex), attended by two women and two standards of Hathor, again stressing the divine nature of their protection. The sides of the brick are decorated with images of protective deities of the same type as are found on birth tusks. The top of the brick is severely damaged, and the excavator suggests this may be due to the wear of a foot repeatedly resting upon it. It was found in the house of the mayor of Thirteenth Dynasty Abydos, within an area that was reserved for the use of the "noblewoman and king's daughter Renseneb," who the excavators suspect was married to the mayor. In the vicinity of the brick

**Figure 2.1** Drawing of birth brick (l. 35.0 cm × w. 17.0 cm) (courtesy of Sam Channer).

were found fragments of birth tusks, confirming that these objects were all related and probably used during the birth process and during the dangerous years of infancy. Although birth bricks were not found at Lahun, a brickmaker's mold has been found. Since the birth bricks were the same size as traditional housing bricks, the inhabitants of Lahun certainly had the means to create birth bricks as well.

The role of birth attendants was of course not only symbolic but eminently practical. Medical texts from the Late Middle Kingdom and later include a diverse range of prescriptions to help hasten the birth of a child, encourage contractions, and loosen a child from the womb.[13] There are also treatments to expel the contents of a "woman's belly," perhaps referring to the placenta or afterbirth. The concoctions were created from a variety of ingredients, some of which would have been readily available, such as ground emmer seed (a type of wheat common in the Near East), onion, and milk, while others were more specialized. Whether they would have been part of a midwife's kit to be available for any birth, or whether they would have been accessible only to specialists who were called upon in case of complications, is unknown.

The location where childbirth took place is unclear. Hospitals were not an option in those ancient times, and there is no archaeological or textual evidence of any specialized structure devoted to this critical process. In the New Kingdom workman's village of Deir el-Medina and the city of Amarna the remains of many homes contain structures that some Egyptologists have called "birthing beds." Made of mud-brick and usually placed in rear of the first room of the house, these consist of enclosed platforms (approximately 1.7 m long, 0.8 m wide and 0.7 m high) that were accessed by a few steps.[14] Their decoration, consisting of paintings of vines, women, and deities such as Bes and Taweret, has prompted many scholars to suggest that they were used as conjugal beds, birthing beds, or places for the seclusion of new mothers and neonates.[15] But the placement in the first room of the house seems at odds with the latter two suggestions in particular. Egyptians feared the entry of potentially hostile entities including demons, and so painted their doors red, a color of power and protection, as an added deterrent. Florence Friedman has noted that it is unlikely that this area would have been reserved solely for an event that could take place on no more than an annual basis.[16] It is more reasonable to propose that the structure was multifunctional, and that as the need arose it could serve as an altar, a site for postpartum purification rites, a secure location for infant care, or a household shrine for petitions related to fertility and safe childbirth.

On the basis of drawings on ostraka (scraps of pottery or stone), temporary outdoor structures have also been suggested as places where birthing occurred. A typical image is that of a women with a distinctive hairstyle nursing or holding a child on her lap, with a servant offering a kohl stick and mirror to her. Both are usually shown in a structure that seems to be made of poles with big-leafed vines hanging down.[17] These structures also appear in other contexts, and may be associated with celebrations rather than birthing.[18] It is also considered that in either event, these images are symbolic – they do not necessarily depict a real structure, but are an artistic convention to encode the symbolism of celebration. In any case, these slim shards of evidence are known only from the New Kingdom and not the time with which we are concerned. In the Middle Kingdom, the most likely place for childbirth would have been the bedroom of the home, whether it be the shared bedroom, or one in the "women's quarters" as is suggested for many of the larger estates. At the mayor's estate at Abydos, it is precisely within an area that seems to be devoted to women's quarters that the birth brick was found.[19] This location is set well at the back of the residence, away from potential dangers lurking in the outside. While the houses of the middle class at Lahun were significantly smaller, it is likely that the birthing area in those was also in the private living quarters in rear. This would provide a safe location for a woman like Dedet to give birth to her child.

## Protecting the Process and Product

It is obvious that the Egyptians were well aware of the many hazards related to pregnancy, motherhood, and infancy. Lahun provides us with the earliest known manuscript concerning predictions of a successful birth and methods of dealing with and diagnosing physical problems during pregnancy and childbirth. The archaeological record reveals a plethora of artifacts that seem to be related to ensuring a successful delivery and the further survival of both mother and child. During Hedjerit's birth and for the many months during which she was largely immobile and particularly vulnerable to accidents, illness, and disease, she and

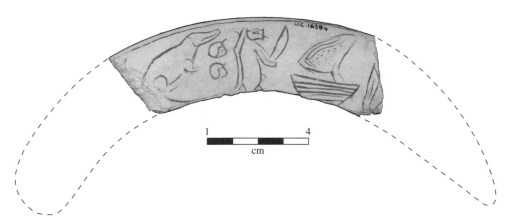

**Figure 2.2** Hippopotamus birth tusk fragment UC16384 (l. 10.6 cm) (courtesy of the Petrie Museum of Archaeology) and reconstruction of probable shape (courtesy of JJ Shirley).

her mother would likely have been guarded by objects designed to keep away the hostile entities that were usually blamed for misfortunes. Judging from the numbers that have survived of rods and birth tusks (often called "wands"), these objects were believed to be particularly efficacious in the Middle Kingdom.[20] The use of the term "wand" in Egyptological literature is unfortunate, as it conjures up the image of a stick or staff. Sometimes they are called "knives," but Stephen Quirke calls them "birth hippopotamus-tusks,"[21] which is a more accurate description of their material, function, and form (Fig. 2.2). They are nearly always made of ivory, the source of which in Egypt was usually hippopotamus tusks. These implements were formed by cutting a tusk longitudinally into two halves, and thus the finished product retains a recognizable tusk shape. This shape, coupled with the wear pattern on some of the tusks, suggests that they may have been used to draw a defensive perimeter around the mother and the child, while she was giving birth. The tusks may also have been used while the infant was sleeping in the day or night, by drawing a protective circle around the area and perhaps placing the tusks upon it. This scenario is particularly feasible at night, when presumably the infant(s) slept with the mother in the bedroom. The sleeping area would thus have been enclosed within a defensive perimeter delineated by the tusk with the protective force perhaps activated by a spell.

The choice of ivory as material for this apotropaic instrument is not random, but reflects the nature of the hippopotamus – what was one of the deadliest animals in Egypt. The female hippo is ferocious when defending her young, even against male hippos,[22] and therefore this form is the one assumed by two deities that were specially devoted to the protection of the vulnerable: Taweret ("The Great One") and Ipet.[23] The hippo goddess is frequently depicted as standing on her hind legs with a pendulous belly and breasts (thus emphasizing the link with pregnant women), the paws of a lioness, and on her back another exceedingly dangerous animal – the crocodile. The hippo is also an animal closely linked with liminality: hippos are quadrupeds and walk on the earth, but they spend most of their time in the water. Indeed, baby hippos can even suckle while fully submerged, and yet emerge unharmed and whole. The waters of the Nile river were thought to be a channel between earthly life and the *duat*, what we might call the afterlife or the farworld, which was inhabited by the dead, the gods, and hostile demons. The ability of the hippo to safely traverse this boundary zone may have added to her potency against malignant forces that might cross over into the human sphere and cause illness or disease. Embodied in a creature closely related to both the divine and the demonic, Taweret was eminently suited to protection of the most vulnerable individuals – mothers and infants.

The length of many of the tusks suggests that perhaps most if not all originated from the teeth of male hippopotami.[24] The male hippo was also a dangerous animal, and was associated with Seth.[25] This link is explained in myths dealing with the battles between Seth and Horus for the rule of Egypt. In the myths, Seth believed that the right to the throne should be his, as he was one of the nine original deities, a child of Geb (the earth) and Nut (the sky), as well as being the brother of Osiris (the first ruler of Egypt). Horus, as the son of Osiris (the first ruler) and of the great magician Isis, claimed the throne by birthright. The two gods engaged in a number of struggles, which often seem to stress the cleverness and trickery of Horus and the brute strength of Seth. In one, Seth was goaded by Horus into engaging in a water race in stone boats. Horus cheated by making his from papyrus and painting it to look like stone. As the race started, the real stone boat of Seth sank to the bottom of the Nile, where in a rage he transformed into a hippopotamus. Unfortunately for him he was harpooned by Horus, but was saved from being killed by the tribunal of the gods. Horus was awarded kingship of Egypt, while Seth served as a protector.

Spells in the Book of the Dead and compositions found in royal tombs called the Royal Books of the Afterlife[26] depict the god Seth as protecting the sun god Ra from his ultimate enemy Apep, serpent of chaos. As he was the most powerful of the gods, if one of his avatars was the hippo, then an object created from a part of this creature would be charged with the god's supreme power and strength.[27] An ivory tusk, carved from the very teeth of a hippo, whether male or female, was thus automatically imbued with the aggressive protection of the animal and the deity, whether used for the defense of mothers and children, or for other religious purposes.[28]

To further their potency, the birth tusks were additionally charged by the addition of carved images of a whole range of fierce creatures, some of which emphasize their apotropaic roles, such as crocodiles, lions, and snakes, as well as fantastic hybrids such as griffins,[29] serpopards,[30] and sphinxes. Many of these wield daggers and snakes to emphasize the aggression with which they will combat any assault on their ward; others seem to be seizing the snakes with their hands and biting them. These same entities protect the sun god on his journey, and thus the child is identified with the nascent sun god himself. Indeed, it could be that in the delivery process, the mother squatting on two birth bricks with the child emerging between them recreates the birth of the sun in the horizon, which in Egyptian iconography is depicted as the sun coming forth from two mountains.[31]

Another prominent image on these tusks is that of a bow-legged, forward-facing dwarf wielding a pair of snakes, who is labeled as *aha* "the fighter."[32] This iconography is used to designate a number of related deities, the best known being Bes. This "Bes-image" is associated with birth and the young right through the Roman Period.[33] Other animals that appear on the tusks seem to be related to pregnancy and successful birth, such as frogs, which are symbolic of multiplicity and fertility. In addition, many of the tusks were inscribed with short protective formulas as well, emphasizing that these were meant to provide divine defenses.[34] A common formula reads "I (or we) have come in order to spread our protection around N." Sometimes the focus is on the children (plural) of a particular woman. Others specify that their sanctuary is geared to repel demonic dangers encountered in life, or in the day and the night. Unlike that of many artifacts, the function of these is therefore relatively transparent. Even when the findspot is a tomb, the function is to ensure a successful rebirth of the deceased.

The identity of the person actually using these, however, is uncertain. They may have been the type of object that one would expect to find in every home, a part of the assemblage of daily life. Whether a new tusk would have been acquired, or whether it would possibly have been passed down as an heirloom, is unknown. The latter might be suggested by examples that were broken and repaired in ancient times, yet continued to be kept in the home.[35] Ivory was a valuable commodity – in terms of effort required to acquire the raw material it represents moderate wealth, but textual evidence suggests that Middle Kingdom Egyptians regarded it as one of the more valued materials.[36]

This does not intrinsically mean that the tusks would have been available to elite women only. Many middle-class burials in the Middle Kingdom contain artifacts usually associated with wealth.[37] Some of the tusks are inscribed with names of women titled *sat nezu* "royal daughter," and many included the title *nebet per*, a female title that translates literally as "lady of the house" but functionally should be considered closer to an "estate manager." It is possible that a *nebet per* would not only have used the artifact for herself and her own children, but might also have allowed it to be shared by others in her household for whom she was responsible, including relatives, employees, and servants. It is also possible that the tusks were used by physicians, priests, or midwives. Indeed, a *nebet per* could have also been a specialist in birth magic. This type of scenario has been suggested by Quirke, who notes that Petrie discovered a number of artifacts that could be associated with defense of infants, including a pair of ivory clappers, a wooden Bes-type figure, and a mask with Bes-type features. These were found in what were probably the bedrooms of two adjoining homes in Lahun, suggesting that they could have been used there, or perhaps were stored there by a specialist skilled in their use and accompanying rituals.[38]

Strikingly, aside from the adult female names, the only other personal names found on the tusks are those of male children, sometimes with the name of their mother included. This phenomenon is not easy to explain. If the tusks were tailor made and inscribed for the named individuals, it does hint that children were named very early on. This fits with the importance of the name in Ancient Egypt as a vital aspect of an individual, and is supported by religious texts that recount the process of naming deities. For example, in a New Kingdom text, Ra states that at his birth both his father and mother told him his name, which had been hidden inside him. In administrative texts from Lahun known as *weput*-lists, a newborn would immediately have been given a main name (in the Old Kingdom this was called the "great name"), as well as a second name "which one calls." As the child developed it might also receive a third name, or a nickname, emphasizing perhaps some identifying characteristic. Many names place the child in the care of a deity, such as *Sasopedu* "Son of Sopedu," or celebrate a popular king such as Senusret. Names like *Dedet* "The one given" reflect the concept of the child as a gift. However, if these tusks were used for the delivery, then we are faced with the scenario that the child in question must have been named before birth, and it would suggest that a male child was hoped for.

A more reasonable possibility is that a name was added to the tusk after it had been used successfully during the birthing process. The proven tusk would then continue to be used during the infancy of that child, and then be passed on for the use of others as well. The lack of female names could reflect an awareness of the possible higher infant mortality rate of male children, suggesting that they needed the tusks more,[39] or it may have been related to the importance that the eldest son had in the family. However, we should not be quick to assume that the tusks were used solely for male children. The fact that some of these objects show evidence of having been repaired intimates that they were used repeatedly. This feature, coupled with the evidence of spells that were specified as being for the use of children (plural) in general, suggest that the tusks would have been used for the protection of children of both sexes.

While none of the surviving examples of birth tusks has Lahun as a confirmed findspot, a number have been found in nearby Lisht. Illahun does, however, provide us with one segment of what was likely a related artifact: a birth rod (Fig. 2.3).[40] The ivory birth rods when complete were made up of separate segments joined by dowels. The segments themselves were carved with apotropaic figurines like those found on the birth tusks. In addition, three-dimensional versions of these creatures could be attached to the top. A wooden lion, crocodile, and baboon found at Illahun may perhaps have been used for this purpose.[41] Surviving rods are attested from the Late Middle Kingdom only; perhaps they were perceived to be less effective than the tusks and the bricks and therefore fell out of use by the New Kingdom.

**Figure 2.3** Rod fragment UC16685 (l. 11.0 cm) (courtesy of the Petrie Museum of Archaeology).

Spoken magic was also prevalent throughout Egypt's history. One of the most familiar sounds to Hedjerit in her early years would have been the intonation of spells being recited or chanted for her protection. Relatively large numbers of spells have been found, testifying to the need to safeguard vulnerable individuals such as expectant mothers, newborns, and infants. They range from utterances designed to guide a woman through a safe delivery, to ones to cure a child who has been bitten by a venomous snake or scorpion, to ones keeping away demons disguised as nurses. Indeed one papyrus dating to the New Kingdom but possibly composed in the Middle Kingdom consists of a series of spells specifically designed to protect a mother and child. "A protective spell for guarding the limbs, to be recited over a child when the sunlight rises," begins one spell. In another a feverish child is addressed: "Spell for a knot for a child, a fledgling: are you hot in the nest? Are you burning in the bush? Your mother is not with you?"[42] The spell is to be spoken over an amulet made of gold and bread pellets, linen, and a seal inscribed with a crocodile and a hand, which is then worn by the child as a protection.

## Infant and Maternal Mortality

The Egyptians went to great lengths to protect pregnant women, neonates, and young infants in response to the harsh reality of high mortality rates of both infants and mothers. Infants that did survive the delivery process itself still were subject to birth defects, accidents, and lower immunity to diseases and illnesses (diarrhea in neonates is frequently fatal). Lethal heart defects often are not apparent for several days, and the time when the larynx is descending (four to six months of age) is also critical for the very young.[43] The actual infant mortality rate[44] for Late Middle Kingdom Egypt is difficult to establish with any certainty, in particular because of the lack of infant remains in cemeteries (this will be discussed below), and the numbers are usually estimated on more modern rates.[45] But even today, the rates vary tremendously; not only may they depend on the country in which the infant is born, but there can also be great disparity within a single country. Relevant factors include the mother's status, ethnicity, wealth, nutrition, and health, as well as the quality of pre-natal care.[46] And while the temptation is to assume that rates are lower today than they were in Ancient Egypt, this is not necessarily the case, and in some countries today the numbers are startlingly high.[47]

Maternal mortality rates are even more elusive.[48] Recent attempts to quantify them are hampered by problems related both to definitions and to methods of measurement. Most definitions rely on temporal parameters, so if a woman dies within a specified time period after giving birth due to pregnancy-related complications or the after-effects of the delivery process itself and the involvement of any aides, it is classified as a maternal death.[49] The lifetime risk of maternal death during a woman's reproductive years today is estimated in some countries as being as low as 1 in 29,800, and in others as being as high as 1 in 6.[50]

However, the extreme difficulties of gathering the data and determining the cause of death of a woman of reproductive age, and the practicality of monitoring individuals, precludes the use of these estimates for anything but the most general analysis of trends even in the modern world.[51] Applying these methods to any ancient civilization is unlikely to achieve reliable results, because of both the small sample numbers, and the lack of detailed documentation regarding the lives of individual women. It is obviously very difficult to assign a cause of death to a woman of reproductive age in Ancient Egypt – the Egyptians did not record the agent of death, nor is it always apparent from skeletal data.[52]

The problem is compounded by the fact that early archaeologists for the most part did not invest their energies in the systematic recording and interpretation of mortuary data from Ancient Egypt, and much potential information has thus been lost.[53] Recent professional work does suggest that Ancient Egypt suffered from a relatively high infant and possibly maternal mortality rate as well. W. Benson Harer suggests a figure of 1 percent for maternal mortality and 20 percent mortality for infants under one month in age.[54] Preliminary cemetery analyses of the Ptolemaic through Roman periods disclose a much higher mortality rate for adult women than men. Out of 60 mummies studied in Douch, there were 9 women for every 3 men between the ages of 10 and 40, while in Aïn el-Labakha, out of 70 mummies there were 10 women for every 5 men between the ages of 20 and 40.[55] However, this may be a later trend, as it is not reflected in analyses of a recent sample of Middle Kingdom cemeteries, which show approximately equal numbers of female and male adult deaths.[56]

Bones can also provide hints as to the cause of higher infant and maternal mortality rates. One explanation for the difficulties that women had giving birth may be found in the New Kingdom cemetery data indicating that the skeletal structure of women was in reality as strikingly gracile as their representation in tomb paintings.[57] The narrowness of their hips may have created problems in successfully giving birth and would have increased the dangers to the health and survival of the mother. Ironically, it may be that the increase in quality of life in dynastic Egypt led to a decrease in the physical constitution of women in terms of their ability to successfully bear children. The few major studies of mortuary data on skeletal remains from sites that span centuries (if not millennia) are consistently revealing that in the dynastic levels, the bodies of women of child-bearing age were generally very slender, and the width of the pelvic region was conspicuously below the average of women in the Predynastic Period and modern Ethiopian populations.[58] Thus, in a twist to natural selection, the attractiveness of these slender women for marriage led to an increasing decline in ability to successfully give birth. The health of mothers and that of infants are thus closely linked, and have an impact on the larger social groups and the population as a whole.[59] To cope with the reality of infant death, special burial practices often develop, and Ancient Egypt was no exception.

## Infant Burials

The prevalent custom among families from a range of classes, from the elite to the poor, was that of burying infants within settlements rather than cemeteries.[60] Baby burials, many of newborns and infants under the age of 12 months, have been found in various sites throughout Egypt, including the First Intermediate Period and Middle Kingdom levels at Lisht,[61] Elephantine, Abydos,[62] Tell ed-Daba, and Lahun, to the extent that what was once suggested to be a custom based on foreign influence now appears to have been native.[63] It also helps to explain the striking scarcity of child burials in relationship to adults noted at some Middle Kingdom cemeteries. For example, in Riqqa in Lower Egypt, the excavator recorded 116 adult females, 124 adult males, and only 10 children as part of his Middle Kingdom sample.[64]

The practice of burying infants outside of the general community burial grounds is not uncommon and is attested in prehistoric and historic cultures, and in areas separated geographically, such as Great Britain and France[65] (Neolithic, Roman, as well as twentieth-century AD), the Near East, France, Hungary, Bulgaria, Italy,[66] and Catal Huyuk.[67] Infants have been found within settlements close to the walls, close to homes, within the homes (sometimes in houses that have been disused) below the floor level, near hearths and ovens, and under buildings as foundation deposits.

All of these locations are where young infants have been found in Ancient Egypt as well, buried in shallow graves, as well as in pottery jars, bowls, and amphoras. Artifacts such as amulets, necklaces, and pottery found with infants reveal that they were buried with care.[68] In the town of Lahun, they were found buried beneath the floorboards of homes in boxes that had previously been used for another purpose rather than specially built coffins. For example, the lid of one box that held an infant and a vase was painted white with red lines in a three by ten grid, and may have been used as a game-board.[69] Sometimes they were buried alone, but as many as three might be placed together in the same box.[70]

The question remains as to why some infants were buried separately from older children and adults. The practice is not consistent, for infants are occasionally found in cemeteries,[71] and adults can be found buried in settlements. The situation becomes even more unclear when we realize that archaeologists do not use any consistent definitions or terminology. Excavation reports and articles mention child and infant burials, but generally fail to state what the criteria are for labeling one skeleton a "newborn," another an "infant," another a "child." Is it based on physiological characteristics of the skeleton, or size, or estimated age? These are rarely explicitly delineated, making analysis even more difficult. It is only recently that a work has been published specifically focusing on a systematic methodology for analyzing the bones of infants and children in an archaeological context.[72] On the basis of burials at Abydos and Dakhla Oasis, those scholars divided individuals into the categories of Fetal Tremester (1st, 2nd, 3rd), Infant (0–0.5 and 0.5–1 years), Young Child (1–3 and 3–6), Older Child (6–9 and 9–12), Adolescent (12–15 and 15–20), and Young Adult (20–5 and 25–30).[73]

In any case, an important point to bear in mind is that the existence of separate burials for infants and young children does not intrinsically suggest infanticide. While infanticide has been an accepted practice in many cultures, it is usually only visible if some sort of material evidence remains, whether it be skeletal or textual. In the case of Ancient Egypt, we have no corroborating evidence. The place of burial may be separated from that of other members of the community because an infant of a very young age had not yet attained the status of "person." Some cultures are specific in terms of the precise age at which an infant can be considered fully human. For Romans it was 40 days. For other cultures, it was more generalized, and in some it is related to the idea of speaking.[74] Greco-Roman cemeteries in Egypt that lack burials of infants below the age of 12–18 months suggest that perhaps those unable to walk or talk yet were not due the same rituals as those older, though they were not discarded either.[75] Indeed the careful burials of fetuses, even if not in the same area as adults, proves that in Ancient Egypt they were valued as living entities from Neolithic to Roman times.[76]

While newborns were certainly valued and even already named, what they may have lacked at this stage was any sort of social status.[77] If infants were not quite members of the adult human social world yet, perhaps they were considered as closer to the society of the divine world. As we shall see later and have mentioned above, in many spells, the healer is the embodiment of Isis, and the patient her son Horus. The many dangers of infancy resulted in a large number of spells designed to aid infants, based on re-enactments of myths. In these it is the child who embodies Horus. Perhaps by keeping the remains of individuals who were in a liminal state, still closer to the divine world than the human, in the home or at least still within the settlement,[78] the family would have a more direct conduit to the gods.[79]

The death of newborn and young infants must have been a part of the daily life of all members of an Ancient Egyptian community, whether the individual who was affected by that death was a relative such as a sibling, aunt, uncle, cousin, or parent, or even completely unrelated by blood. There were times, particularly for accounting and registration purposes, that the death of an offspring was recorded,[80] but these were not specifically noted as being children. It may be that until an individual was old enough to be part of the labor force, the death would not have been officially registered. Nevertheless, although an infant's death was not necessarily recorded, somebody had to be responsible for carefully wrapping the infant and placing it in a specific position with selected objects in the burial spot close to the home.[81] Perhaps that person was one of the parents, or both of them, or another designated individual.

## Post-partum

A successful birth was cause for a celebration, and there is evidence that at least in the New Kingdom, an assortment of food and beverages was brought to the grateful father, probably by friends and relatives.[82] In the Middle Kingdom, although we do not have any evidence of celebrations to commemorate birthdays, we do have evidence that birthdays were at least remembered. One individual records that he was born in the reign of Amenemhat I, another that he was born in year 27 of the reign of Amenemhat II.[83]

After the drama of her birth, with her mother squatting on two birth bricks amid chanting nurses or midwives wielding birth tusks and rods, a child such as Hedjerit would have stayed in close contact with her mother for at least the first weeks of her life. In the *Tales of Wonder*, probably composed in the Middle Kingdom, after the queen, Redjedjet, had given birth to triplets, she "purified herself by (means of) a purification of 14 days." The word used here, *wab*, means to wash or bathe, but also to purify, signifying a transformation from one state to another. This passage may indicate that after delivery women were secluded for the first 14 days to remain pure, and to help lessen the chance of infection, disease, or intrusion by demons while the new mother and child were still in a transformative and vulnerable state.[84] If there were a period of post-partum confinement, this could be interpreted as a sign of the respect and esteem accorded a successful mother in Ancient Egypt. Recent ethnographic research by Morsey has shown that even in the small village in modern Egypt,[85] "contrary to male anthropologists' description of ritual pollution as indicative of females' devalued status, the enforcement of confinement rituals in the FatiHa is an indication of valuable social status. It is an index of women's culturally specific valuation rather than their inferiority."

It is unclear how sequestered the neonate would have been, but her world would nevertheless have likely been filled with the touch of her mother, surrounded by artifacts charged with protective power, and with the sound of soothing voices and magical spells spoken or sung by her mother and perhaps members of the extended family or nurses. Lullabies may have been sung for her while she was still in the womb, though if so they have left no trace in the archaeological record, nor would we necessarily expect to find any evidence of songs that are usually memorized at an early age and left unrecorded. As a newborn and infant, Hedjerit would have seen the comforting protective figures of deities adorning apotropaic bricks, tusks, and rods. These objects and their associated incantations would have been a natural and familiar part of the immediate environment of a Middle Kingdom child such as Hedjerit.

Another individual whose touch was likely familiar to Hedjerit was a nurse. In the Middle Kingdom there were three known titles for nurses:[86] *atjyt*, *menat*, and *khenmetet*. The last is attested mostly from the New Kingdom on and with a single exception usually refers to a divine nurse (male or female). Images depicting the use of birth tusks are rare indeed, but one Eighteenth Dynasty tomb includes representations of women labeled as *khenmetet* "nurses" each holding a serpent staff and tusk in front of the tomb owners.[87] In itself, this image is not strong enough evidence to confirm that in the Middle Kingdom the tusk would have been wielded by a nurse, but it is a possibility.

The first two titles, *atjyt* and *menat*,[88] are more prevalent in the Middle Kingdom, but their precise meaning is uncertain. Because they appear together in certain texts, their function must differ. Ward has shown that *atjyt* can appear in contexts with the word "to suckle" (*seneq*), but it is usually written with the child on a lap determinative, suggesting that it refers to a dry nurse, so not necessarily someone who was lactating herself.

In contrast, the title *menat* is most often determined with a breast, hinting that it refers to a wet nurse. In a letter from Lahun written by the servant of the personal estate Panetyni to an unidentified lord concerning a delivery of clothing, the *menat* nurse is mentioned: "On the seal of this humble servant: 1 to/of the nurse Iy [. . .] (cattle/leather?) 1 since he spoke of it at the house of nurses."[89] In another letter, the servant of the estate reports "Look, I have had sent: honey, a *hin*; [some commodity], [oil] issued as a requisition from the 'house of nurses'."[90] The word *menat*, determined with the sign for breast, is used both for the nurse herself (Iy is determined by the standard woman sign) and for the house of nurses in both letters. However, there are examples where the title is used by men, indicating that it could also refer to an individual who had a broader role in the raising of a child – what we might call a nursemaid or nanny.

It is possible that one or two nurses would have played an important role in Hedjerit's birth and immediate aftercare. If she had been a child of the elite, her mother might even have chosen a wet nurse to suckle her instead. The role of a wet nurse was certainly critically important for the survival of children whose own mother had died during delivery or shortly thereafter. Evidence from Deir el-Medina shows that single or widowed men could raise their own children, but they would need help for feeding a newborn, whether from lactating relatives or a non-related wet nurse. Conversely, a woman who had lost her own child was in a position to help feed somebody else's.[91] Middle Kingdom stelae often incorporate the name of the nurse along with those of other family members, thus granting these individuals the same piece of immortality afforded to the relatives of the donor.[92] In Egypt, a nanny or nurse would play a vital role in childrearing, and was considered an integral part of the daily life of the family.

## Family Size

Determining family size is equally complex. The probable age of the onset of menstruation for an Egyptian girl would have been 14 – significantly later than that of girls in the modern western nations.[93] If the average age of death for women was roughly 30 years of age and birth-spacing at an average of every 33 months was practiced,[94] assuming the woman did not become pregnant immediately after the onset of her first menstruation,[95] there might have been four to seven birth attempts in her lifetime.[96] One scholar analyzing differences between world populations in the pre- and post-industrial eras has suggested that "the typical woman before 1800 thus had 2.02 children who survived to reproductive age."[97] Estimates for Roman Egypt suggest that women gave birth to an average of six children.[98] In effect, even though a woman may have attempted to give birth to four to six children the actual number of children surviving to a reproductive age would have fluctuated, and the family size as well. An average size for our purposes here, for a non-elite family, is two to three children surviving to a reproductive age of about 15.

Corroborating data is again elusive. Textual sources are difficult to analyze in terms of family structures. Complications include the prevalence of popular names repeating themselves across generations and between contemporaneous individuals unrelated to each other, as well as the lack of specificity in kinship terms themselves.[99] The only clear terms are "wife" (*hemet*) and "husband" (*hay*). The terms we usually translate as "mother" (*mut*) and and "father" (*jt*) could be used for two generations of lineal[100] ascendants as well as what we would term "in-laws", while "daughter" (*sat*) and "son" (*sa*) were used for two generations of lineal descendants. The words commonly translated as sister (*senet*) and brother (*sen*) were used to refer to collateral kin[101] of at least three generations. For example, the word *senet* could refer to the individual's sister or aunt (either the mother's sister or father's sister) or their daughter (what we call a "cousin"), as well as the daughter of either a brother or a sister ("niece"), perhaps even a sister-in-law, as well as an unrelated female friend or lover.

An Ancient Egyptian household could comprise members other than solely the parents and children. A series of letters written by a land-owner and farmer, Heqanakht, while he was away on business, indicate the size of an Early Middle Kingdom rural household.[102] Heqanakht had five sons and a new wife – though whether all the sons were from the first marriage is unclear. Three girls who are mentioned may have been his daughters or were otherwise related. The household also included Heqanakht's mother, another female relative of some kind (perhaps aunt or sister), and male and female servants. The impression given is that of a large, boisterous, and bickering extended family surrounding Heqnakaht.

Accounting texts from Late Middle Kingdom Lahun also provide clues. In one census, the head of the household, Hori, is living with his wife and their infant son, his mother, and her five daughters.[103] His mother, therefore, had six children, though whether they were fathered by the same person, and whether any could be grandchildren, is unknown. In the next census, Hori has disappeared, and the focus is on his son, seemingly the only child he had. Another text that lists the personal staff of a priest seems to be selective as to which children are identified.[104] The priest himself has a son and a daughter, and apparently his wife is dead. With the exception of one adult male, the priest's extensive list of dependents includes only women, and most of them have between one and three daughters, some of which are listed as infants. These women and daughters probably worked for the priest, but after finishing their duties returned to their own homes, where they may have had other children waiting for them.

More complete census lists can provide clearer clues as to the size of families. Demographic research is currently underway based on such documents from the New Kingdom planned settlement of Deir el-Medina. Although the research is not yet complete, Toivari-Viitala, in her work on women in that community, reported that a sample of 30 households included one couple with four children, five couples with three children, a man with three children (from two different wives), six couples with two children, seven couples with one child, four childless couples, and six "bachelors."[105]

These figures must be treated carefully, as they pertain to a settlement that perhaps should be considered as atypical. Nevertheless, it raises the possibility that in Lahun, which was also a planned community, families usually consisted of one to three children – fewer than usually proposed on the basis of modern ethnographic evidence. The appearance in the census of a solo man raising children on his own is to be expected given the posited high maternal mortality rate.

Representations also tend to be difficult to decipher.[106] For example, Old Kingdom figurines often depict a couple with one child or two (in the case of two, generally one is male and one is female). But these may be abbreviated versions of a larger family size. In the Middle Kingdom tomb scenes often summarize, showing only the eldest son. In scenes where more family members are depicted, it is unclear which are alive and which are deceased. It is entirely possible that a tomb listing and depicting children of the tomb owner may include deceased relatives, including children. Therefore the offspring of one couple named Ukhhotep and Djehutyhotep seems to include four sons and one daughter, but it is unclear if they all survived to reproductive age, or whether some of the children survived infancy but died after a certain age.[107] The fact that deceased infants (before being weaned or capable of independent mobility) are not represented visually is no surprise, as this was the case in most cultures until the nineteenth century AD.[108]

## Birth

Just surviving birth and infancy was an accomplishment for the mother and the child, and both were greatly valued. The respect accorded motherhood was apparent in many ways in Ancient Egypt, from the frequent representations of the tomb owner with his mother to literary texts. In one New Kingdom text, a son is reminded to support his mother because

> She had a heavy load in you, but she did not abandon you.
> When you were born after your months, she was yet yoked to you, her breast in your mouth for three years.
> As you grew and your excrement disgusted, she was not disgusted, saying: "What shall I do!"[109]

This respect for mothers is also apparent in many documents in the fact that when the individual records his parentage, the mother is often emphasized. In one study of Middle Kingdom documents, "out of a total of nearly 600 cases, 48% name both parents, 46% name the mother alone, and only 5% name the father alone."[110] This close bond between Hedjerit and her mother was formed early on, and was retained as she grew and developed. As the scope of her activities expanded from sucking at her mother's breast to eating solid food and playing with other children, she would form new connections with others in her family and community.

## Notes

1   Egyptian dates were recorded relative to the beginning of a king's reign, and by listing the day of the month of the season. There were three seasons of four months each in a year.

2   The "Great Cackler" was part of a creation myth wherein Amun, as creator god, arises from the out of the watery Nun on the primeval mound, appearing as a great white goose just before the first moment of creation, when in the world there was nothing but utter, complete stillness. As the Great Cackler, *Ngeg-wer*, he breaks the primordial silence for the first time with his loud honk, causing the newly generated deities to open their eyes and begin to see, while the very earth remains in silent astonishment at the sound of his voice. "He commenced to speak in the midst of silence. He opened all eyes, and caused them to behold. He began to cry aloud while the earth was dumbfounded" (P. Leiden, ch. 90 IV, 6–IV, 7 in Gardiner 1905, 12–42; Assmann 1975, 136).

3   The jerboa is a gerbil-like rodent of the Egyptian desert.

4   Although scholars are not completely agreed on the identification of the animal known in Egyptian as "*hedjerit*" it mostly likely refers to the "jerboa" (Westendorf 1999, 503). The name is listed in Ranke and Baumgartner 1935 vol. I, 261. It is also attested as the name of one of the weaving women in Lahun in UC32094A (Collier and Quirke 2006, 144–5) and in UC32099E (Collier and Quirke 2006, 156–7).

5   See Roth and Roehrig 2002. I would like to thank Josef Wegner for allowing me access to his article (forthcoming), which provides an extensive discussion of the comparative and ethnographic data.

6   The creator god Khnum is also present at the royal births.

7   Fischer 2000, 27.

8   Often represented as a frog.

9   Nephthys was one of the original nine gods and the sister of Isis.

10   The birth brick discovered at Abydos confirms this, as the mother and the attendants are depicted with blue hair (a marker of divinity), rather than black (human), while the mother is seated on a divine throne (Wegner forthcoming).

11   The word *meskhenet* also refers to a birth brick. Thus the deity may be considered as a personification of the brick itself, and indeed can be represented as a brick with the head of a goddess. In the Papyrus Westcar (on which is written *The Tales of Wonder*) this goddess foretells the future of one of the children.

12   Wegner 2002.

13   Westendorf 1999 vol. 1, 411–38; Nunn 1996, 194–5.

14   The equivalent of 5.5′ × 2.5′ × 2.5′ (F. Friedman 1994, 97).

15   For a discussion see F. Friedman 1994, 97–111.

16   F. Friedman 1994, 97–111.

17   These are identified as convolvulus or morning glory vines.

18   See for example TT51 the 19th Dynasty tomb of Userhat and Shepset.

19   Wegner 2004.

20   The main publication is still Altenmüller 1965.

21   Quirke 2006, 100.

22   Female hippos can kill male hippos as they attack the vulnerable side of the male, whereas male-to-male fights are usually head-on – ritualistic but not necessarily lethal.

23   For the hippopotamus in Ancient Egypt see Behrmann 1989, 1996, especially vol. 2, 59–95.

24   The tusk of females was usually about 20 cm, while that of males was considerably longer, up to 50 cm. As an example of some of the lengths see UC16379 at 42 cm; UC16380, broken but with a length of 31 cm; UC16382, in two pieces measuring 15.5 and 14.5 cm, with at least two further pieces missing; and a tusk at the Egyptian Collection of the Museum of Fine Arts Budapest measuring 32 cm. A 20-cm fragment of an unworked tusk was found at Lahun (EGY125).

25   Seth is one of the original nine gods, the others being the primeval creator god Atum, Shu, Tefnut, Geb, Nut, Osiris, Isis, and Nephthys.

26   While the Book of the Dead consisted of funerary texts primarily for the non-elite, composed from the New Kingdom through the Roman Period, the Royal Books of the Afterlife were composed for New Kingdom pharaohs.

27   Seth, wielding snakes, also appears on some of the birth tusks (UC16383).

28   See EGY180a,b, ivory tusks with an incised pattern.

29   A cross between a lion and an eagle or other large bird.

30   A cross between a serpent and a leopard, also commonly depicted in Mesopotamia.

31   Wegner forthcoming.

32   Polz and Voß 1999, 390–9.

33  Romano 1989.
34  Altenmüller 1965.
35  Jeffreys 2003.
36  Richards (2005, 111) in her table of wealth indices ranks ivory as 8 out of a high of 19 on the scale of effort expenditure, and 10 out of 14 on the scale based on indigenous Egyptian attitudes.
37  Richards 2005, 118.
38  Quirke 2006, 81–4.
39  It has recently been shown that genetically, females have some added health benefits in infancy, and the rate of infant mortality in males is generally greater than that of females (Harer 1993, 20; Luy 2003).
40  Quirke 2006, 99–100. For the rods in general, see the important discussion of Ritner's theory regarding these artifacts in Wegner forthcoming.
41  Quirke 2006, 99–100.
42  Parkinson 1991, 129–30.
43  Scott 1999, 31–2.
44  This is defined as the death of a child before reaching the first birthday and is calculated as the ratio of deaths per 1,000 live births.
45  For an overview of the complex nature of the issue see Golden 2004, 147–50; Adetunji 1996.
46  In the United States from 1980 to 2000, for mothers classified as "white" the rates fell from 10.9 to 5.7. For those classified as "other" the rates fell from 20.2 to 11.4 but remained high; of these, for mothers classified as "black" the rates fell from 22.2 to 14.1 (Centers for Disease Control and Prevention 2002). Education and wealth seemed to have surprisingly little bearing on the likelihood of survival.
47  CIA estimates of infant mortality rates, based on data from 206 countries in 2005, give a range from a low of only 2.29 deaths per 1,000 live births in Singapore to a high of 187.49 per 1,000 live births in Angola (Central Intelligence Agency 2006).
48  See for example Boerma 1987.
49  World Health Organization 2000, 3–4.
50  The low rate is for Sweden, while the high rate is for Sierra Leone and Afghanistan according to the World Health Organization 2000.
51  As an example, the range of uncertainty in the maternal mortality rate estimates for Sierra Leone are 510 to 3,800 maternal deaths per 100,000 live births (World Health Organization 2000).
52  A notable exception is in the case of the body of a woman in Abydos whose skeletal remains leave little doubt that her demise was caused by bodily violence (Baker 1997, 111).
53  This is a great pity, as fecundity is indicated in pelvic remains (see for example Angel 1972, 97.)
54  Harer 1993, 20.
55  Dunand 2004, 22.
56  Richards 2005, 170.
57  Toivari-Viitala 2001, 170–1.
58  See recent review of the data in Kraus 2004, 206–8.

59  Goodman and Armelagos 1989.

60  Richards (2005, 170) notes that in the Middle Kingdom towns of Abydos and South Abydos the practice occurs in elite and non-elite settings as well. The lack of neonates in cemeteries is also evident at Greco-Roman cemeteries (Dunand 2004.)

61  F. Arnold 1996, 15.

62  Picardo 2006.

63  For references see Richards 2005, 66, 169,170; von Pilgrim 1996a, particularly 36, 81–3; Feucht 1995, 124–34. For Deir el-Medina see Meskell 1999; 1994.

64  Richards 2005, 97.

65  Laubenheimer 2004.

66  Scott 1999, 90–123.

67  Moses 2004.

68  See EGY157a, described in the catalogue as "string of blue faience and carnelian beads, with one amethyst bead. Bead shapes include grape bunches, a lion, and a falcon."

69  See EGY073 (this is the lid only; the box has not been found).

70  Petrie et al. 1890, 24.

71  In Greco-Roman Egypt neonates and infants were buried in separate areas of cemeteries at Douch (ranging from fetuses of 6 months to children of 6 years). At Aïn el-Labakha and Nag el-Deir, while children of 1–12 years are attested, neonates are not. In these cemeteries the children were mummified and sent to the afterlife with grave goods as adults would be (Dunand 2004).

72  Baker et al. 2005.

73  Baker et al. 2005, 158–60.

74  Scott (1999, 49) notes that the word "'infant' means 'unable to speak.'"

75  Dunand 2004.

76  Dunand 2004, 23; Feucht 2004, 44–46, and see nn. 72–8 there for references.

77  At Middle Kingdom Tell el-Daba, only infants buried in pots and individuals in simple pit burials did not receive the benefits of offering deposits, which suggests that this form of grave good was linked to social status (Müller 1998).

78  Some of the burials in Elephantine that have been the object of careful modern archaeological and stratigraphic analysis indicate that the infants were placed beneath homes that were uninhabited at the time (von Pilgrim 1996a). We cannot tell if this was the case in Lahun as well.

79  In Elephantine, most of the skeletons whose sex could be classified were judged probably male. It may that it was male infants who were specifically selected to be buried close to home (von Pilgrim 1996a). For the divinity of children in other cultures see also Wileman 2005, 95–117.

80  Collier and Quirke 2004, 116–17; UC32153 in Collier and Quirke 2006, 268–9; See the discussions in Kraus 2004, 86, and Kóthay 2001, 356 concerning the use of the Egyptian term "*em aw*" to record a death.

81  In one burial at Abydos, the excavator notes a burial that was carefully arranged with a two-year-old child positioned with a newborn tucked under its chin below an overturned bowl in a pit under the house floor (Adams 1998, 25).

82  Feucht 1995, 103.

83  Feucht 1995, 114.

84 As mentioned above, ostraka and plaster from the walls of New Kingdom settlements provide depictions of what some scholars suggest were confinement shelters (Pinch 1983). If this interpretation is correct the scenes could represent the preparations for the end of the period of seclusion and a reintroduction of the mother and child to society. However, there are no comparable scenes from the Middle Kingdom, and they may be manifestations of a practice prevalent only in the New Kingdom, and perhaps only in Upper Egypt.

85 Morsy 1982, 173.

86 Ward 1986, 3, 8, 12.

87 Ritner 2006, 212.

88 An administrative text from Lahun shows traces of the determinative of the breast and possibly the text referred to a *menat* here, but too little remains to be certain (UC 32143A in Collier and Quirke 2002, 177).

89 Paraphrased from UC 32216 in Collier and Quirke 2002, 153.

90 UC 32124 in Collier and Quirke 2002, 61.

91 Toivari-Viitala 201, 190

92 Feucht 1995, 154.

93 There is consensus among the medical community that the modern western age of menarche (a girl's first menstruation) is unusually low and is continuing to fall because of better nutrition, among other factors. Research by Tanner 1978 showed that the age of onset dropped from an average of 17 in 1830 to 12.8 in 1962. The soundness of his research has been questioned because of his small and selective sample size. All studies, however, show that there is a significant difference in the age of onset between girls in wealthier urban areas and girls from a poorer rural background, with the onset of menarche for the latter significantly later. Strassman's research on the Dogon (1996, 1999b) also suggests we need to rethink fertility norms for the ancient world. Dogon women generally begin menstruating at the age of 16, and have only approximately seven periods a year until they reach their twenties, at which point they marry and begin to bear children. Since this book is focusing on the middle class of Ancient Egypt, I have selected a median age.

94 I am using as a model a non-elite woman who did not make use of a wet nurse, and would thus have breast-fed for an average of three years. This does not assume that breast-feeding would physically prevent pregnancies but that this would have been combined with other methods such as contraception and abstinence (to be discussed later) to create a spacing of nearly three years.

95 This in itself is an unknown factor. In many cultures there is a delay of a minimum of one to two years between onset of menarche and conception of first child. Bagnall and Frier (1994, 114) suggest that the mean age for marriage in Roman Egypt was just over 17.

96 This takes into account the fact that the interval between births tends to be lower after an infant death. See for example Ronsmans 1996.

97 Clark 2005, ch. 2, p. 3. A figure of an average of five birth attempts with two surviving children is also cited by Angel 1972, 98.

98 Bagnall and Frier 1994.

99 Lustig 1997.

100 "Lineal" refers to "consanguines connected by a line of descent. Two such relatives are never from the same generation" (Lustig 1997, 46).

101 "Collateral" refers to "consanguines not directly connected by descent to the next generation. Thus, of two such relatives, neither need be directly related to the other as ancestor or descendant, although there is a line of descent to a common ancestor. Collateral relatives may be of the same or of different generations" (Lustig 1997, 47).

102 Parkinson 1991, 101–7, and see now J. Allen 2002

103 Parkinson 1991, 111–12; UC32163 and UC32164 in Collier and Quirke 2006, 110–15.

104 UC32166 in Collier and Quirke 2006, 116–17; Kraus 2004, 75–99.

105 Toivari-Viitala 2001, 190.

106 For family scenes in early New Kingdom tombs see Whale 1989.

107 For an example of the different interpretations possible of kinship relations in a single tomb see the case of the Middle Kingdom Meir Tomb B-4 described in Lustig 1997, 44, fig. 4.2.

108 Dunand 2004, 30–2.

109 Lichtheim 1976, 141.

110 Fischer 2000, 59–60 n. 50.

# 3

# Close to Home

*When I was yet an infant, I sat in the shelter of my mother's lap, a sling holding me close while she spun her thread. Then I stretched my arms to discover what I might put in my mouth. I found grapes and dates there, all sorts of fine vegetables, and figs, both notched and unnotched. I stuffed one of these dates in my mouth, and dropped the rest because I had too much in my arms. My mother laughed, and then she placed a crocodile of clay into my hands and told me not to be greedy.*[1]

## Weaning

The daily life of an infant like Hedjerit in many ways would have been similar to that of infants today. Egyptian texts consistently establish that infants were breast-fed for approximately three years. Human mother's milk is the most complete food for infants, providing not only nutrition but also antibodies boosting the child's immune system. Hedjerit's first introduction to solid food likely occurred early on, around six months of age, while she was still being breast-fed, and indeed at this time the composition of the milk (whether it was produced by the birth mother or by a wet nurse) would have changed in response to changing needs. At first Hedjerit may have been introduced to pureed or mashed fruit, grains, and vegetables. Research carried out on infant feces at an Upper Egyptian Paleolithic site has shown that about the time they began to crawl, infants there were weaned on ground and mashed vegetables.[2] Determining which plants were eaten in Lahun is tricky, and depends on our correct translation of Egyptian words for foods, and correct identification of archaeological remains that have been carefully recorded in a secure context. Without a lexical list or dictionary it can be difficult to identify the meaning of a word. Classification systems vary from culture to culture, and different names may be applied to a food depending on color, whether it is cooked or not, use, even size or appearance.

Meanings also vary over time and location. Thus today, in the USA the word "corn" is understood to refer to a specific grain, "maize," while in the UK the word refers to "grain" in general (causing the occasional egregious interpretive error). Sometimes a plant has been identified by textual evidence, but does not appear in the surviving archaeological record. An example is "emmer," the most common grain in Egypt and the ancient Near East, for which we surprisingly have no evidence in Lahun. That we have any idea at all as to the flora of Lahun in large part is due to the foresight of the Egyptologist Percy Newberry, who identified and recorded the many different types of plants found in tombs – an important and relatively rare undertaking for the time. Unfortunately, Lahun was excavated at the end of the nineteenth century, and determining the correct context of the finds today is exceedingly difficult. By modern standards the recording of finds at that time was insufficient and inconsistent; the supervisor of the excavation, Sir William Flinders Petrie, had multiple concurrent excavations, many of which were of necessity left unsupervised; and some of the flora identified by Newberry are now shown to have come from a different habitation layer.[3] A particularly illustrative example of the latter has been given by Germer in her recent reanalysis of plant remains, explaining that "red- and blue-dyed wool, so often cited as Middle Kingdom, was recently dated by C14 to c.AD 1200–1400."[4] That is a difference of approximately 3,100 years!

So what would have been the first solid food eaten by Hedjerit? She would not have been fed meat, for at that stage in life it is difficult to digest. In addition, meat was likely a rare dish for the non-elite, who would have received more than enough protein from legumes, let alone the fish to which they had access. Indeed different kinds of fish are the most commonly listed goods in administrative texts. Fruits have been found, particularly in tombs where the dry air helped preservation. In particular, fruits from three species of palm trees might have been used: the dom palm and argun palm, both of which are attested by material remains, and the date palm, which is another example of a plant mentioned in textual records from Lahun, but with no surviving material trace. Plum-like fruits called "balanites," sycamore figs, and Christ's thorn fruits provided tasty sweet treats.[5] Barley has been found in Lahun, but as mentioned above, there was surprisingly no trace of protein-rich emmer. Once the child's digestive system had matured a bit, the simple addition of combinations of legumes and groundnuts would have raised the protein levels of cereals dramatically. Evidence for peas has been found in Lahun, but it is unknown if these were wild peas or specifically cultivated. In either case, they could have been easily cooked and included in a baby's puree. Lentils and faba beans may have been cooked, mashed, and added to the diet as well. Carob fruit has also been found, which would add not only a chocolate-like sweet flavor, but protein.

For a teething child, the gums might have been rubbed with honey, a practice that is known in the Islamic world. Modern western dental practice discourages

46

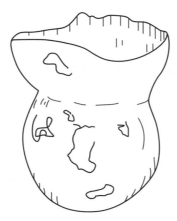

**Figure 3.1** Drawing of pinched vase, The Manchester Museum, The University of Manchester, EGY413 (h. 8.0 cm × w. 6.8 cm) (courtesy of Sam Channer).

the use of any sugary substance for teething as it can lead to tooth decay. But honey was a popular medicinal product in Ancient Egypt and is well attested in Lahun, and we even have the remains of pottery beehives surviving from this site. Note that one of the Lahun letters mentions honey being requisitioned from the "house of nurses," perhaps for this purpose.[6] Hedjerit's brother, Senbubu, would likely have experimentally offered her a taste of liquids that he himself enjoyed as well, sometimes perhaps from the tips of his fingers that infants naturally suck, thus introducing her slowly to the foods she would eventually be reliant upon for survival. As she got older, she could have been fed from a simple clay vessel with pinched sides so the contents would have less chance of spillage. Petrie found a number of bowls of this kind within the town of Lahun.[7] The cups are small and are made of common Nile-silt clay, which is what we would expect for vessels for everyday use. Conceivably, they could have been used for the feeding of infants and small children, as well as that of anyone who was debilitated or infirm. Two can be firmly dated, as they were found together with seals bearing the name of Senusret III in a box (Fig. 3.1). The box was probably used for the burial of a baby,[8] and it may be that the vessels were provided to ensure the infant could receive proper nourishment in the afterlife.

The elite cemetery at nearby Lisht has also yielded a more elaborate version of a small feeding cup that provides further clues that it was intended for the very young. While the ones in Lahun were made of undecorated clay, this one was made of blue faience and rather than being pinched, it had a little spout (Fig. 3.2).[9] The outside was painted with a parade of powerful and apotropaic

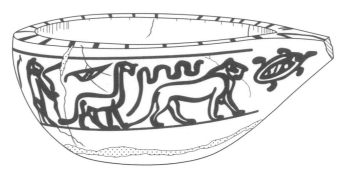

**Figure 3.2** Drawing of baby cup in J. P. Allen 2005, 30–1, object #23 (h. 3.5 cm × w. 8.0 cm) (courtesy of Sam Channer).

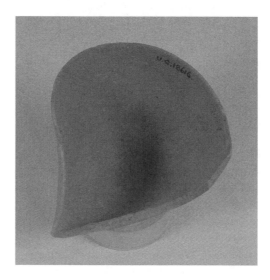

**Figure 3.3** Clay pinched bowl UC18616 (h. 5.1 cm × w. 10.2 cm (courtesy of the Petrie Museum of Egyptian Archaeology).

creatures that are already familiar to us from the hippopotamus birth tusks. These include: a turtle, snakes, a serapod, a crocodile, lions, and two serpent-wielding Bes- or Beset-images (Beset is the female counterpart of Bes). The depiction of a hippopotamus and the *sa*-sign, which means "protection," confirms that the function of the apotropaic figures was to protect the contents of the vessel, thus safeguarding the health of the child. A vessel from Lahun is a bit larger, but it is roughly the same shape (Fig. 3.3). Although it might look like a lamp, it does not have any traces of oil.

Many diseases and conditions caused by poor diet in childhood are visible even in the human remains of adults. An analysis of bone and teeth[10] in particular can help indicate childhood stress and what the dietary intake of infants might have been. For example, excessive porosity in the bones of an adult indicates chronic ill-health that may have stemmed from conditions prevalent during childhood.[11] Harris lines in bones appear as shadows in X-rays and indicate periods of arrested growth due to malnutrition and illness during the individual's youth. Unfortunately, the skeletons at Haraga, which may have been the main burial ground for the inhabitants of Lahun, were not examined by a forensic anthropologist. This would not only have enabled us to learn about the general health of the populace, but could have enhanced our understanding of their access to proper nutrition, and perhaps provide further clues as to what sorts of foods a child such as Hedjerit would have been weaned on and had access to later.

A new form of analysis to answer the question of foods used for weaning was performed on a sample from a Roman-Period cemetery at Dakleh Oasis.[12] By using stable nitrogen and carbon isotope analysis of the remains of skeletons, fauna, and flora in the area, scholars concluded that the weaning process would have begun at about six months of age by introducing millet-fed goat's or cow's milk. This forensic evidence was confirmed by the Roman textual sources that provide guidelines on weaning practices, thus concurrently reflecting the extent to which this particular Egyptian community adopted Roman practices. Hopefully more analyses of this kind on Middle Kingdom Egyptian populations will be undertaken in the future.


## Child Care

Before becoming self-sufficiently mobile, Hedjerit would have needed to be carried. In some cultures, newborns are placed in cradleboards or swaddled for ease of transportation, as well as for safety and comfort. In Ancient Egypt, however, there is no representational or material evidence for the use of swaddling or of cradleboards. The Egyptian word *tjam*[13] with the determinative for linen or cloth refers to covering or binding, and from the New Kingdom on it can be used in reference to small children. This could be translated as swaddling, but it could also denote a sling. It is likely that Ancient Egyptian infants were carried by their mother or caregiver close to the body in a sling.[14] From the Predynastic Period on, images in both sculpture and painting depict infants being held in the arms of their mother (or nurse) and carried just to the side, on her hip, or on her belly, legs wrapped around her waist, ready to suckle. These can be contrasted with Middle Kingdom images of Asiatics carrying their infants on their back. One New Kingdom tomb painting depicts the tomb owner watching over laborers working on his fields. In the background, under a tree, sits a woman picking fruit with her child on her lap held in place by a sling.[15] From the sling, the child reaches up to fiddle with her caregiver's ear.

The woman may be the child's mother, but she could also be a nurse or a relative. In any case, though there is no direct Middle Kingdom material evidence, slings are used around the world to keep children close and safe while their caregiver engages in daily activities and work, and were likely used in Ancient Egypt as well. The Egyptians recognized that the protection, care, and raising of a child were a serious and difficult responsibility, and textual evidence confirms that in this culture mothers were highly respected and praised as powerful and important individuals.

While fathers were also depicted in close familial relationships with their children, these are usually more formal. The Middle Kingdom funerary stela of Dedusobek shows the deceased sitting on a chair with his dog beneath and his son on his lap. His wife is also depicted giving him offerings, while his daughter and another son are named but not depicted. The practice of naming but not necessarily showing the family members was common, and reminds us that the images should not be taken at face value. It may be that it was especially important to immortalize the eldest son on a relief, as this would ensure that the opening of the mouth ritual (to be discussed in chapter 9) would be properly performed and the deceased would be able to successfully enter the afterlife.

In terms of caring for the children, it is likely that all members of the extended family participated, including the fathers. Older children, in particular those between the ages of six and ten,[16] enjoy playing with and taking care of younger children, and the data suggests that in Lahun homes were inhabited by extended family units as well as the nuclear family, and servants were in abundance as well. Lists of workers as well as legal contracts reveal that many of these servants were foreigners, in particular those called *Aamu* or Asiatics by the Egyptians.

Most of these would have come from the Levant – the region of Canaan and Palestine – but trade was also known as far north as Syria. If we assume that at least some of these foreigners were relative newcomers to Egypt, like immigrants everywhere they may have retained their native language, as well as learning the Egyptian spoken by the majority. One of the best-attested jobs held by foreign women was that of servant, and some lived with their children in the home of their master or mistress. From a very young age, some children would have been exposed to at least one other language from hearing the servants and playing with other children, and some (particularly those of foreign descent) might have been fully bilingual, able to switch from one language to another with ease. Unfortunately this is another aspect of life invisible in the archaeological record, and for which we must rely on ethnographic evidence and our understanding of childhood language learning behaviors.

The children of Lahun seem to have been integrated into the daily life of the town, and letters to officials often acknowledge the children. These letters are unfortunately often very fragmentary, but enough remains to give us an idea of the concerns expressed in them. In one, Dedusobek, who is the "servant of the personal estate," writes to the overseer of the temple, and mentions "Moreover, as for the . . . about it along with the children of the lord l.p.h."[17] On the reverse

**Figure 3.4** Girl with sidelock of youth from the tomb-chapel of Ukhotpe, after A. M. Blackman and Apted 1953, plate 15 (courtesy of the Egypt Exploration Society).

of the fragment we can read "Do? your children want . . . ?"[18] One long letter written to the temple-overseer, Ptahpuwah, retains the address, giving us the name of the sender, the date it was sent, and the delivery person: "The lord l.p.h. The temple-overseer Ptahpuwah. From Iemiatib, Month 1 of *akhet* day 15. Brought by the cultivator Neni"; it also includes a standard greeting: "And greet the children of/and the entire estate."[19] Another letter apparently concerns an allocation of grain that has not been provided to a child ". . . without them giving the cereal-thereof to the child belonging to us yet they requested it on account of him. You should thus write about it to the overseer of singers Senwosret about having. . . ."[20] At the very least, the letters reveal a society that did not ignore its children, but acknowledged them as active and dynamic members of society.

Children thus had a place in representations of an ideal life that was meant to last for eternity. Throughout most of Egypt's history they were represented with three characteristics distinguishing them from adults: they were usually completely naked or wore a bit of jewelry, both males and females sported sidelocks of hair, and they often had a finger to the mouth (Fig. 3.4). Janssen has noted

51

that the Middle Kingdom children at this time are often shown in dress similar to that of the adults portrayed.[21] This is unlikely to represent a change in practice, but rather reflects a temporary change in artistic convention and canons. However, it is likely that the standard representations do reflect reality to a large extent. Both boys and girls in all time periods are shown as having their heads shaved or close-cropped, except for a single wide braid or two or more pigtails. Jewelry and pendants are sometimes depicted as being worn in the sidelock, and this may have been how some of the amuletic pendants that have been found in Middle Kingdom sites were worn.

This practice is confirmed, albeit by a young woman rather than a child, by one of the *Tales of Wonder*, a series of tales told to amuse the king. Although set in the Old Kingdom, they are now thought to have been composed in the Middle Kingdom. In one of the stories, to cheer himself up, the king, on the advice of his magician, goes out on the lake in a boat rowed by 20 young women unclothed but for fish-nets. A wonderful time is had until suddenly, a turquoise fish-pendant drops from the braid of one of the women.[22] Amusingly, she refuses to row until it is retrieved by the magician, who is able to part the waters to find it. For the elite and the lower classes, the sidelock would have been a convenient means of keeping the child's hair out of the way, but more importantly, it represented childhood as a stage of life. As will be discussed below, hair played an important role in rituals, and the childhood sidelock was no exception.

Depending on the religious and cultural restrictions, clothing and diapers can be optional during the day in hot climates such as that of Egypt. The practice of allowing children to be naked continues today in many areas of African, Asia, and Middle and South America, and in the day during the summer months even in colder climes. Examples of children's clothing, including simple tunics that resemble bags with slits for arms and small neck holes, as well as sleeves that could be added to other garments, have survived from Ancient Egypt, and these would perhaps have been reserved for colder nights as well as festive or ritual occasions.[23] Leaving children minimally dressed would also aid in toilet training. In cultures where the mother remains close to the infant on a daily basis and learns to recognize the signals that the infant needs to eliminate, potty training begins as early as one to three months of age.[24] By the time Hedjerit was able to move around and play outside with other children, she would have been familiar with the appropriate places to squat and relieve herself.[25] As discussed previously, the larger estates had small rooms that were possibly used as bathrooms or lavatories behind the bedrooms; the smaller homes did not have such extra rooms. In these homes, it is possible that the equivalent of chamber pots could have been used at night. These would be difficult to identify in the archaeological record, as any sort of old pot, or for that matter for the outdoors a pot-stand, would do. This type of toilet training would also have eliminated a medical problem that is common in the modern western world – diaper rash. For all the myriad health problems that afflicted Ancient Egyptian babies, ranging from anemia to diarrhea to snakebites, and any one of dozens of ailments that were blamed on hostile entities, this is one that they did not have to deal with.

## Play

The remains of homes in Lahun do not show any obvious evidence of separate segregated sleeping or playing areas for the children. Infants would probably have slept with their parents and with their siblings in the bedrooms, likely located in the more private rear of the house away from the front door. While still unable to walk, infants would have been carried close to their mother in slings, but once they became mobile, there would have been plenty of room to play with other children outside in the warmth. The streets of Lahun were fairly broad – the main streets were five meters wide, and the side streets three or four meters.[26] Even at a very young age, once she was mobile Hedjerit would have played out in the streets with the other young neighborhood children. Rather than keeping an eye on her constantly, her mother likely charged Hedjerit's older brother to watch over his younger sister. Women in Lahun may also have shared supervisory duties, with mothers or servants taking turns watching over groups of children, leaving others free to perform different activities. This type of communal caregiving, which is common in many parts of the world, including Africa, would be a natural development in a town with homes at close quarters such as Lahun.

Playing games is also a natural childhood activity, which exercises children's physical, mental, and imaginative faculties, and instills local social values as well. Depictions on tomb walls suggest that many of the games involved much physical activity, and some of the older children are shown playing with balls, examples of which have been found in Lahun.[27] There is, unfortunately, little data available to indicate interaction and play during early childhood years – this phase of life was not usually depicted in images. We do not know if boys and girls were separated or played together, whether competitive, co-operative, or helpful games were encouraged, whether different skill sets were encouraged according to gender, or whether social distinctions were established, such as might be the case if servants were not allowed to romp with the householder's children.[28] As will be discussed later, Middle Kingdom tombs do depict games and dances performed by older children or young adults, but the very young are not included. However, Egyptian art was not meant to represent reality, and children, whether they are represented as doing so or not, imitate their elders. Versions of games such as those may well have been played in the streets of Lahun by children like Hedjerit and Senbubu.

Childhood is a time of intensive learning, and values, traditions, customs, and beliefs become deeply ingrained, and are then re-enacted and eventually passed on again later in life. This enculturation occurs during observation of adults, through work and play activities, and also through interaction with accessible artifacts, including toys. Specifically designed toys for the sole use of children were probably few and far between, and the concept of an industry devoted to

**Figure 3.5** Toy top UC7147 (l. 6.3 cm) (courtesy of the Petrie Museum of Egyptian Archaeology).

this purpose again reflects a modern western practice. Lahun does provide us with a few examples of objects the primary use of which was probably as toys, such as colorful "whip tops" – conical pieces of wood that would be continuously twirled by whipping with twine or string (Fig. 3.5).[29]

Other artifacts have been found at Lahun that seem to have been used in games. On the basis of English parallels, almond-shaped pieces of wood ranging in size from 6.9 cm to 16 cm and wooden pointed sticks about 25–40 cm in length have been interpreted as equipment for playing an ancient version of "tipcat."[30] This game, popular during England's Industrial Revolution, consists of a player attempting to make the almond-shaped piece of wood jump into the air by hitting it with the longer pointed stick. This is of course only one of numerous possible interpretations for these objects, which were discovered by the English excavator Petrie.[31] If these wooden artifacts had initially been excavated by a scholar from another country, they might have been interpreted in a completely different way on the basis of customs and practices familiar to that excavator. A sling that was found could have been used as a toy, as a weapon for hunting small game, or in practice combat games.[32]

Even in the case of these seemingly obvious objects that look so familiar to the modern eye, caution must be maintained in determining their use without any visual or textual corroborating evidence. In most rural areas of the world children play with objects that surround them, be they spoons, or sticks, or pottery shards, or stones that are naturally in the shape of people or animals. Children also use their imaginations and create their own playthings. In Egypt, mud would have been an ideal and plentiful substance for children to use. Indeed mud objects in the shape of animals have been found in Lahun that were originally described as toys. For the most part the animals are quadrupeds; some are

**Figure 3.6** Mud pig UC7186 (l. 8.9 cm)
(courtesy of the Petrie Museum of Egyptian
Archaeology).

**Figure 3.7** Mud bird UC7189 (l. 5.2 cm)
(courtesy of the Petrie Museum of Egyptian
Archaeology).

clearly crocodiles, some seem to be hippopotami, some might be pigs, apes, or birds, while others are more difficult to identify (Figs. 3.6 and 3.7).

Female figurines have also been found of mud, wood, or fired clay, and these were also initially labeled as dolls and categorized as toys (Fig. 3.8). Determining the function of all these objects, and indeed how to classify them, is no simple matter.[33] Many of the female dolls have their genital areas clearly emphasized in some way. For example, most of the faience and wooden examples have a series of dots in a reverse triangle formation over the pubic region. Some of the mud examples have no arms or legs, some have clearly marked breasts, others have none; but all have the pelvis emphasized, some with a grain of corn embedded within a triangle.

Figure 3.8 Mud female UC7156 (h. 12 cm) (courtesy of the Petrie Museum of Egyptian Archaeology).

That some of these categories of artifacts[34] were not toys, at least not purely, is proved by their being discovered in contexts unrelated to children, such as the tombs of both men and women, shrines, and military structures such as forts. It is now thought that the wooden, faience, and fired clay female figurines with marked genitalia operated to reflect the value placed on women as stimulators of fertility (which in Ancient Egypt was the male's responsibility) for both birth in this life and rebirth in the afterlife.[35]

The grain of corn embedded in the pelvis of some mud figurines seems to be a transparent marker of the womb as being the source of new growth and emergent life. The Egyptians were aware that the source of conception was male seed (the source of fertility) placed in a woman's womb, and the mud female figurines seem to virtually spell out this idea. While these objects likely were used to magically enhance a woman's ability to successfully conceive and give birth, they also would have functioned as impromptu teaching tools. Children are naturally attracted to objects that represent the human form, and being exposed to objects like this, perhaps being allowed to help create them, even if only by gathering clay and watching their formation, or seeing them in household shrines, children would have been exposed to and enculturated into their gender roles from a very early age.[36]

**Figure 3.9** Mud crocodile UC7196 (l. 5 cm) (courtesy of the Petrie Museum of Egyptian Archaeology).

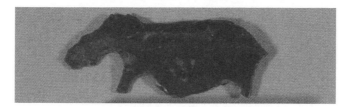

**Figure 3.10** Flint hippopotamus UC16780 (l. 5 cm) (courtesy of the Petrie Museum of Egyptian Archaeology).

There is also some question as to whether these dolls were not at times clothed rather than in the naked condition we usually find them. One such figure was found shaped in the form of a woman holding a smaller female, with linen wrapped around them both.[37] Both figures are made of clay, and the larger one has hair woven into a series of holes at the top her head. The smaller figure has the holes, but the hair itself is missing. She also features a hole around the ear area, a large necklace of clay around her neck, and prominent breasts. The larger figure is tapered at the bottom, which would make the pair easy to hold, or alternatively to stick into the ground. The linen is wrapped around both of them keeping them tightly bound. While this doll and others of the same shape date to the early New Kingdom, dolls could have been "dressed" in the Middle Kingdom as well. Perhaps these were indeed played with by children. After all, dolls often show their sex, and the female sexual characteristics are the ones more easily rendered.

Equally possible is a scenario whereby although these objects were initially created with a more ritualistic use in mind, they were secondarily used as toys or cast off and appropriated by children. The animal figurines, for example, tend to represent powerful creatures such as crocodiles and hippos that also played an important religious role in the area of Illahun (Figs. 3.9 and 3.10). The crocodile was the icon of the god Sobek, who was particularly worshiped in the region of the Fayum. Indeed, the name of the main lake in the Fayum was *she-sobek* "Lake of Sobek," and a temple founded by Amenemhat III and his son Amenemhat IV and dedicated to a triad consisting of the god Sobek, the goddess Renenutet (represented as a serpent or a snake with the head of a woman), and Horus can be found in Medinet Madi.

The sacred significance of the hippopotamus has already been discussed, in particular its association with the protective goddesses of fertility Taweret and Ipet. Similar figures of the same animals (along with figures of other animals such as birds and fish, vessels, and clay figurines of females in both Egyptian and Nubian style) formed from unfired mud are also found in the Middle Kingdom multicultural fortress settlement of Askut in Nubia.[38] These and other remains found in domestic contexts at Askut may suggest an intermingling of Nubian culture (possibly through Nubian wives) with that of the colonial Egyptian inhabitants, with largely Egyptian religious practices. Similar finds at military sites lacking an obvious familial context, such as Uronarti, also seem to point toward the objects having a primarily ritual use, and this is certainly one plausible scenario.[39]

Again, however, we need to keep in mind the multivalent nature of objects. Playing with these artifacts would have familiarized children with the religious icons that would have such an important role at the level of both household cults and more formal religion.[40] All family members may also have participated in cultic rituals from an early age, for example by being responsible for depositing a votive offering, such as a mud crocodile, to the god Sobek. Figurines also help to re-enact and pass on myths, as well as stories and tales. One can imagine children playing out a mock battle between a mud crocodile and hippo, parallel to scenes that appear on the walls of Old Kingdom tombs.

Animal shapes are relatively easy formations to manage for budding artists and craftsmen, and it would be difficult if not impossible to differentiate the work of inexperienced older apprentices from that of children imitating their elders and preparing to be productive members of the labor force.[41] We must also keep in mind that children tend to carry around artifacts and deposit them in unexpected areas (though not necessarily randomly). This creates even more problems for archaeologists attempting to determine original context, function, and purpose thousands of years later.

Finally, to label an artifact as a toy is not to belittle its function. Even if they are basic by today's standards, toys are an important means of passing on traditions and cultural mores, and even of instilling fears, desires, and social expectations into each successive generation. Toys could even have been made by older children for younger children. On the other hand, we must not think of children as simply passive absorbers of information – they are active participants in the community. Children are themselves inventive and can come up with their own ways of adapting to their environment and dealing with the people around them. They are not simply smaller versions of adults, but even at a young age have their own agendas. Recent anthropological work on childhood reminds us that "even though children's play may reproduce features of adult roles and activities, the intent may have been to mock, make fun of, and even challenge the social order."[42]

## Playing with Pets

In addition to playing with each other and with toys, children would also have played with animals, especially dogs.[43] In the Old Kingdom the Egyptians experimented with the domestication of various wild animals, but most of these attempts proved unsuccessful. One of the earliest animals to be depicted as domesticated in Egypt was the dog. From the Predynastic Period dogs are shown with collars and leashes close to humans, mostly in hunting scenes. By the Middle Kingdom, at least three distinct types or breeds of dogs were common, and they were included on tomb walls, complete with names to ensure their survival in the afterlife with their owners. A famous example comes from the stela of WahAnkh Intef II, a king of Dynasty 11 who included reliefs and names of his five dogs in his own mortuary chapel. WahAnkh immortalized his dogs by listing their names, which were of Libyan origin (some of them were translated on the stela into Egyptian): "Behkai, that is to say: Gazelle," "Abaqer" (likely Berber "hound"), "Pehtes, that is to say Black One," "Teqru, that is to say Khenfet-kettle," and "Tekenru."[44]

One of the main types of dog was the hound – depicted with classic deep-chested hound bodies and long legs. Some with perky ears and curly tails resemble basenjis, a hunting dog from Africa, while others have floppy ears or looser tails, and bring to mind greyhounds, salukis, ibizan hounds, and pharaoh hounds (Fig. 3.11). Other dogs were more short-legged and squat, while spotted dogs were particularly popular in the Middle Kingdom. These white dogs with large black spots make a regular appearance in Middle Kingdom tombs as pets, and even as guardian deities in later religious compositions. In the Middle Kingdom tomb of Djehutyhotep in Beni Hassan we find a large, bulky spotty

**Figure 3.11** Dogs from the Middle Kingdom tomb of Sarenput I at Aswan (courtesy of Ken Griffin).

**Figure 3.12**  Spotted dog based on the Middle Kingdom coffin of Khui of Asyut, now in the Cairo Museum (courtesy of JJ Shirley).

dog named "Ankhu" (Living One) among a row of tribute-bearers as well as under the tomb owner's chair,[45] while in other tombs and coffins in the same region we find spotted hunting dogs (Fig. 3.12).

The Egyptians employed different words to refer to dogs, although determining the exact meaning of these terms is difficult. They may have grouped dogs by physical type, or by function, or by phase of life. In general, it is thought that the word *tjezem* refers to a hound type, or perhaps the hunting dogs. This word is used in a literary text from Lahun, ". . . as a dog [circles?] his master . . . ,"[46] in what is likely an analogy similar to that found in the Middle Kingdom text the *Instruction of Amenemhat I*, where the king states that he "made the Asiatics do the dog walk." Here, the pharaoh is describing the Asiatics as being under his control like obedient and subservient dogs. Dogs also appear in the earliest veterinary text known, also found in Lahun. One small fragment possibly concerns a dog's toothache, and reads:[47]

> [. . .] of its teeth, aching
> [. . .] . . . in pain (?) [. . .]
> [. . .] its [ . . . ] it is tired [. . .]
> [. . .] hound (?) of . . . [. . .]

In this text, another word for dog is used: "*iu.*" This may be an onomatopoeic word imitating the "*iuu iuu*" sound that dogs and puppies make. Again, we cannot be certain of what the distinction was between these two words – all we can say is that there was one. Although hunting was their primary use in the

Middle Kingdom (there is evidence of the use of dogs for policing as well in the New Kingdom, and as mascots for the king in battle), they were also kept as pets, and we can realistically imagine that puppies would have had a special appeal for children, as would kittens.

The town of Lahun had granaries within the larger estates, and where there is grain there are rats. Petrie noted that nearly all the homes in Lahun had holes in the walls from rats, and these holes still bore the evidence of having been stuffed up in an attempt to keep out the rodents.[48] An odd, rectangular artifact made of fired clay with air slits and sliding door, which was originally described as a chicken coop, has more recently been described as possibly a rat trap.[49] In areas where there are rats, we usually find that there are cats. Again, evidence of the use of cats to help in the elimination of vermin is found in Ancient Egypt, but evidence for the domestication of cats as pets does not appear until the New Kingdom. It is only then that we have a reference to a cat being named. The word for cat is also onomatopoeic: "*miu*," obviously reproducing the sound that cats make. In any case, it is highly likely that cats would have been a familiar sight in the town of Lahun, even if they were not strictly speaking kept as pets.

The streets of Lahun would thus have been filled with the sound of barking dogs, the braying of donkeys, pigeons cooing, babies crying when hungry, and children laughing as they played. Hedjerit and other children who survived weaning learned about their world and their role within it by interacting with their environment, its animals, and its people. In the next chapter, the role that material culture played in the life experience of an Ancient Egyptian, especially in terms of forming and reflecting social identity and cultural norms, will be developed.

## Notes

1   Crocodiles were associated with greed (and with officials) in Ancient Egypt.
2   Wileman 2005, 20.
3   Germer 1998.
4   Germer 1998, 84.
5   See Germer 1998, 86–8.
6   UC 32124 in Collier and Quirke 2004, 61.
7   Petrie et al. 1890, 20, pl. XIII 89, 90; See also EGY412–18.
8   Petrie et al. 1890, 25, pl. XIV 18, 20; Quirke 2006, 102.
9   Allen 2005, 30–31, object #23.
10  Rose et al. 1993.
11  Rose 2006, 73–6; Wapler et al. 2004.
12  Dupras et al. 2001.
13  *Wb* V, 354.
14  R. Janssen and Janssen 1990, 20.
15  From TT69, the tomb of Menna.
16  Kamp 2001, 16.

17 "l.p.h." is a standard epithet meaning "life, prosperity, health." UC 32119F Fragment ii in Collier and Quirke 2002, 45.

18 UC 32119F verso Fragment ii in Collier and Quirke 2002, 45.

19 Slightly adapted from UC 32198 Fragment ii in Collier and Quirke 2002, 45.

20 UC 32116F in Collier and Quirke 2002, 45.

21 R. Janssen and Janssen 1990, 26.

22 One fish-pendant that may have been worn in a sidelock from Haraga was found in the grave of a child "about 10 years old" (Engelbach 1923, pl. X, 14.).

23 For examples see R. Janssen and Janssen 1990, 32–7.

24 See in particular the East African Digo, who complete toilet training when the child is five or six months old (deVries and deVries 1977).

25 Some cultures leave the child naked, others dress them in skirts, dresses, or crotchless trousers that open when the child squats.

26 Quirke 2006, 48.

27 For an overview of games that might have been played in general see R. Janssen and Janssen 1990, 55–66.

28 Kamp 2001, 14.

29 Examples still showing the groove can be found in Petrie et al. 1890, 30 and see UC7147 and UC7148.

30 See for example David 1986, 163. Examples of the almond-shaped sticks are UC7146, and the pointed sticks UC7144 and UC7145.

31 Petrie et al. 1890, 30.

32 Petrie et al. 1890, 30.

33 For the following see Quirke 1998a.

34 See Pinch 1993.

35 Roth 2000.

36 Kamp 2001, 12–14.

37 Hayes 1959 vol. 2, 17.

38 Smith 2003, 131–5.

39 Quirke 1998a.

40 This should come as no surprise, for we can easily find outlets today that mass produce biblical action figures (even available in a variety of skin tones). See for example www.trainupachild.com.

41 Wileman 2005, 59–60.

42 Schwarzman 2006, 127.

43 Rice 2006.

44 Parkinson 1991, 113.

45 An image can be seen at www.osirisnet.net/tombes/el_bersheh/djehoutyhotep/ e_djehoutyhotep_02.htm.

46 UC 32117C in Collier and Quirke 2004, 41.

47 UC 32036 Fragment D in Collier and Quirke 2004, 57. The veterinary papyrus was originally published by Griffith, who interpreted another segment as a treatment for a dog with worms in his eyes (Griffith 1898, 13), which could make sense if Fragment D belonged to the long segment. However, in Collier and Quirke's revised edition there is no indication that the two fragments are linked, or that the long section concerns dogs, and indeed the next two treatments are for bulls. I cannot see any sign related to dogs in the images of the papyrus fragment itself. The

treatment suggests a rectal examination by hand, which would also be more realistically accomplished on a bull than a dog.

48   Petrie et al. 1891, 8.
49   UC 16773. A three-dimensional reconstruction can be found at www.kahun.man. ac.uk/school_rattrap.htm.

# 4

# The Stuff of Life

*One day, when Ra had already appeared in glory in the horizon, I awoke and my heart was filled with joy at the fragrance of barley and bread. My belly hungered, and I went forth to find my mother baking and singing. When she saw me her heart was happy more than anything and she sat me down. She reached over to a wooden box, opened it, and removed a comb and a fish-pendant of new turquoise. Placing me on her lap, she combed my sidelock of youth until it shone like lapis-lazuli,[1] and placed the beautiful fish-pendant in my hair. She then removed the "living one"[2] from the box, and allowed me to see my face in it.*

Children watch their parents' preparations for daily activities and in the process assimilate the associated embedded social values and norms of behavior. Even apparently mundane processes such as the application of cosmetics and the selection and donning of specific clothing and jewelry are not only practical, but can function as external articulations of current status, gender, age, role, class, and ethnicity that are transparent to those sharing the common cultural code. These codes are not only culturally bound, but are shaped by geography, time period, and social group. The same seemingly innocuous accessory can convey a dramatically different message when moved to a different context.

One modern example is the wearing of a handkerchief. Functionally, a handkerchief is simply a square piece of fabric that may be white or colored, embroidered, or otherwise decorated. Its initial function was that of maintaining personal hygiene in a decorous manner – to wipe one's hands, blow one's nose, trap a cough, or dry tears. However, it can also be used as a clothing accessory that signals the wearer as a fashion-conscious individual, as a member of a particular gang, or as having specific sexual preferences, depending on the culture within which it is worn. To an individual who has never experienced those contexts, these uses might not even be conceivable. That same hanky, placed by itself in an exhibit case, conveys none of these meanings. The viewer is left without any hint as to who used it, for what purpose, when, or what meaning it held for that individual. Without the clues provided by context, our understanding of the object remains limited.

This is an issue constantly confronting anyone attempting to interpret the past. Even when trying to reconstruct the activities of everyday life, we must rely on the scattered physical remains and what little information we have on the original context. Comparative anthropology and research into the range of uses of similar items in other cultures can help broaden the questions we ask concerning function, symbolism, and meaning, but the ultimate reconstruction must be based on theories derived from the internal evidence. In terms of personal preparation for daily activities, we are lucky that the settlement of Lahun has left us with a variety of physical remains, as well as textual references. The chapter will focus on some the prevalent domestic items that would have helped Hedjerit learn about her cultures, its customs, and its norms.

## Cosmetics

Cosmetic jars are a type of artifact that was found in relative abundance in the private sections of homes in Lahun. Usually made of stone or pottery, they have survived the centuries, and some still contain the residual remains of their contents (Fig. 4.1).[3] When dealing with any vessels, the form and material provide initial clues as to use. From an early age, Hedjerit would have learnt to recognize that the squat, round-bodied vessels with a pronounced flat perpendicular rim

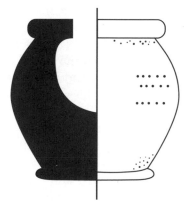

**Figure 4.1** Drawing of kohl pot after The Manchester Museum, The University of Manchester, EGY151a (h. 4.7 cm × w. 5.9 cm) (courtesy of Sam Channer).

**Figure 4.2** Drawing of kohl pot and lid after The Manchester Museum, The University of Manchester, EGY149 (h. 2.9 cm × w. 4.3 cm) (courtesy of Sam Channer).

(sometimes the rims are separate as in Fig. 4.2) and flat lids (sometimes grooved to ensure a tighter fit) often held kohl, the eye-liner still used in Egypt. Examples of kohl pots from Lahun have been found made of pottery[4] and faience,[5] as well as stone[6] such as porphyry, greywacke, basalt, and calcite. Some tubes found in Ancient Egypt contained two compartments, one that would hold black kohl, the other green.[7]

Hedjerit would have become familiar with the contents through watching both parents apply the kohl to their eyes by dipping a stick into the container, mixing the powder with fat, placing the kohl stick between the lids, closing the eye, and then gently running the stick across, thus coating the inside of both lids with the black or green eye-liner. Examples of kohl applicators made of wood, hematite,[8] and ivory[9] have survived. Green kohl, which can also be seen on statues in the Old Kingdom, was made from the mineral malachite. Black kohl, however, was made from a type of lead mineral called galena, which has many anti-bacterial properties and keeps away flies, and because black absorbs light it was also used to resist the glare of the sun.[10] Unfortunately kohl is absorbed into the body, with the result that the galena can cause lead poisoning.[11] This is especially dangerous for children, and if kohl was applied to the eyes of children in Lahun as it is today in Egypt, this would have exacerbated their health problems.

That kohl was an important item to the Egyptians for more than just its cosmetic properties is confirmed clearly by the appearance of the black eye-paint (in Egyptian *mesdemet*) in offering lists to the deceased and in medical texts, as well as in administrative lists. Examples from Lahun include inventories of "items taken in the removal." It is not known from where the items were removed, or for what purpose. One of the modern editors of the removal lists suggests that they could have been a list of provisions for a journey, perhaps a boat journey or a pleasure trip to the Fayum by a member of an elite couple.[12] Clues to the presence of a woman include the listing of the "seal of a woman," as well as a mirror case. Two of these removal lists include a small wooden box that contained something made of gold, amethyst, silver, and a bag of eye-paint.[13] This suggests that these materials were apportioned from a storehouse or residence; thus a stock of kohl would be provided in a bag, and then its new owner would place it in a jar for daily use.

Other small jars would have held unguents or oil of vegetable and animal origin. Numerous small unguent vessels of various materials have been found in Lahun, as well as being mentioned in removal lists. For personal use, the oil would likely have been based on vegetable oil scented with flowers or resins, and could have been used both for preparing cosmetics and for moisturizing skin, which can easily turn dry in the hot climate of Egypt. This oil appears in letters such as this request from the mistress of the house Iku: "Have sent to me a little oil from [. . .] bring to you oil. . . ."[14] Oil also had a medicinal purpose, appearing frequently in the Lahun Gynecological Papyrus,[15] as well as in a letter confirming the delivery of oil to the house of nurses, perhaps to help soothe the chafed skin of a wet nurse.[16]

# Hair

Oils could also have been used on hair. The Egyptians paid great attention to their hair and it stands out as a readily visible marker of age, gender, ethnicity, class, rank, role, and even emotional state. For example, female mourners in funeral processions are usually shown wearing wigs of long locks, cast over the front of their face as they weep.[17] Young children, whether male or female, are instantly recognizable by their sidelock. Men of the Late Middle Kingdom are usually depicted as beardless and clean-shaven. The hair of Hedjerit's parents was probably kept closely cropped. This is verified by the presence of hair on human remains, and by depictions of natural hair peeking out below wigs. Hairstyles were easily changed through the use of extensions and of wigs, examples of which have been found in Lahun. The hair of these examples seems to be thick and only lightly curled, while another bunch of surviving hair has been plaited into individual braids and decorated with beads.[18]

Both of these examples are of human hair, though others have been found made of animal hair. Some of the wigs have a thatched pad underneath, which would also have helped keep the scalp cool. A wide range of styles can be found in the Middle Kingdom, and the following is just a sample. In the Late Middle Kingdom, the prestige wig for men seems to have been either of shoulder length and worn tucked behind the ears, or closely cropped. The close-cropped look appears often on relatives, friends, and co-workers of the deceased, again emphasizing that in art the hairstyle is indicative of rank or status. Women also wore rather short wigs with a slight curl,[19] as well as long straight ones arranged both on the back and over each shoulder down the chest. Dancers are shown with a single long pony tail with a large bead or ball at the end. A style that was later associated with the goddess Hathor – a straight part in the center with the hair tucked behind the ears and a pronounced flip or curl at the bottom of each side

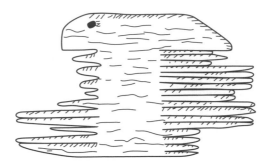

**Figure 4.3** Drawing of comb after The Manchester Museum, The University of Manchester, EGY225a (h. 6.9 cm × w. 4.0 cm) (courtesy of Sam Channer).

– can also be seen, particularly on Late Middle Kingdom statues of women.[20] Priests on the other hand were bald, but since at this time the priesthood was a part-time profession, Hedjerit could easily have watched her mother put on a special dancer's wig for work at the temple, while her father removed his to signify his role as priest.

The importance of hair in the life of the people of Lahun is again supported by textual evidence. The same commodity lists discussed above also mention hair: specifically 20 hair braids and two wigs.[21] A woman named Inu, depicted plaiting a braid or extension in a well-known relief in the tomb of an Eleventh Dynasty queen, has the title "one who does hair." While hairdressers such as Inu seem to have been proud of their profession, a rather disparaging view of barbers is presented in the Middle Kingdom *Satire of the Trades*: "And the barber is (still) shaving at evening's end. To the town he takes himself; to his corner he takes himself; from street to street he takes himself to search for people to shave. He is vigorous with his arms to fill his belly, like a bee which can eat (only) as it has worked."[22]

On a practical level, keeping the hair short would have helped to deal with head lice, a perennial problem that has been confirmed by the presence of lice in the hair of mummies and on combs dating to the fifth to sixth centuries AD.[23] Many of the combs are double-sided, with narrower teeth on one side. It is this narrower side that would have been most useful in running through hair to remove nits and their tenacious eggs, while the large side could untangle and smooth the thick Egyptian hair. Numerous wooden combs remarkably similar to those of millennia later have been found in Lahun (Fig. 4.3).[24]

Hair and wigs were also decorated with beads of carnelian, faience, or gold, and held in place by hairpins. Many of the hairpins from Lahun were decorated with incised lines, or shaped with the head of an animal or a human hand at one end (Fig. 4.4), and made of ivory – a material which has already been discussed

**Figure 4.4** Ivory hairpin UC16681 (l. 7.6 cm) (courtesy of the Petrie Museum of Egyptian Archaeology).

as a substance that is usually associated with "luxury" items. The fact that it is prevalent in Lahun indicates that its use was not restricted, and finds such as these ivory pins as well as bronze mirrors should not lead us to assume that their owners were necessarily wealthy or elite.

## Mirrors

To arrange their hair and makeup Hedjerit's parents would have used a mirror. The disk would be made of bronze and polished to create a high-quality reflective surface, as has been verified by experiments.[25] Some of the surfaces of the mirrors are curved, which could be either the result of warping over time or intentional curving at the time of manufacture.[26] One mirror now in the British Museum had a convex and a concave side, possibly providing a larger reflection on one side for detailed work such as shaving, applying cosmetics, or tweezing.[27] The most common shape for handles in the Late Middle Kingdom was the open or closed papyrus column, which could be made in wood, ivory, pottery, stone, and even metal.[28] Examples have also survived with the top of the column carved with the face of a leopard or the cow-eared Hathor, and later falcons and rearing snakes were added to the ones with faces. A so far unique example (Fig. 4.5), found in a house in Lahun, was made of wood and was shaped like the face of Hathor, wearing her distinctive wig with curled ends, surmounting a plain papyrus column.[29]

Many of the mirrors from all periods in Ancient Egypt show the remains or impressions of cloth on them, indicating that they were stored carefully.[30] In the Middle Kingdom, tomb reliefs, coffin paintings, and wooden models[31] show mirrors carried within a strapped carrying case either over the shoulder (Fig. 4.6) or in the hands of servants who bring offerings to the deceased, who may be male or female.[32] Although no remains have been found, the representations indicate that these cases were made of brightly colored basketry or leather.[33] Indeed one tomb painting of leatherworkers shows a basket case as one of the finished products. That these cases were also used in the daily life of the townspeople of Lahun is further indicated by both the physical evidence of wear on the handles,[34] and textual evidence, as they are listed in removal inventories.[35]

Mirrors and reflective surfaces are found in tombs from the Old Kingdom on, usually placed under or by the head of both women and men.[36] While it is often

**Figure 4.5**   Drawing of mirror after The Manchester Museum, The University of Manchester, EGY189 (l. 27.1 cm × w. 12.2 cm) (courtesy of Sam Channer).

stated that this occurs more often in the graves of women than in those of men, as Bourriau points out when it comes to their use as funerary goods, "this evidence is sometimes vitiated by the fact that the excavator has used the presence or absence of a mirror to indicate the sex of the occupant of the grave!"[37] Nevertheless, in the case of the Late Middle Kingdom, Lilyquist has demonstrated that while men do appear with and owned mirrors, on the basis of both tomb representations and inscriptions on actual mirrors and handles, mirrors were more

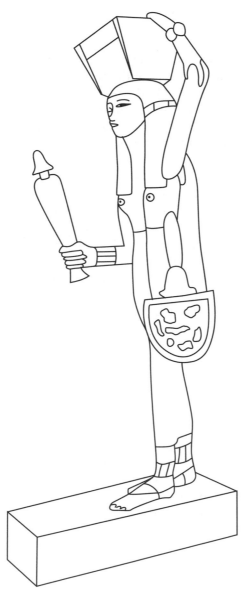

**Figure 4.6** Drawing of woman with mirror case after Roth and Roehrig 1989, 8, Fig. 7 (courtesy of Sam Channer).

often associated with women than men.[38] She notes as well that the mirrors probably held a different meaning for male than female owners.

Possessing a mirror indicated a certain degree of status, and in the *Admonitions of Ipuwer*, a text of uncertain date that is a prime example of one of the favorite Egyptian themes of chaos temporarily overturning order, we find a hint that poorer women would have used water to view their reflection: "A woman who (once) had to gaze on her face in the water now has a mirror."[39] That some of the mirrors were inscribed with the titles of priests and priestesses raises the possibility that they could have been used in connection with formal temple or shrine rituals.[40] The only possibly corroborating evidence is representations of females holding mirrors and wands carved in the shape of a hand, and performing a dance that has been interpreted as a ritual connected with Hathor.[41]

Reflective surfaces confirm an individual's appearance and identity and may have been necessary for a fully successful rebirth in the afterlife. This may help explain the frequent depiction on tomb paintings of mirrors being brought to the deceased by family or servants. Mirrors were also included with other important items under the deceased's chair, on a table as part of the heap of offerings, in registers depicting burial goods, or even painted on the inside of coffins, alongside other items deemed necessary for the maintenance of the individual in the afterlife. There are a number of possible explanations for the frequent appearance of mirrors in a funerary context.[42] They are often shown in tandem with unguent jars and materials that were used in rituals of rebirth. The mirror may also have been associated with the sun and thus may have been important in ensuring full vision in the afterlife. The fact that the handle of the mirror itself can be shaped in the image of the face of Hathor, combined with its frequent depiction in association with objects associated with Hathor, also points to the possibility that this goddess played a vital role in the successful resurrection of the individual.

Would an individual living in Lahun be aware of all these multivalent layers of meaning? It is not unreasonable to suggest that a woman (or man) using the Hathor-handled mirror would be reminded of the goddess and see the analogy between the disk of the mirror, polished almost to gold, and the disk of the sun itself that rests upon the head of the goddess. Again, these objects would also function as an aid to the transmission of beliefs, for a child's curious questions as to the shape of the handle would provide the opportunity for describing the religious beliefs and ideology prevalent in that culture.

## Boxes

All of these items, along with palettes for grinding pigment for cosmetics,[43] pigment,[44] and tweezers (which were not only useful for plucking stray hair and for removing splinters, but were also an important medical tool),[45] would have been stored in a wooden box. One small box excavated at Lahun was found to contain a kohl stick, 30 juniper berries, and powdered red ocher;[46] another beads and a scarab.[47] Many of the boxes were of a manageable size, rectangular and about 30–60 cm in length,[48] although some were circular.[49] They could easily have held a mirror and various jars as well as clothing (as suggested by another box that still had stray scraps of linen stuck to it).[50] Some were painted red,[51] some white,[52] and some were inlaid with ivory strips,[53] again testifying that high-status materials were available to the non-elite of Lahun. Surviving lids allow us to learn that they were closed by tying a string from a knob on one end of the lid to a knob on the box.[54]

Boxes were included in the commodity lists of Lahun, along with a list of their contents, but unfortunately there is no indication of whether they were being distributed from a central source or for what purpose. Along with boxes, the remains of linen bags[55] and baskets made of palm leaf[56] or bundles of rushes[57] were excavated at Lahun. One was found containing a number of copper tools: two chisels, two axe-heads, and a bowl, with a copper knife just to the side of the basket,[58] perhaps belonging to a metal-worker. Another basket was discovered having been repaired with a strip of linen in antiquity, testifying to the expected reuse of items.[59]

## Clothing

If Hedjerit had rummaged around in the boxes, she would also have come across clothing worn by her parents. The most commonly found item of clothing that has survived from Lahun was footwear. A variety of types of sandals have been found in a range of archaeological contexts, including domestic and funerary, as well as in accounting lists.[60] At Lahun, the most commonly discovered were sandals carefully woven of palm fiber, though sandals of leather have also been found.[61] The simple unisex design, with a thong passing through a hole in the sandal between the first and second toes[62] and then inserted into two holes near the end of the sandal, was ideal for walking in the sand and on hard dirt floors in hot weather. The palm-fiber material would also help cool the feet, and be easy to shake out. Because palm trees were common throughout Egypt, and many varieties grow very quickly, this was a popular material to use.

A number of leather soles and sandals have also been found, suitable for more sustained use.[63] Some of the leather soles and heels may have lined and strength-ened the shoes made up of palm rush,[64] while others may have been used for all-leather footwear. One unusual shoe has survived that still uses the toe thong to keep the shoe on, but was designed with a leather upper part stitched to the sole to cover the toes (resembling a modern slipper).[65] The leather was still furry on the inside, and while it covered the toes, the back of the foot would have been exposed, with the shoe held in place at the back by a leather ankle strap. Foreigners in Middle Kingdom Egypt are usually depicted wearing a different type of footgear than the Egyptians.[66] These unusual (though not unique) shoes could have belonged to someone of other than Egyptian native origin living in Lahun, or they could have had a specialized use, perhaps for traversing rugged terrain such as during military ventures. An analysis of the hide used for any these sandals has not yet been performed, so we cannot be sure which animals' skins would have been used, but we cannot rule out sheep, goats, or cattle.

Although in terms of cost it is unlikely that sandals were a luxury item,[67] it seems that on most occasions townsfolk such as Hedjerit and her family would have gone barefoot, reserving the use of sandals for special occasions or when performing certain duties or tasks. Even though tomb representations in terms of many details are meant to be symbolic rather than representational, the consistent depiction of bare feet versus sandals in tombs of all periods may reflect reality to some extent. In Middle Kingdom tombs such as that of Djehutyhotep in el-Bersha[68] (a high official and nomarch under the reigns of Amenemhat II through Senusret III), this becomes obvious. Not only are most of the lay people depicted with bare feet, including laborers hauling a giant statue of the noble, hunters, fishermen, herders, soldiers, priests, and his wife, but Djehutyhotep himself in all but the most prestigious of scenes has bare feet.

In stark contrast to the abundant sandal survivals, clothes are rare in the archaeological record of Lahun although references to cloth abound in the textual sources. Even weaving and sewing tools survive, but no linen.[69] To a great extent this is due to the high perishability of linen, yet this cannot be a complete explanation. As has been noted, sandals and other fragile objects of organic material survived and were discovered during excavations, as did items that were considered more precious and might have been attractive to looters, such as copper tools and ivory ornaments. Linen and cloth were valuable to the villagers, however, and may have been recycled for use as covering for tools, utensils, and mirrors, and even as wicks for lamps. The town of Lahun was seemingly abandoned for reasons as yet unknown, but it is difficult to find an explanation for the total lack of clothing in light of the presence of other items. To a large extent, to determine the clothes that would have been worn by the members of a family such as Hedjerit's, we must therefore rely on representational records.

While small children had little need of much clothing, Hedjerit's parents would have worn dress appropriate to their work and status. The most commonly depicted style of clothing for elite women in the Middle Kingdom was an ankle-length linen dress that either started above or had broad straps that covered the breasts. While reliefs and paintings sometimes show the breasts exposed, statues and examples of dresses that have survived clarify that this was an artistic convention to emphasize the gender of the individual, but did not necessarily reflect reality. Depending on the nature of her employment, a woman would have changed into more specialized garb. For example, weaving women in the tomb of Khnumhotep II at Beni Hassan are shown wearing either the long gown or a topless short kilt.

In general, however, the range of styles of clothing in the Late Middle Kingdom was much greater for men than for women. The standard piece of clothing was a linen kilt that reached to just the knees or mid-calf. This was sometimes folded to create a triangular, pointed, stiff front-piece, conveying the message that the wearer was of higher rank. For more formal occasions longer kilts could be worn, as well as pleated shawls over the shoulders. At the other end of the scale of status, herdsmen are often shown wearing much less clothing

Mourners

*Sem* priest

**Figure 4.7** *Sem* priest from the New Kingdom tomb of Roy (TT255) (courtesy of Ken Griffin).

– at most a loincloth. When Hedjerit's father was on duty as a priest in the local temple, he would don regalia appropriate to that role. His wig would remain at home, and he would be shaved. The lowest rank of priest, the *wab* (meaning "pure"), would wear a long kilt; a *khery kheb* (a literate ritual priest) wore a kilt with one diagonal sash crossing his shoulder; while a *sem* priest (a funerary priest – a role often played by the eldest son) would wear a distinctive leopard skin around his shoulders (Fig. 4.7).

Clothing and sandals were prestige items, and not only had an obvious practical purpose, but also served to convey a certain status, projected role, and even ethnicity. Egyptian representations of foreigners focused on emphasizing differences in hairstyles, features, clothing, and footwear that were easily identifiable and consistent within one cultural group. Clothing is still an important marker of ethnicity today, and specific types of clothing are associated with different countries.[70] In Ancient Egypt, while sandals were unisex in style, clothing differed according to the gender of the individual as well. This is clear not only in the form, but also in the greater variations of style for men, at least according to our representational sources. This may reflect the wider range of jobs and roles that could be held by men, as well as the more fluid mobility available to males relative to the more restricted domains accessible to women of the Middle Kingdom. Even today, clothing is an important outward manifestation of an individual's self-identity. As we change roles throughout the day we don different outfits appropriate to the situation and the image we wish to project. While the changes in clothing were not as drastic in Ancient Egypt as they are today, nevertheless, by watching her parents dress, a young child such as Hedjerit would have learnt to decode the signals embedded within her culture, and would have incorporated them into her own life and eventually transferred them to her own children as well.

# Jewelry

Jewelry is another accessory that contains embedded within it multiple layers of meaning and value, which will usually remain invisible to archaeologists and scholars interpreting them outside of their primary context. Jewelry can be a particularly intimate class of object, yet the wealth of sentimental attachments, memories, and significance that an individual assigns to a particular item is often impossible for anyone else to discern, even in the modern world. Sometimes we may be able to catch a glimpse of the emotional resonance of an artifact, such as in the case of the string of beads found inside one of the box infant burials at Lahun.[71] Most of the beads were made of faience, some shaped like bunches of grapes, as well as carnelian, one shaped like a hawk, one like a recumbent lion, and there was a single bead of amethyst. Why was this string of beads buried with the infant? Did it belong to the infant, or perhaps to the parents? Was it selected because it was a favorite, or was it selected because it was redundant? Was it worn as it was found, or was it restrung for the burial? Are the shapes significant? The lion and the hawk are also found on the birth rods – were they chosen for a religious reason? Were they meant to protect the baby, or to protect the living from the potentially harmful dead? At the moment these questions are unanswerable. Clues may be found by an overarching study of the objects found in other infant burials in the Middle Kingdom. Patterns and consistencies may suggest a common practice and underlying beliefs. Lack of constancy in forms may indicate that the choice was purely personal. Because so many infant burials did contain beads, at the moment we can at least acknowledge that thought and care went into the interment of infants, and that the accompanying beads were included for a reason other than as simply attractive adornment.

In the case of the Lahun burial, the string of beads was fairly typical of the type of jewelry found elsewhere in the settlement. Strings of beads are the most common, but because many were found loose we cannot always be sure if they were meant to be worn as necklaces or bracelets. Most are made up of faience beads in a variety of shapes including narrow cylindrical, thicker barrel, and even a diamond-shaped one.[72] During the Middle Kingdom, blue-green faience was the most common, although white faience beads were also used.[73] Red carnelian was also frequently used, as well as other semi-precious stones that were found in Egypt, such as amethyst, garnet, green jasper, and quartz,[74] while other imaginative materials included shell, ivory, and wood. Any of these could be shaped, and in Lahun examples have been found representing animals such as hawks and crocodiles or deities such as Bes and Taweret.[75] Each of these amulets has religious connotations as well; the hawk can represent the distant deities Ra-Harakhty or Horus,[76] while the crocodile represents the god Sobek-Ra, whose cult center was nearby. Bes and Taweret are both protectors of the vulnerable, especially, as we have seen earlier, pregnant women and children. None of these objects in and of itself provides enough clues to indicate who would have worn it or when. They are not gender specific, not even the ones with Bes and Taweret, for these deities could have protected any vulnerable individuals. It is conceivable that necklaces with amulets might have been worn much of the time. In addition, it is impossible to determine if objects such as these would have continued to be worn and considered as valuable, sentimental, or simply attractive adornments even after their initial amuletic function had been fulfilled.

Other types of jewelry, such as finger rings and earrings, that one might expect either have not survived or were not used in Lahun. An exception is what appears to be a round ivory ear-stud that would have been placed within a hole pierced in the earlobe.[77] Another unusual item found was a bronze torque – a necklace formed of a solid rounded roll of bronze with the ends flattened to rest more comfortably on the collarbone. Because torques are rarely found in Ancient Egyptian sites, as opposed to the Near East (Byblos in particular seems to have been a production center for torques),[78] this specific find has been interpreted as a material manifestation of a foreign presence in Egypt, and as perhaps having been owned by an Asiatic woman married to an Egyptian man.[79] While this is one interpretation, others are possible: it could have been a gift, payment, or a reward for service. The torque could equally well have been worn by a man or a woman. Without other substantiating markers of ethnicity, it is also difficult to assign either a native or foreign background to the presumed owner on the basis of this single piece of jewelry.

Unlike so many of the finds from Lahun, the torque was not an isolated find, but was discovered by Petrie as one of a group of artifacts known as "Group 9" in a "house on the south side of the second street from the top, in the workmens' western quarter."[80] He notes that the "date of the group is not well fixed" and that some of the artifacts are forms typical of in the Twelfth or Thirteenth Dynasties. However, he also noted that some of the homes in the western quarter were reused in the New Kingdom, and it is possible that this house was as well, and that this entire group of artifacts should be dated to the New Kingdom.[81]

The assemblage itself is of interest and included: the torque; the mirror with the Hathor handle (discussed above); five stone vases; two chisels with wooden handles; a flint knife with a fiber binding around the handle (found in the adjoining room along with the disk of the mirror) and another broken flint knife; a small whetstone; a piercer set in a nut handle, along with two others with their handles missing; a wooden box; and finally a leather bag that contained a copper piercer, seven flakes of flint, a pierced piece of wood, a wooden spoon with the remains of a humanoid figure on it, and some nuts and roots.[82] An assemblage such as this can, to a degree, help us to reconstruct life in this home. We can imagine the mirror being used by men or women to apply their cosmetics from one of the vases. On the other hand, mirrors also played a role in religious rituals, as did travertine vases of a shape similar to three of the ones found in the group.

Perhaps these were work-related objects belonging to a woman who worked at the temple. The piercers, flint, and chisels could suggest a husband who worked as a craftsman, or perhaps these were tools that would have been found in most homes. Because the survival of this conglomeration of artifacts was unique in Lahun, we are not in a position to judge whether or not it should be considered as typical of what we should expect to find in the house of a family in the western sector, such as Hedjerit's. On the basis of the fact that numerous similar items have been found in the town, we may tentatively suggest that this grouping is not unusual, and would have been familiar to Egyptians living in Lahun.

Knives of flint, whetstones, copper needles, spoons, cosmetics, combs, sandals, clothing, jewelry, mirrors, and boxes and bags in which to keep them all made up the stuff of everyday life in town like Lahun. The were used by people like Hedjerit and her family, and many of them embody meaning and value to the user beyond simply their usefulness. Some may have triggered painful memories, while others may have been sentimentally kept long after they had served their initial purpose. While still a child, Hedjerit was learning how and with which objects she should interact, and concurrently was introduced to the norms, customs, and signals of the culture in which she lived. She was learning how to be a citizeness of Lahun. Next, she would need to learn skills that she would use in her work.

# Notes

1   Black hair shining as if it were blue was a desirable trait, and the hair of the gods is described as being of lapis-lazuli.
2   One of the words that was used for a "mirror" in the Late Middle Kingdom was *ankh* "the living one," and another was *maa heru* "one who sees the face" (Lilyquist 1979, 68–71).
3   From Lahun, EGY149 is an example of a kohl pot with the kohl still inside.
4   EGY419, 420.
5   See EGY153b which is made of blue faience decorated with a black lotus pattern; EGY164a–b.
6   For examples of pots see EGY143, EGY144a–e; for lids see EGY144f, 145a–l; for pots with matching lids see EGY146a–b, EGY151a–c
7   See for example J. Allen 2005, 19–20.
8   Bourriau 1988, 144.
9   See for example the kohl stick found in box EGY75.
10  Similarly American football players use eye-black grease or apply black tape to their upper cheeks in order to cut glare (as well as to look more intimidating to their opponents).
11  True kohl is, therefore, not recommended for use today.
12  My thanks to Stephen Quirke for discussing these with me.
13  UC32179 verso 5, 11, and UC32183 recto2, 16, in Collier and Quirke 2006, 29, 33. Although these commodity lists appear on different fragments of papyri, they are nearly identical, suggesting that they might be drafts of a single list.

14 UC32209 verso 3 in Collier and Quirke 2002, 131.
15 UC32057 in Collier and Quirke 2004.
16 UC32124 recto in Collier and Quirke 2002, 61.
17 See the Middle Kingdom coffin from Abydos in Bourriau 1988, 95.
18 See EGY13785; UC 7053i believed to be Late Middle Kingdom from Lahun.
19 Green 2001, 74.
20 Bourriau 1988, 49, and in particular 71.
21 UC32179 and UC32183 in Collier and Quirke 2006, 31, 35.
22 Parkinson 1991, 74.
23 www.headlice.org/news/classics/nitsonthenile.htm.
24 See for example EGY223a–c, EGY224a–b, EGY225a–b.
25 Bourriau 1988, 161–2.
26 Lilyquist 1979, 50.
27 Bourriau 1988, 162.
28 Lilyquist 1979, 60–3.
29 See EGY189.
30 Lilyquist 1979, 63.
31 Roth and Roehrig 1989.
32 Lilyquist 1979, 63–5.
33 Lilyquist 1979, 63–5, fig. 104.
34 Lilyquist 1979, 97.
35 Two are listed directly after entries for hair braids and a wig in UC32179 3 in Collier and Quirke 2006, 30–1.
36 See for example the Dynasty 6 Qau tomb 1089, within which is the skeleton of a man surrounded by pottery and with a mirror carefully placed by his head (now UC17668 in the Petrie museum), and the numerous examples cited by Lilyquist 1979, 96.
37 Bourriau 1988, 161.
38 Lilyquist 1979, 97.
39 *Admonitions of Ipuwer* 8, 5. Translation that of Assmann 2005, 138.
40 Lilyquist 1979, 97–8, figs. 105–6.
41 For this argument and for an example of a New Kingdom hand wand see Capel and Markoe 1996, 101–2, fig. 36b; Hickmann 1956.
42 Lilyquist 1979, 98–9; Derriks 2001, 421–2.
43 See EGY137a–e, EGY138–40a.
44 See EGY231.
45 See for example EGY252b and UC7087. The broad tips of the latter suggest a use other than that of plucking hairs.
46 A red mineral that could also have been used to make cosmetics to redden cheeks, fingernails, or lips. See box EGY075.
47 See EGY076a.
48 See EGY255 (24 × 30 × 27 cm) and EGY254a (25 × 26 × 42 cm).
48 See EGY077, the circular lid of which was incised with a flower pattern with green paint, and EGY078.
50 See EGY255, EGY257.
51 See EGY256.
52 See EGY257, EGY259.

53   See EGY179a–b.
54   See EGY254, and EGY073; the lid was painted as a game-board but the box held a baby burial and vase. For an animation of the box opening and closing, see www.kahun.man.ac.uk/lesson4.htm.
55   See EGY108.
56   See EGY116, EGY121.
57   See EGY200.
58   See EGY201-6.
59   See EGY117.
60   UC32135B in Collier and Quirke 2006, 127.
61   See EGY90a, EGY92b.
62   During the Amarna period of the New Kingdom, sculptors showed these two toes as splayed and clearly separated, which is what happens when one wears thong sandals over a period of time. However, this was not an artistic feature of the Middle Kingdom.
63   See EGY92b–f; UC7497.
64   See UC7499.
65   See EGY91a and the discussion in David 1986, 245–6.
66   See the tomb of Khnumhotep in Beni Hassan for details.
67   The cost of a pair of sandals in the New Kingdom was steady at only 2 deben, the equivalent of one sack of grain, and it likely had a similar assigned value in the Middle Kingdom.
68   Tomb 17L20/1. Photos of the tomb are available online at www.osirisnet.net/tombes/el_bersheh/djehoutyhotep/e_djehoutyhotep_01.htm.
69   David 1986, 247–7.
70   For an amusing example of an online game featuring matching clothing to country visit www.coedu.usf.edu/culture/Activities/match/index.html.
71   See EGY157a. For the difficulties in determining, yet the importance of acknowledging, the emotional undertones see Insoll 2004, 111–15.
72   See EGY157b.
73   See EGY76a; EGY157b.
74   See IPSMG R.1920–81.51 in the Ipswich Museum.
75   See EGY157c; UC51426; UC51699; UC51856.
76   Respectively, the form of the sun god during the day and kingship.
77   See EGY176.
78   For another example excavated in Abydos see no. 22b in Capel and Markoe 1996.
79   David 1986, 135–6.
80   Petrie et al. 1891, 12, pl. XIII 1–18.
81   Quirke 2006, 97.
82   Petrie et al. 1891, 12–13. The leather bag is in the Manchester Museum as EGY199a–c.

# 5

# Crafts and Trades

*My mother sent me forth from the house one morning with my brother so she could finish her spinning. He took me to another street where we saw a carpenter wielding a chisel, but he looked wearier than a field-laborer. We then went to the house of the potter — his clothes were stiff from clay. Then he said to me: "Do not fear, do not fear now that you have come to me." And then he took some mud and pounded it with straw and a little water. He showed me how to roll it into a ball in the manner of Khepri himself,[1] and then he shaped it into a little mouse. With my own two hands I added its ears upon it, and when it was finished, it was excellent. Never had the like been done before!*

Many of the objects found in the homes of Lahun would have been manufactured right in the town itself. As Hedjerit toddled or was carried about the town, she would have passed by many of these places where items that she used everyday were produced. In the modern western world much of the production is hidden from view or even carried out in foreign countries, but in Ancient Egypt it was mostly local and visible. The production of textiles, for example, is well attested within Middle Kingdom settlements, while a range of archaeological, representational, and textual evidence illuminates the processes for us.

## Textiles

Much has been written elsewhere on the details of textile production, and therefore only an outline will be provided here.[2] In Ancient Egypt the most popular material for cloth was linen, which is made from flax. Colored wool was also found in Lahun, but as it has been recently dated to the medieval period, and was probably moved into the earlier levels by nesting animals, the lack of any other examples suggests that wool was not used at this time in Egypt. But paintings on the walls of four Middle Kingdom rock-cut tombs of Beni Hassan,[3] as well as a model found in the tomb of Meket-Re in Thebes, provide us with the details of the process of growing, harvesting, and preparing the flax, and of spinning and weaving the linen. Because the representational details are supported by archaeological evidence found at Lahun we can assert with some confidence that the depictions are fairly accurate.[4]

The two main stages of textile production, namely preparation of raw material and manipulation of the material into the final product, seem to have been strictly gendered, with men involved in the first agricultural stage, and women the second manufacturing stage. Men were responsible for growing the flax plants in the winter, harvesting them by pulling up bunches, and then setting them out to dry. The rough outer portions would be stripped and the flax would be soaked in water for up to 14 days before being beaten with specially designed wooden toothed beaters.[5] The final stage in making the plant fibers themselves into material useful for making fabrics was scouring the flax, and bleaching it.

The next stage in the process, that of spinning, seems to have been the expertise of women (the details of the personnel and hierarchy will be discussed below). Once they were supplied with the prepared flax, it still had to be spun into workable long threads. This could be done either by hand, or by means of spindles (basically a stick pointed at one end and with a spiral groove at the other) and whorls (a wooden circular disc with a hole in the center for the spindle).[6] With one hand the spindle is quickly rotated while the material is passed through the spindle groove and pulled out with the other hand as yarn or thread. The ball of material could be kept wet also by running it through a loop in the bottom of a pottery spinning bowl filled with water. Not only did this prevent the ball from rolling away, but the wetness made the material more manageable. By controlling the thread and the extent and direction of the twist, the spinner created thread that was appropriate for different products. Different types of thread were found at Lahun – some of it was coarse, most of it was medium fine, and some was even very fine.

Once the thread was spun, the weaving could begin. Again, according to depictions and text, in the Middle Kingdom this seems to have been an activity that was performed by women rather than men.[7] From the Predynastic Period on, the apparatus of choice for weaving was the large horizontal loom.[8] Not only is this represented in the Beni Hassan tombs (Fig. 5.1) and the model of Meket-Re, but parts of looms and accessories have been found in Lahun. These include jacks (known as heddle-jacks) made of stone or wood,[9] a straight bar,[10] loom weights,[11] heddle-rods, and a weaving sword.

Once the thread had been woven into cloth, this then had to be washed and bleached. Here, men played a role. All the evidence we have from Ancient Egypt points to men, rather than women, as doing the laundry. Indeed, washing was a small industry with a hierarchical structure, as is indicated by titles such as "the overseer of washermen Sidjehuty."[12] Men were responsible for the washing of many different types of material, from large cloths such as the freshly woven items

**Figure 5.1**   Drawing of weaving women in the Middle Kingdom tomb of Khnumhotep II (Beni Hassan tomb 3) (courtesy of Sam Channer).

at Lahun to smaller, more private garments such as loincloths and even the "towels" that were worn by menstruating women.[13] This may be because cloth is very heavy when wet, or because it was an outdoor activity, but many of the activities that women engaged in also involved heavy weights, such as carrying children, pounding grain for bread or beer, and indeed, weaving. If the laundry was done outside the confines of the town itself, as was the growing and processing of the flax, then this could also have been a deciding factor, at least initially. Most of the titles of the Middle Kingdom, and the artistic convention of painting the skin of men as darker than that of women, attest to a division of labor based on men working outdoors and women indoors. However, gender allocations of tasks quickly become embedded in a culture's traditions and customs, even when the original reasons, whether they were practical or not, are lost, and this may have been the case here.

In any event, after the cloth had been bleached to the desired shade, it would be polished with a tool made of a thick, round piece of leather doubled over into an oval, stuffed and stitched with leather.[14] With the exception of fringes and the occasional patterned cloth, most Egyptian clothing was left undecorated except for pleating. Because pleating is best done when the cloth is wet, it too was likely the responsibility of the men doing the laundry.[15]

The cloth was now ready to be refined for a number of uses. Besides its obvious use for clothing, linen was used to make the slings for carrying infants, to wrap the handles of tools, and for wrapping the dead after mummification. Medical texts prescribe the use of cloth in a variety of ways to heal the living: from bandaging, to soaking and burning for fumigation, to inscribing and placing on the ailing part of the body, to charms to protect the bearer.[16] Coarse linen was used as sackcloth and as bedsheets for poorer individuals, while very fine linen would be used for the beds of royalty, for rituals (when it was sometimes dyed red), and as votive offerings to a deity. Even slings have been found that could have been used as children's toys or weapons for hunting birds and other small animals.

The threads, even before they were woven, were also used for one of the most important items for the inhabitants of Lahun: nets. The number of wooden netting needles and bodkins found in Lahun testifies to the popularity of nets, which would be used for fishing at the nearby lakes in the Fayum, and for trapping various animals such as birds as well as mammals that would be driven into the trap. Over 40 net fragments have been found at Lahun, all with a diamond-shaped mesh, but with different signs of wear. Bundles of net have also been found – one even had a fish hook still embedded in it. Smaller nets were used for transporting and supporting pottery vessels. The fiber from flax, as well as palm, was used as well for making rope.

Finally, cloth would be recycled in the home. Ironically, no clothing was found at Lahun, but a dozen pieces of fabric survived from the town, all of them having been reused. Even from these scraps it was obvious that they were typical of other complete cloths that have been found in burials dating to the Middle Kingdom and early New Kingdom. Excavations in the homes also uncovered numerous copper needles with an eye at one end.[17] Even a needle case has survived, made of a bird bone (which is hollow) wrapped with cloth and reeds; it still contained a threaded copper needle and a wooden bodkin. These were not used for making clothing – most garments were made by taking larger pieces of linen and tying them on. Instead, the needles and scraps of cloth were kept in the home for patching and repairing various items, such as bags, boxes, and baskets. There is little evidence as to who performed this sewing, and Hedjerit might have watched either her mother or her father or indeed any of her siblings or the servants sewing the cloth onto damaged goods, and thus learned how to do it herself in the future.

Hedjerit would could also have become familiar with the process of spinning at an early age. Spinning requires less skill than does weaving, but it would take as many as three spinners to supply thread for a single horizontal loom worked by two weavers.[18] Spinning is a social activity and one that can be performed while engaged in other tasks in the home. It takes up little room and could have been performed inside the home, or even on a cool rooftop. Hedjerit might have helped her mother as well as other relatives or servants with the spinning, thus acquiring and practicing the skills she would later use herself. Whether her mother worked in the same area as the weavers or would bring the threads to the weaving area, Hedjerit would likely have accompanied her, and again have tried to imitate the activities of her elders. If she were particularly adept, one of the weavers might have allowed her to work with her as an apprentice.

An accounting text from Lahun lists six weaving women (including one named Hedjerit), and specifies that one is accompanied by her sister, and one by her daughter.[19] Tomb paintings show girls helping in the spinning process, and their small stature is emphasized by their being shown standing on platforms so that they would be able to reach the spindles and thread. Although boys are more often depicted in scenes of flax harvesting, in one instance a young boy is also shown helping the spinners,[20] while perhaps simultaneously learning a skill that was traditionally associated with men in Egypt – making rope.[21] These scenes emphasize that in Ancient Egypt children were integrated into the community at large, as well as contributing to the local economy.

Within the town of Lahun there is also evidence of rigorous regulation of the production, distribution, and ultimate consumption of both flax and cloth. The range of quality of cloth found at Lahun suggests that the women who spun and wove there would have likely traded their products either as bulk material or as finished products to buyers, who would then sell them either for further refinement or to their final destination. Here, both letters and administrative texts provide us with dramatic insights into the daily working life of the inhabitants. Bundles of flax were tabulated and inventoried, as were different qualities of threads, kilts, and cloth, with deliveries carefully monitored.[22] In one letter, a man threatens to cease his production of linen until he receives at least one payment that is due him. Another letter, written by the "lady of the estate" Irer to the lord, reveals that women were also involved at the management level. Irer informs the lord that all is well, but that they have not received any message from him in some time. Indeed, the frustrated Irer refers to the "neglectfulness of the lord l.p.h." and then proceeds to report to him a labor problem with the weaving women:

> This is a communication to the lord l.p.h. about the servant-women who are here without getting down to weaving (clothes). . . . Your humble servant[23] could hardly have come herself, since the fact is that your humble servant entered into the temple on day 20 to purify for the month.
>
> So, perhaps, the lord l.p.h. could bring them himself. It was a mistake assigning responsibility to the minor Haremhab about the arrival of Qemaw. The lord l.p.h. really should spend some time here. Look, there aren't any clothes, because my responsibility is directed to the temple – the threads have been set up, but cannot be woven![24]

These workers obviously feel confident enough to assert themselves, and temporarily at least stop their labor.

I have here emphasized the production and distribution of linen because out of all the daily commodities, it was the most expensive,[25] and thus of paramount importance to the town of Lahun as well as the general Ancient Egyptian economy. In the Late Middle Kingdom, the textile industry involved the expertise of personnel at all levels of society, of both genders, and of all ages. At all stages, it relied upon the skills of women and children, who were recognized as essential contributors to the maintenance of *maat* in Ancient Egypt. Rather than their being marginalized minorities, their efforts in this respect were valued and woven into the fabric of Egyptian life.

# Crafts

Of course the production of cloth was not the only business activity in Lahun. Although other craftsmen are not as evident in the textual evidence, during Hedjerit's toddles around the town she will have seen numerous of them at work. Carpentry, bricklaying, basketry, stone-masonry, flint-knapping, and the creation of pottery, jewelry, and metal items are all attested in the archaeological record from Lahun. Many of the finished products found there would have been produced elsewhere (the foreign pottery is one obvious example, which will be discussed later), but the plethora of tools attests to the activity of craftsmen in the town itself.[26]

Many of the tools were made of a combination of metal (bronze or copper) and wood (often for the handles), sometimes bound together with leather. Other tools were made of stone, in particular flint. This was a favorite material for knives; flint is sharper for certain tasks than metal, can be reworked when broken or dulled rather than having to be discarded, and as a raw material is readily available. Flint nodules can easily be found on the surface of the desert in Egypt even today, and higher-quality flint was quarried at sites such as are found in Upper Egypt near the Qena bend of the Nile. Examples of flint knives have been found; some with straight backs and a single cutting edge,[27] some curved, with a double cutting edge.[28] Flint scrapers and axes have been found, as well as agricultural saws, sickles, and woodworking tools such as adzes. Rough and unfinished pieces made of flint also survived, as well as worked and unworked flint flakes. The cast-off from flint-knapping can often be worked itself, and if it is too small it remains as a pile of debris – a give-away to archaeologists. Thus the presence of what many early archaeologists would have considered useless garbage indicates instead the presence of local production, and that in Lahun, flint was indeed actually knapped in the town by local craftsmen, rather than having to be imported.

Some of the tools were made by hand, and some would have been made in molds, depending on the material. Flint and other stone objects cannot be made in a mold, but metal, faience, and clay objects can, which greatly helps in the large-scale production of similar objects. When molds are found, it indicates that the finished products were created there with raw material that may or may not have been produced locally. In Lahun, pottery molds have been found that would have been used for casting metal objects such as axes, chisels, and knives, some

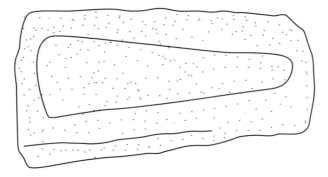

**Figure 5.2** Drawing of chisel mold after The Manchester Museum, The University of Manchester, EGY219 (l. 20.0 cm × w. 9.7 cm) (courtesy of Sam Channer).

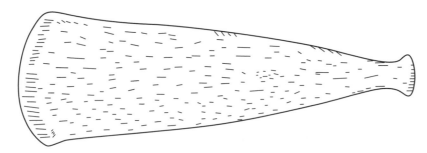

**Figure 5.3** Drawing of copper chisel after The Manchester Museum, The University of Manchester, EGY203 (l. 20.0 cm × w. 7.0 cm) (courtesy of Sam Channer).

of which have also serendipitously been found as well. Figures 5.2 and 5.3 show chisel molds and similarly shaped copper chisels. Made of fired clay, the molds often had a coating of clay and fine ash on them, presumably to create a smoother finish. Copper tools that have been found and would have been used by other townspeople include knives with curved blades and ones with single edges, tweezers, needles, fish hooks, piercers (which could have been used for leatherwork), bowls, and mirrors, as well as "model" tools such as chisels and knives. Some of these tools (two axe-heads and two chisels) and a hammered copper bowl were found in a basket, with a knife just next to the basket, perhaps all waiting to be delivered from the caster to their destination, which may have been a workshop where they would be distributed for use.

The "model" tools are an intriguing phenomenon. Their final destination may have been a tomb, as miniature metal tools have been found in tombs for use by the deceased or the deceased's workers in the afterlife. Thus the term "model" is often assigned to them, as it assumes they were not used in daily life. However, depending on the context, the smaller size may indicate that they were used by younger apprentices with smaller hands. The miniature tools in Lahun, however, were found in the foundation deposits of the temple; these particular tools were used in the important rituals associated with the erection of sacred buildings.

That tools were cast in Lahun is certain from the discovery of completed metal tools (some in a basket, as described above) and five molds together in one house/workshop. The presence of raw materials such as copper ore and iron flux, coupled with evidence of local copper mines, indicates that the metal itself might have been smelted at Lahun.[29] The lack of slag or crucibles within the confines of the town itself does not necessarily suggest a lack of smelting in the area. Metal production is a messy business, and it is possible that the workshops would have been carefully placed somewhere south of Lahun. The prevailing winds in Egypt blow from north to south, so this location would have ensured that the noxious fumes would have blown away from the town. As this area has not been excavated, this must remain speculative.

Carpenters also worked in Lahun and their tools, such as axes, chisels, adzes, drills, mallets, and nails, have survived. Accurate measurement was ensured by the use of right-angle tools and plummets made of stone and wood. To bore holes in wood they made use of bow-drills, which were also used for stone or beads. While carpenters would have created furnishings for homes, such as doors, seats, beds, and boxes, the houses themselves were built by bricklayers and finished by plasterers and painters. The bricks were made of local mud and water formed in wooden molds, an example of which was found at Lahun. In addition, a plasterer's float was found, with bits of plaster on tools, walls, artifacts, and furniture that were attached to walls, as well as pigments and palettes for containing and mixing paint. Stone-masons would have been busy preparing blocks of stone for building the temples and pyramids, as well as fashioning vessels and cultic objects for use in the temples and in the homes. Stone-masons' tools have been found as well, and include wooden wedges, clamps, and triplets of sticks used for facing the stone (all of these could have been created by the local carpenters). Basketry and matting were also likely practiced in the village. Baskets, sandals, ropes, vessel handles, bedding, pillows, and door blinds were made of the fibers of date palm, rush, and papyrus, which were all available locally.

One of the more unusual workshops found in the town of Lahun was that of what was originally dubbed a "doll-maker." This attribution is largely based on a store of locks of hair found in a single room. Petrie describes the hair as follows: "five threads placed together, about 6 inches long, had pellets of mud rolled on them by the fingers, 12 or 14 in the length, and a conical lump at the end: this may have been copied from the actual dressings of girls' hair with pellets of mud at the ends as in Nubia at present."[30] The hair is similar to that found on female figurines from Thebes and would perhaps have been attached to analogous figurines in Lahun. Mud figurines with hair have also been found at Lahun,[31] but as discussed in the previous chapter, we should hesitate before assuming they were toys for children. The marked emphasis on the pubic region, within which was placed a grain of corn, suggests that they had a more symbolic use, probably related to fertility. Some of the wooden figures that had jointed limbs also seem to represent foreigners, and could have been used in execration rituals. Regardless, the presence of a repository for fake hair in a single location does suggest that an inhabitant of Lahun was a specialist in making hair for figurines.

Another popular craft practiced in the town would have been that of pottery. Most of the vessels that would have been found in Hedjerit's home would have been made of fired clay, specifically of a type of clay called Nile silt. As the name suggests, this is clay that was prepared from the alluvial mud from the river. Another type is known as marl clay. This was a finer clay that needed to be quarried rather than gathered locally, had a very different consistency, required a different process to form vessels, and had a different firing temperature. In Lahun, only one specific type of marl clay was found (marl C), and it was a type that is not particularly suitable for throwing on a wheel – with the exception of some rims and handles, the bulk of the marl C vessels were formed by hand, usually by coiling.[32] It may be that these marl vessels were not even produced in Lahun at all, but in the area of the quarries in Upper Egypt near the Qena bend, and consequently traded to the Delta region.

In either case, once the raw material for clay had been gathered, it was then soaked in water to help refine it in a process called "levigation." As the mud sits in the water, the smaller particles float upwards, leaving the heavier clay at the bottom. This procedure is not often documented in Egyptian sources, but in an official journal that has survived from Lahun, we find levigation mentioned as part of a division of land among the recorded activities and conscriptions that took place during the thirty-fourth year of the reign of Amenemehat III.[33] Later, the same text mentions a division of land that again seems to include clay and molding bricks.

Once it had reached a desired consistency, the clay would be trodden and pounded, then be further processed by adding a variety of materials including straw, chaff, and even dung or old bits of broken pottery as "temper." The amount and type of material added would depend on the consistency, hardness, and texture of the final product desired. A porous vessel, such a "zir" or water jug, would have coarse temper added in order to help the water stay cool by the process of evaporation. However, a plate that was meant to serve runny and hot foods would have a finer texture. The clay was then further pounded, moistened if necessary, and formed either by hand, or with the aid of a turntable.[34]

High volumes of similar objects would be formed with the aid of cores[35] – the most obvious example of these being the ubiquitous ceramic bread molds. Objects could be left plain, burnished, or decorated at this point by carving into them, or adding a bit of color with slip or a wash, or the decoration could be left until after firing. Many of the potsherds found in Lahun have potters' marks on them: a simple stamp or incision on the vessel to indicate the potter or workshop from which it originated. Representations on Middle Kingdom tomb walls illustrate the entire process for us, as well as informing us as to the design of kilns. Although many examples of kilns have survived from other sites in Ancient Egypt (including one in Hierakonpolis, where apparently the potter had an accident and burnt down his entire house), none has been found in Lahun. Perhaps they too were just outside the town walls, or in the unexcavated section of the town. Pottery workshops themselves are not always easily discernible, even to archaeologists,[36] and Lahun's remain undetected. There is no doubt, however, that pottery was one of the fundamental materials of daily life in Ancient Egypt at all periods of time.

That Lahun had its own local ceramic industry is attested by chemical analyses that have been performed on pottery that was brought by the excavators to England,[37] but also by papyrus fragments from the town. One fragment, dated to year 38 of the reign of Amenemhat III, provides a listing of pottery supplies, amounts that had been produced, and amounts still required, as well as the name of one of the potters: Kemniu.[38] Not all the pottery found at Lahun was locally made, however. Pots that have been identified as cooking bowls by their shape and the presence of smoke residue from fires, for example, were all imported from the east Delta region. It is also possible that some of the ceramics made in Lahun were exported to other Middle Kingdom settlements. Some of them seem to have been unique to this town, such as the lamps or burners that will be discussed below. Whereas the residents of other towns seem to have simply used ordinary small dishes with pinched rims as lamps (filled with oil, perhaps olive oil, which is particularly well suited for lamps,[39] and lit with a cloth or fiber wick), many of Lahun's lamps are in the shape of arms coming out of a wall, or pillars, or small men, and are currently without any known parallels. It may be that they had a specific function associated with the temple(s), or perhaps the large residence structure that would have housed the mayor.

Even more intriguingly, a number of potsherds were immediately recognized by the excavators as being completely non-Egyptian. The fragments were brightly colored and decorated with swirls and geometric patterns characteristic of the Aegean. Neutron activation analyses of fragments have confirmed that most were imports from Crete (17 fragments were identified as coming from Phaistos, two from Mesara, and one from Knossos), but some were local imitations – made of native clay but in all other respects appearing to be Aegean.[40] Their presence in Lahun remains unexplained. They were not leftovers from large containers for transporting commodities, but mostly tableware: cups and small pots with handles, indicating that the value of the objects was intrinsic, rather than in anything that they held. They have been relatively precisely dated, to a 50-year timespan, suggestive of a single batch of imports.

Their findspot is not particularly illuminating, as many were found in a rubbish dump near the larger estates in the northern section of Lahun, but some were found in the chambers of both large and smaller homes (Petrie was not much more specific in his recording than this). Possible scenarios abound for their presence. They may indicate a group of Aegeans living in the town, using their own utensils. It has been suggested that they represent the favorite tableware of the Cretan wife of an Egyptian. They may represent a particular fondness on the part of some of the residents in Lahun for exotic and foreign goods, perhaps initially brought to the town by a trader, soldier, or diplomat. A definitive answer remains elusive.

A question that requires further research is the extent to which the different types of craftsmen and artists pooled their efforts and worked together.[41] For example, in some cases a potter may also have had some skill in painting, and would have decorated his own vessels. Others may have turned to specialists in order to create a quality product. The organization of these craftsmen is also uncertain. The title "chief craftsman" does appear in what appears to be an account of distribution of fish,[42] and it is likely that the fairly rigid hierarchy seen in other professions was also the model for craftsmen.

All of these craftsmen would have produced artifacts for all three of the main spheres of life in Illahun: the religious dimension, represented by the temples; the afterlife, typified by the pyramids and tombs; and the daily life of the residents of the settlement. Many of the items produced locally and abroad would have been found in Hedjerit's home, perhaps traded for the products of her mother's spinning or weaving. The ones with which Hedjerit would have been most familiar would probably have been those associated with the basic concern of people everywhere: food and drink.

## Food

An alarming number of discussions on food in Ancient Egypt are derived from evidence found in tombs. This can, however, create a skewed reconstruction of daily life. The food and drink that were depicted on tomb walls, listed in offering formulas, spells, and prayers, or physically left inside the tomb, either in petrified form or as models, were not meant to represent reality, but rather what the deceased would prefer to eat in the idealized world of the afterlife. The depictions, therefore, present us with cuts of meat, breads, beer, wine, and a few classic vegetables. Most are included because of their symbolic and religious resonances, rather than their nutritional value or actual use in daily life. For example, lettuce is often represented, not because of a love of salad, but because of its association with the fertility god Min. On the other hand, neither pigs nor fish are represented even though archaeological evidence verifies that they were both consumed, and fish in particular was a staple of workmen's diets.

To build a more accurate picture of subsistence patterns in Ancient Egypt, we need to examine the archaeological remains and lists of supplies from settlements instead. Even then, there will be many questions that will remain unanswered. For example, in England today, three standard meals are eaten. For a business worker the following schedule of meals is typical; before going to work (which usually starts at 9:00 a.m.) breakfast is eaten, followed by a lunch at 1:00 p.m., and upon returning home, perhaps at 7:00 p.m., a dinner is served. Yet variations abound and the conventions can be confusing for those unfamiliar with the culture. For example, the word "dinner" can be used for lunch, and dinner can be called "tea," even though that meal may not feature any tea at all. The use of these terms is also deemed to indicate someone from a particular class. In the past, "tea" was a snack taken at approximately 4:00 p.m. by the upper classes and consisted of actual tea and little sandwiches.

The etiquette and codes of behavior associated with foodways are culturally and ethnically bound and can be difficult to discern without a guide. In some cultures it is traditional for children and adults to be seated separately, and some also prescribe rules for the order in which individuals are served. Ancient Egypt has left us with no books of etiquette, recipes, or feeding schedules, even though there were standards of behavior. We do not know how many meals were eaten, though three or four seem to be the norm worldwide and would seem reasonable for a family like Hedjerit's. Glimpses of etiquette, at least for the upper class, can be found in the "instruction texts" that began to be composed in the Middle Kingdom. These often purport to be written from a father to his son, and consist of guidelines for good behavior designed to help the boy (and they are gender specific) to act as a good citizen, to earn promotions, and to rise in society and rank. Some of these document in writing etiquette that would have been transmitted orally in households of the middle class as well. Hedjerit's brother, for example, might have been advised on how to behave properly were he ever to be privileged enough to eat with his superiors:

> If you are one among guests
> At the table of one greater than you,
> Take what he gives as it is set before you;
> Look at what is before you,
> Don't shoot many glances at him,
> Molesting him offends the *ka*.[43]

The satirical Middle Kingdom text now called *The Teaching of Khety*[44] warns against greediness and overindulgence at the table: "If you have eaten three loaves, drunk two jugs of beer, and the belly is not yet sated, restrain it!"[45] This advice may sound familiar to us and it emphasizes an attitude of humbleness, quiet, and moderation that was considered virtuous in Ancient Egypt. It does not, however, provide insights into anything more than the most general practice of table manners, nor does it inform us of what was eaten, or who prepared the food or cleaned up afterwards. It is probable that women, being generally in charge of the household, would have been responsible for food management as well. In the *Tale of the Eloquent Peasant*, before leaving on his trip the protagonist exhorts his wife: "Look, you have twenty gallons of barley as food for you and your children. Now make for me these six gallons of barley into bread and beer for every day in which I shall travel."[46] However, others may have been involved in the cooking process as well, in particular servants, for those households that had them.

In matters of food and drink, children would have actively learned by watching and helping their elders. One of the first lessons learned by young girls and boys would have been the recognition of various vessels and their specific purposes. The fact that vessels are created in such a way as to best conform to their function helps archaeologists determine their use as well. Large, wide-mouthed, rounded vessels and bottles with grooved necks, as well as medium-sized ovoid jars and jugs, all bearing potters' marks and made of marl clay, were found in Lahun.[47] The finer quality of marl clay makes it particularly suitable for storage vessels, especially those containing liquids, while the spouts on some of them suggest that they may have been used in the cooking process as well. Other large bottles that could be sealed with mud lids were used to hold liquids such as water, wine, and beer, and were made of Nile silt and decorated with a red slip as well as black bands after the reign of Amenemhat III. While the bottoms of most storage jars were flat, these large decorated bottles were more pointed and required the use of pot-stands, also made of Nile silt. Tableware designed for fluids was made of a finer Nile silt clay, and consisted of water jars, small dishes, bowl and cup sets, and triangular, pinched, and standard cups (useful for both drinking and feeding).

Pottery from Lahun also included plates and platters that were hastily hand-formed of coarse Nile silt, and not very well fired. Both their shape and their porous material make them unsuitable for use as receptacles for wet food, but were ideal for the presentation of bulkier and drier foods such as breads, legumes, fruit, and vegetables that probably formed a large part of the Egyptian diet. One type of vessel not represented in the samples taken from Lahun, but so common in other settlements that it is likely that it was used there as well, is a small conical vessel made of coarse Nile silt. The remains of bones found in examples from other sites inform us that they were used to hold allocations of meat. In terms of cutlery, we find wooden spoons[48] (often with decorated ends) and flint or metal knives, but forks were not invented until centuries later, and were not required for the Ancient Egyptian dishes.

The most common cooking accessories for mass production, found not only in Lahun but in settlements all over Egypt and throughout its history, were bread molds. These come in a variety of shapes depending on the time period, but in Lahun they were shaped like tubes with a narrower closed end. Dough would be placed in the tubes of fired clay, which were then placed in the oven. When the bread was ready, the loaf would be removed from the mold. Because many types of molds had a tendency to break easily when the loaf was removed, usually only shards remain today.[49] Luckily, complete examples are found that were used as foundation deposits in temples and significant buildings, and their original shape is therefore certain. For private home use, bread could also have been cooked over coals without the need for molds.

Bread was a staple of the Ancient Egyptian diet. Not only did it provide fiber, but also grain is an excellent source of necessary usable protein when combined with legumes, vegetables, or nuts and seeds – all of which were readily available in Lahun. The main grains of Egypt were barley and emmer wheat – both of which are well attested in the textual record. Numerous accounts and letters document the disbursement to and from Lahun of large quantities of processed barley and emmer, often listed in units of sacks, barrels, and double barrels. One journal from the thirty-fourth year of Amenemhat III notes the "Arrival of sealer Senbi ferrying fodder in the ship of Captain Ketity. Brought in this ship: fodder, sacks 100. Arrival of sealer Nebirut in barge of Captain Kemtu on a mission. Arrival, sacks 100."[50] Another cargo list notes double barrels of processed barley, malted grain, and dates, as well as loaves that may have come from Upper Egypt to Lower Egypt.[51]

Accounts further suggest that Lahun provided grain for its own inhabitants and perhaps other parts of Egypt as well. One report mentions processed barley, perhaps going downstream, and on the other side of the papyrus we read: ". . . coming from the threshing-floors in this district: processed barley barrels, emmer barrels, given flax bundles,"[52] suggesting that flax was traded in return. The presence of farmers and agrarian workers in Lahun is confirmed by the survival of large numbers of agricultural implements such as hoes,[53] rakes,[54] winnowing scoops,[55] and sickles.[56] Intriguingly, while both barley and emmer are found in the textual record, in contrast to the barley that Petrie found in large amounts in Lahun, he does not seem to have found any actual remains of emmer, at least not as far as we can tell from his records or those of his botanical specialist Percy E. Newberry.[57]

Everybody consumed grain; it was the main form of payment for workers, while the bread and beer produced from grain were in huge demand not only from the residents of the town, but from the temples as well, where they were used in religious celebrations. Texts verify that barrels of grain were dispersed to various sectors of the town such as the "house of the pyramidion" and the "southern storerooms of the canal,"[58] as well as to estate owners who in turn would use the grain to produce provisions as festival offerings. One letter lists the different types and quantities as "deliveries of the mayor . . . as festival offerings . . . *bit*-loaves 50 100 *pesen*-loaves 10 100. . . ."[59] These estates contained within them sets of large granaries that may have helped supply the poorer residents in smaller homes, but would also store the grain that was required to produce the large quantities of temple offerings expected. Scholars have suggested there would be enough grain stored in these Lahun granaries to feed a population of between 5,000 and 9,000.[60] But Kemp has noted that these figures are inconsistent with the population density based on the size of houses, which is estimated at 3,000. An explanation may be, therefore, that much of the bread and beer produced by the estates went to temples, or to other areas in the region. Some of the smaller homes had a single small granary as well, and reconstructions place this either on the rooftop, or in the courtyard near the hearth.[61]

Different varieties of bread were known and attested in the documentary record as well as from bread molds of different shapes. Because there is not necessarily an English equivalent of these varieties, the type is mostly left untranslated here. Certain kinds of bread seem to be particularly associated with festival offerings and appear in the accounting texts:[62] *bit-*, *pat-*, *pesen-*, *bekhsu-*, *seshet-*, along with *t-hedj benben* (which literally means cones of white bread).[63] Other types of bread, perhaps produced for use outside the temple or the palace, include *qefen-*, *benbent-*, and *senu*-loaves.[64] The assortment again emphasizes the importance of bread in Ancient Egypt.

Grain was also provided to the town brewer,[65] as well as being used for household brewing. The beer produced by the grain was a weak beverage that could have been drunk by all, but it had other uses as well. Beer was also used as a medium for medicines, both because many drugs are soluble in alcohol and to mask the taste of bitter herbs. Many of the prescriptions in the Lahun Gynecological Papyrus feature the use of sweet beer.[66] Although it was weak, it was alcoholic, as was wine. In a small town like Lahun, Hedjerit would have certainly seen the negative effects of drinking too much. Inebriation was frowned upon and according to instruction texts was to be avoided. On the other hand, within a religious context the altered states produced by alcohol were condoned. In the Ramesside period in particular the Festival of Drunkenness was well attested. This celebration was associated with the goddess Hathor, and although no named Festival of Drunkenness appears in the texts from Lahun, it is likely that a good deal of drinking went on there during other festivities dedicated to the indulgent goddess.

There is no direct evidence from Lahun that beer would have been drunk by children, but sources suggest that this would have been the case. In the New Kingdom *Instructions of Ani* the father teaches his son to respect his mother because "when she sent you to school, and you were taught to write, she kept watching over you daily, with bread and beer in her house."[67] This phrase should not be taken too literally, for "bread and beer" were such indispensable staples that the phrase came to refer to food in general, much as today we might say that a hard worker is really "earning her bread and butter." Bread and beer, therefore, were also two of the most important provisions for the deceased, and were provided in tombs not necessarily in physical form, but magically via representations and texts. The gods as well needed to be nourished, and temple records list vast deliveries of provisions in the form of loaves of bread and barrels of beer.

One of Hedjerit's favorite foods was also likely grain-based: cake. Although in texts cakes are usually mentioned in a temple context, all the ingredients were there for the making, and children and adults in Ancient Egypt had a sweet tooth.

There is even a letter concerning sending a confectioner somewhere, possibly to or from a governor.[68] The main sweeteners for cakes would have been fruits, particularly dates, and honey. Although there is no archaeological evidence for the date palm in Lahun, dates themselves have been found and are known to have been used as a sweetener, as well as being mentioned in medical prescriptions, commodity lists, and inventories of cargo.[69] Honey too was used for cakes, although the greater effort involved in producing honey indicates that it would not have been as common as a sweetener like dates for the middle and lower classes. Carob was another sweet product and attested among the surviving archaeological remains from Lahun, and these may be some of the earliest known samples from Ancient Egypt. The carob tree was not native to Egypt, but evidence of trade with Palestine during that period allows us to infer that either the trees had been imported by then, or the carob found its way in as a direct import of the dried fruit itself. Other fruits of domestic origin, such as those from the sycamore fig, Christ's thorn bush, the plum-like balanite, and raisins, could all have been used as sweetener for cakes.

Evidence from the New Kingdom shows that householders could grow their own fruits and vegetables in small gardens as well. The layout of most of the homes in Lahun makes it seem unlikely that this occurred within them, even the larger ones. Each of the large estates in the north-east corner of Lahun had a courtyard with a pool and trees, which are thought to have been kept in large planters. Even some of the medium-sized homes show the remains of a small pool in a courtyard, and the trees, likely sycamore figs, may have provided some fruit, as well as shade and oxygen. Vegetables, however, require moist soil, and it is possible that the gardens were located just outside the town. The fact that few vegetables are mentioned in accounts may support the idea that they were locally grown and harvested as needed. They were not part of the major cargoes, and therefore were not included in inventories.

Occasionally letters do mention vegetables and their producers. One letter (of which only the introduction remains) is "about allocating assignments to the vegetable-producers Sire, Iku, Ankhtify, Senwosret, . . ." – all of whom are male.[70] In one endearing letter one brother, Senbu, asks his brother Ankhtify if he will send him a handful of onions: "May Herishef, lord of Nennesu[71] make your mood for you. May you send to me the ? handful, a handful of onions, . . . to your brother-there. It is good if you take note." It would indeed be serendipitous if this Ankhtify were the same person described as a vegetable-producer in the first letter, but there is no way to verify this. Archaeological remains of fruits and vegetables are scarce in Lahun (the aforementioned dates and some watermelon seeds are exceptions), and so it is only by using evidence from other time periods that we may theorize that vegetables and fruits such as lettuce, garlic, celery, and pomegranates would have been included in Hedjerit's diet.[72]

The evidence for legumes is more common, and these, eaten in combination with grain-based foods, would have satisfied the bulk of the protein needs for most families. The remains of lentils, faba beans, and peas were found by Petrie,[73] while a removal inventory includes groundnuts.[74] These basic foods were not included in funerary rituals or distributed as festival offerings, as they were simple and abundant. Their method of preparation is unknown, but there is a good chance that they were cooked down much the same way they are today in Egypt, flavored with spices such as garlic and onion and other herbs that grew wild, and served with bread as the main dish of many meals.

Another source of protein and oils that is mentioned in striking abundance in both temple and town accounts is fish. This should come as no surprise, as Lahun was built next to a large, fertile lake. At least 11 different types of fish are mentioned, some with sub-categories of having been "gutted." The large numbers mentioned in the texts provide a glimpse of the quantities that were consumed. In one account, the names of the different types are missing, but they are listed in substantial numbers "400; 50; 1,490; 100, total 2,000,"[75] while in another we read of 400 *adj*-fish and more than 1,000 gutted *rat*-fish.[76] Stone-haulers are often mentioned in the same accounting texts, and considering that the workman's village for the builders of the pyramids at Giza includes a large fish-processing area, it is likely that laborers such as these who were engaged in hard manual labor were supplied with much of the fish that was caught. Letters can give us an idea of the volume that could be collected in a catch. One missive is written from the servant of the personal estate Khemem to the overseer of the chamber, complaining that he has not received a response to a previous request, and now asks for help having the cargo counted: "Then he requested a cargo-boat to hunt out 10 catches of fish for the lord l.p.h. Then he took 500 gutted fish having brought them in as catch. The reason your humble servant is writing about it is about having it counted at the quay of Per-kheny by the lord l.p.h. Your humble servant has sent Ita about it to have. . . ."[77] Presumably Ita was sent off to count the cargo, and insure its safe arrival.

Lists also note fish that were brought by the fisherman to a separate area to be slit and gutted. The logical place to have such an area would be outside the town, preferably in the south section (though probably not by the temple in the south-west!). The rank smell of fish would have been rampant in that area, and Hedjerit's family may have enjoyed working and playing in areas where they could catch the fresh north wind. This may be part of the reason that fish do not play a role in depictions of provisions for the deceased, who would live forever in an idealized, clean afterlife filled with the divine aroma of gods and incense instead. On earth, however, Hedjerit's family would likely have had fish as part of their diet. Indeed, at Lahun Petrie uncovered a number of uniquely shaped deep oval pottery dishes, decorated on the bottom inside with an incised fish and sometimes with plants such as the water lily on either side.[78] While their function is unknown, it might seem reasonable to suggest that they were used to serve fish for a meal.

While at other Middle Kingdom sites such as that of Elephantine numerous fish bones have been found, these small faunal remains seem to have largely decomposed at Lahun. Exceptionally, small fish bones have been found that were modified and pierced for use as needles.[79] Nevertheless, the settlement provides us with an abundance of tools associated with the local fishing industry. Copper fish hooks[80] and fiber nets[81] were both distinctive tools for fishing. Fowlers, who shared the lake and marshes with the fishermen, could also have used the nets to trap their birds. While fowlers are mentioned in texts, the birds themselves are noticeably absent from both the textual record and, with the exception of bone tools,[82] the archaeological evidence.

Cattle are an energy-intensive commodity and were more carefully tracked, with herds being monitored according to numbers by life-stage (adult, young, calf), expansion by births, and depletion by the livestock being assigned for butchery or redistribution as whole units[83] or by parts.[84] Most of the herds belonged to the estates of temples – Sobek being one of the deities most frequently mentioned – as well as palaces of the pharaoh. The expense of cattle and their importance for rituals meant that the herdsmen had great responsibility. One text records the births that enlarged the herds of a king (name lost) under the "year herdsman" Neferkau, suggesting that those duties or perhaps the census were held annually.[85] In terms of other livestock there is no direct evidence for sheep or pigs in Lahun, though we know that these were common in other settlements.

What is clear is that a variety of foods would have played a part in the daily life of Lahun residents such as Hedjerit. Her diet would mainly have consisted of dishes made with the plentiful and nutritious grains, legumes, fish, vegetables, fruits, and cakes made of dates and maybe honey. Meat would have been reserved for special occasions – notably religious festivals. While the town (probably through the mayor) provided offerings to the gods in the form of nourishment worthy of the gods, such as fine bread, beer, and cattle meat, the priests would take their share, and during large festivals in which the public participated, would redistribute it back to the population. Hedjerit and her family would look forward to these occasions as a taste of the foods they might enjoy in the idealized after-life. At home, however, Hedjerit would have been provided with a nutritious (and hopefully delicious) diet, and would simultaneously have learned how to manage her own home in the future, and provide for her children.

# Notes

1    Khepri is the sun god at dawn, who appears like a dung beetle pushing his round ball of dung up from the eastern horizon into the sky.
2    The following is a summary of J. McDowell 1986; Cartwright et al. 1998.
3    The tombs of the following individuals provide the main sources: Amenemhet (BH2), Khnumhotep II (BH3), Baqt III (BH15), and Khety (BH17).
4    S. Allen 1997.

5   See EGY6859.

6   See EGY30b-c for complete sets. The spindle whorls of Lahun now at the Petrie Museum have been analyzed and were found to be made of both imported and native soft wood (Cartwright et al. 1998).

7   There is no evidence for male weavers in the Middle Kingdom, though they are depicted in New Kingdom scenes.

8   The vertical loom was not known until the Second Intermediate Period, and then men are shown using it.

9   See EGY50a–dd.

10  See EGY34.

11  See EGY37.

12  Letter UC32197 in Collier and Quirke 2002, 90–1.

13  Note that the only direct evidence for the latter is from the New Kingdom (A. McDowell 1999, 59–61).

14  See EGY94a–b.

15  Barber 1994, 198.

16  Raven 1997.

17  More than 35 are now housed in the Manchester and Petrie museums.

18  J. McDowell 1986, 239.

19  UC32094A in Collier and Quirke 2006, 144–5.

20  In the tomb of Khety in Beni Hassan (BH17).

21  Barber 1994, 194.

22  See for example UC32096 C, UC32349, UC32183, UC32360, UC32144 B, UC32137 D in Collier and Quirke 2006, 150–1, 104–5, 32–3, 108–9, 178–9, 238–9; and UC32216 (lot LVII.1) in Collier and Quirke 2002, 152–5.

23  Throughout this book, while Collier and Quirke translate this as "the servant there," I use the more reader-friendly "your humble servant."

24  Paraphrased from UC2203 in Collier and Quirke 2004, 114–17.

25  Quirke 2004b, 72.

26  A detailed overview can be found in David 1986, 164–72.

27  See EGY243.

28  See EGY238, EGY239a–c.

29  Gilmore 1986.

30  Petrie et al. 1890, 30.

31  See UC7156.

32  The best overview of clays in Lahun can be found in Bourriau and Quirke 1998.

33  UC32190 in Collier and Quirke 2006, 12–15.

34  The kickwheel or flywheel was not known in the Middle Kingdom.

35  A core is a solid shape over which a layer of clay is pressed and smoothed until it has the same shape. The clay vessel this created can then be removed from the core (which will be reused for the next vessel) for further refinement.

36  Nicholson and Patterson 1985.

37  Fitton et al. 1998.

38  UC32193 in Collier and Quirk 2006, 70–3.

39  Even if one spills olive oil on a terracotta lamp, only the wick will burn. Olive oil also generates only a little smoke.

40  Fitton et al. 1998.

41  This question has been raised in Dorman (2002) in relation to human-headed canopic jar lids from the New Kingdom, but it is applicable to any time period.

42  UC32144A in Collier and Quirke 2006, 252–3.

43  Lichtheim 1973, 65. The *ka* is one part of what we might think as the "soul" of an individual, and requires sustenance to survive.

44  It is also now known as *The Satire of the Trades*, as in chapter 4 above.

45  Lichtheim 1973, 191.

46  Lichtheim 1973, 170.

47  For the following see Fitton, Hughes, and Quirke 1998.

48  See EGY174a–b, 185.

49  Jaquet-Gordon 1981.

50  UC32190 in Collier and Quirke 2006, 8–11.

51  UC32177 in Collier and Quirke 2006, 106–7.

52  UC32096C in Collier and Quirke 2006, 150–1.

53  See EGY42-8c.

54  See EGY49a–c.

55  See EGY56a–b.

56  See EGY53; EGY700.

57  Germer 1998, 84–5.

58  UC32178 in Collier and Quirke 2006, 54–5.

59  UC32147A in Collier and Quirke 2006, 255–7.

60  Kemp 2005, 215–17.

61  The Manchester Museum "Virtual Kahun: 'Bringing Collections Together,'" www.kahun.man.ac.uk/gallery_town.htm, accessed July 7, 2006.

62  Collier and Quirke 2006, 303–7.

63  The word "benben" also refers to a short, squat obelisk, and to the pyramidion that often capped the pyramids.

64  Collier and Quirke 2002, 185–200.

65  UC32309 in Collier and Quirke 2006, 114–15.

66  UC32057 in Collier and Quirke 2004, 58–64.

67  Lichtheim 1976, 141.

68  UC32151C in Collier and Quirke 2002, 78–9.

69  Germer 1998; UC32057 in Collier and Quirke 2004, 58–64; UC32179 in Collier and Quirke 2006, 26–9; UC32177 in Collier and Quirke 2006, 106–7.

70  UC32098A in Collier and Quirke 2002, 10–11.

71  Herishef was a creator god associated with Herakleopolis (Nennesu).

72  Murray 2000.

73  Germer 1998.

74  UC32179 in Collier and Quirke 2006, 26–9.

75  The total does not of course add up to the total given in the papyrus, but so much is missing that the references are unclear. UC32097B in Collier and Quirke 2006, 152–3.

76  UC32142B in Collier and Quirke 2006, 172–3.

77  UC32205 in Collier and Quirke 2002, 120–3.

78  See EGY477; EGY479.

79  See EGY6170a–c; EGY6180c.

80  UC7251–3.

81  UC7512.
82  See EGY97, the needle case previously discussed.
83  UC32179 in Collier and Quirke 2006, 24–5.
84  See UC32361, which is headed "parts of bull for distribution," in Collier and Quirke 2006, 110–11.
85  UC32179 in Collier and Quirke 2006, 24–5.

# 6

# Learning, Earning,
and Leisure

*When I saw my brother leaving the house with a kit consisting of a palette, reeds, and a small water jug, I wanted to know where he was going. I looked around and found I was alone. Then I set out after him, hiding so as not to be seen, running after him as swiftly as a hare. Just as I saw him leaving the town walls, he turned around. Trembling overtook my body, and I threw myself on my belly, in order that he not see me. But his eyes pierced my hiding place, and he returned to me saying "Little Hedjerit, I go to be a scribe, you know you cannot follow."*

## Education

In the wake of the turbulent First Intermediate Period, the Middle Kingdom rulers focused on reorganizing the administration of the freshly reunified country. New bureaucracies were formed and new policies set into place.[1] A side-effect of this reassertion of the dominance of the central government was a need for the training of more scribes. Among other tasks, people were needed to record transactions, document policies, and chronicle royal events. The ability to read and to write was paramount to upward mobility in the officialdom, administration, and even priesthood. Nevertheless, literacy remained restricted even in the Middle Kingdom.

The topic of literacy is a thorny one and difficult to determine in the ancient world. The term itself is problematic as it glosses over the wide range of abilities that are subsumed under its umbrella. Today, functionally literate individuals may be able to read important road signs, know the alphabet, sign their name, and write simple responses on a form. Others may be able to read captions to graphics, but not be able to handle a newspaper. On the other end of the spectrum are those who not only can read dense tomes, but are able to write fluently as well.

The ability to read and the ability to write, although related, are also not identical. Individuals labeled as illiterate might not be able to write, but may still be able to recognize important signs. While this is not the venue for a discussion of literacy in Ancient Egypt, it is important to recognize that literacy was a range in that culture as well, and abilities were influenced by geographical and temporal constraints, accessibility to education, and the opportunity to practice. Thus some people estimate literacy at only 1–5 percent,[2] while others note the potential for a wider range.[3] As in the modern world, there was likely a large difference between individuals in the rural environment and those living in cosmopolitan communities such as Deir el-Medina and Lahun. Because these settlements were developed specifically for the development and administration of state-sponsored projects, the literacy levels were relatively high; thus these are towns which supply most of the textual data.

In addition, there is the added complication of registers of language, and a major difference in scripts. Registers of language exist today as well – for example, an individual well versed in literary texts may well struggle with a technical manual designed for engineers. In terms of script, even today it is far easier to read typescript rather than an individual's handwriting. In the Middle Kingdom, Egyptian texts were written in either the hieroglyphic script (the one that is most familiar to us, wherein the characters retain their shape as recognizable pictorial forms) or hieratic, which was a faster handwriting. Hieroglyphs were called *medu netjer* "divine words," and were used frequently for religious texts, decrees, autobiographies, and hymns, which were carved or painted on materials such as stone that were meant to last for eternity (Fig. 6.1). Because of the fuzzy boundary between hieroglyphs and images, hieroglyphic texts were also integrated as architectural elements and could be written left to right, right to left, or vertically top to bottom – always in a way that reflected order and aesthetics. In contrast, hieratic (Fig. 6.2) was usually written from right to left or in columns on papyrus or ostraka.

A wide variety of texts was written in hieratic, including letters, accounts, inventories, legal, magical, medical, and religious texts, and beginning in the Middle Kingdom what we think of as literary texts. Discussions of genre and categorization of Egyptian literature are ongoing, but are complicated by the Egyptian delight in incorporating what we consider different genres into a single document.[4] For example, the *Tale of Sinuhe* is a wonderful story that incorporates a hymn as well, and the entire tale is set within the framework of a tomb autobiography. Indeed, early scholars tried in vain to find an actual tomb of Sinuhe, not realizing that this was a device for the story. While most scribes can perhaps better be described as secretaries, many of the scribes of the Middle Kingdom were also inventive and skilled composers. This time period gave rise to genres such as instruction texts (framed as advice given from a father to his son), discourses (reflective ponderings on such matters as kingship and life itself), laments (which usually feature the theme of chaos overcoming order), hymns (praises to a deity or the king), and tales (what we might call fictional stories). Many of

**Figure 6.1** Sample of hiero-glyphs from the tomb-chapel of Ukhotpe, after A. M. Blackman and Apted 1953, plate 15 (courtesy of the Egypt Exploration Society).

these present an idealized, elite view of the world that cannot be accepted at face value, nor be considered as a reflection of daily life. For example, even the laments convey a horror at a world that has been disordered by a reversal of the social order, with the poor gaining access to previously restricted privileges – obviously this was only negative from the standpoint of the upper classes, and not that of those who would benefit. Nevertheless, not only the written products but the authors themselves would have had an impact on the daily life of an inhabitant of Lahun.

The large body of textual evidence found in both elite and non-elite contexts in the town attests to the widespread presence of scribes. There does not seem to have been a class restriction in Ancient Egypt on who could become a scribe, and because it would lead to higher-status positions it was likely the goal of many a young boy, and indeed the hope of his parents. In the Middle Kingdom texts proclaiming the benefits of becoming a scribe began to be composed that some have suggested were used as part of a large-scale recruitment process. Composi-tions such as the *Teaching of Khety* (mentioned above in chapter 5) promote the

**Figure 6.2** Sample of hieratic
(author's hand).

idea of being a scribe as the ideal route to success while vehemently denigrating
other trades. Again, this contrasts with what we know of the respect with which
professionals in some of the other trades were actually treated, but we should
remember that the text was also a literary exercise of sorts, skillfully and elo-
quently written. It begins as a teaching, then proceeds to list a series of trades in
menial and horrifying terms, and then finishes with a paean of praise for the
profession of scribe.

Beginning of the Instruction made by the man of Sile whose name is Dua-Khety,
for his son called Pepi, as he journeyed south to the residence to place him in the
school for scribes, among the sons of magistrates, with the elite of the residence.
He said to him:

"I have seen many beatings – set your heart on books! I watched those seized for
labor – There's nothing better than books! It's like a boat on water. . . . I'll make
you love scribedom more than your mother, I'll make its beauties stand before you;
it's the greatest of all callings, there's none like it in the land. Barely grown, still a
child, he is greeted, sent on errands, hardly returned he wears a gown. I never saw
a sculptor as envoy, nor is a goldsmith ever sent; but I have seen the smith at work
at the opening of his furnace; with fingers like claws of a crocodile he stinks more
than fish roe."[5]

The text was composed by a scribe and is obviously heavily biased, but it may have appealed to many a young Egyptian male. Certainly there seems to have been a rise in the number of scribes in the Middle Kingdom. Unfortunately, we have little evidence for the process of educating scribes.[6] The text above mentions the boy being sent to a "writing school" and therefore we know that there was a location where some children were formally educated. Whether Lahun itself had a school for scribes is uncertain, or whether students studied part-time in or near the village on their days off, as seems to have been the case in Deir el-Medina, is unknown,[7] but there is much evidence for the existence of scribes.

The presence of teachers is suggested by a papyrus containing a series of nine model letters, some with corrections in red ink.[8] These seem to have been designed to give practice in the skills a scribe would need when acting as a personal secretary to an estate manager writing to the estate owner. Most include a platitude to a deity, as well as the request. One typical example reads: "The servant of the personal estate Ser says to [. . .] l.p.h. in the favor of Sobek lord of Kheny as the servant there wishes. It is a communication to the lord l.p.h. to have brought to me some roasted grain to the servant there." In this example, there follows an indication of what should be written in red ink: "hearing clause." This is followed by the clause itself, presumably filled in by the apprentice scribe: "May your hearing be good."

Other surviving equipment, such as a writing tablet prepared for use[9] and what appears to be a board used for teaching counting,[10] confirms the presence at least of students. Most of the information that has survived concerning the educational system comes from the New Kingdom, specifically the village of Deir el-Medina. From there we find student exercises that were written on ostraka or on writing boards covered in plaster. Some have the remains of corrections in red ink which were once thought to have been those of a teacher, but have now been shown to be in the handwriting of the scribe himself.[11] In addition we have a series of texts called *The Miscellanies* that seem to consist of materials written by teachers for students, although the quality of writing of these suggests that they represent the efforts of advanced students or apprentices who were taught not in groups, but individually by a tutor.[12] As is still the case, students would have learned to write by repetitively copying these texts from a written example and also from dictation. Students would memorize and write and write, until an entire passage was completed.[13] The phrases might include proverbs, or quotations from classic works, or word lists organized by native Egyptian categories ("onomastica"). As they were writing, the young Egyptians would also be absorbing the values of the society in which they lived and codes of good conduct. Along with being copied in writing, the texts would have been recited as well. The Egyptian word for "read" is the same as the one for "recite," emphasizing the common practice of reading aloud, rather than silently. Indeed, one Middle Kingdom text, *The Instruction for Merikare*, advised "do not kill anyone whose good side you know, with whom you once chanted the writings," revealing that this could be done in groups.[14]

The first script that was learnt was hieratic – hieroglyphs were reserved for those who would specialize in carving them onto monuments. Hieratic, however, was used for the subjects that needed to be formally learned and that would be useful for bureaucratic and civil service careers. These subjects included mathematics and the geography of Egypt and of the Ancient Near East – an area that had close contact with Ancient Egypt and was politically important. It is unlikely that any foreign languages were learned, although there is a possibility that in the New Kingdom some scribes may have learned Akkadian – the language that was used for political correspondence throughout the Near East at that time. These subjects were not learned separately; the knowledge was acquired and disseminated by means of the word lists and teachings that were copied by the apprentice scribes.

The teachers were scribes themselves, and individuals with a specialty would have taught that particular subject. Along with repetition, they may have encouraged student learning with a bit of corporal punishment. One of the *Miscellanies* informs us that "a boy's ears [are] on his back,"[15] while the word for "teach" is determined by the hieroglyph of a man holding a stick. All of the texts refer to the students as "boys," never as girls. This does not necessarily mean that all women were illiterate. It is likely that royal women were schooled as well with private tutors. As for non-elite women, although the title "scribe" is rare, it does exist.[16] Moreover, the letters that remain suggest that some women were able to write. An argument has been made that they would have hired a scribe to pen the letters for them, but some of the ones from Deir el-Medina are mundane requests that could just as easily have been delivered orally and in person, rather than necessitating the sender hiring a scribe to pen the letter. Letters were also written by women in Lahun, such as the one already discussed concerning weavers. Literacy has many levels, and while most women were perhaps not schooled in the formal arts of writing poetry and eloquent tales, many may have learnt the rudiments from their schooled relatives. Indeed, if the same model was followed at Lahun as was apparently followed at Deir el-Medina, then it becomes clear that the instruction could have been performed by inhabitants of the village itself.[17] If the individual were literate he would teach his own son(s) or grand(sons), and if not, the children would be sent to someone else who was literate, and usually of higher rank. The students themselves did not necessarily hold the bureaucratic jobs that are normally associated with literacy; in Deir el-Medina, among the students was one "who would never rise above the rank of stone cutter, and possibly also one woman."[18]

While some of the skills of some scribes would have remained at the level of copyist, talented ones would have been the authors of original compositions. Indeed, while most of the authors remained anonymous, some of the most eloquent Old and Middle Kingdom composers were remembered later in poems and songs. One New Kingdom student miscellany laments:

Is there any here like Hordedef? Is there another like Imhotep? There is none among our people like Neferti, or Khety their chief. I shall make you know the name of Ptahemdjehuty and Khakheperresonbe. Is there another like Ptahhotep, or likewise, Kaires? . . . Departing life has made their names forgotten: it is writings which make them remembered.[19]

Texts such as these emphasize the importance of writing in the Egyptian ideal world, and the elite status that could be held by those who were privileged to acquire that skill. The range of scribal titles in documents from Lahun is impressive, as the following list demonstrates.[20] Each title begins with the Egyptian word "*sesh*", meaning "scribe of" or "secretary of," followed by: fisherman, the army, the town, in charge of the seal, in charge of the seal of the bureau issuing people, in charge of the seal of Gesiab, the assessor, the board, of the fields, of accounts, resins, provisions, trappers, estate of . . . , herds, the temple, Hetep-Senusret (the town of Lahun), the Outer Palace, district councilor, the vizier, as well as chief secretary, and just general secretary. The range of departments for which a scribe or secretary was needed shows the high level of bureaucracy that was prevalent. Within these departments, there were many other positions that would have required literacy, in particular the many overseers would have been able to read and write in order to properly supervise. Officials could also work part-time as priests, and within this line of work, certain levels required a high standard of literacy. Even within the military (which is well attested at Lahun as well), while a low-ranking soldier or even an elite archer had no need of writing or reading skills, commanders certainly did. In addition, scribes were brought on campaigns to keep accounts, and there is also evidence for specialized translators for forays into other lands, such as those of Nubia or Asia. For a boy of Lahun such as Hedjerit's brother Senbubu, who was skilled in writing, reading, and proper conduct, there were thus many possibilities for advancement in administration.

For women of the Middle Kingdom, however, the situation was markedly different. As mentioned above, formal schooling does not seem to have been generally available for non-royal women. Nevertheless, titles are attested that suggest that women could still hold administrative roles, even though these were uncommon. In his work on feminine titles in the Middle Kingdom,[21] Ward has collected examples of various ranks. Some of them are not surprising, such as nurse, housemaid, cleaning-woman, various attendants, domestic servant (literally "she who is allowed to walk through the house"),[22] and maidservant (there are two different terms used for this, and one may have been associated with kitchen work, while the other was more general). Other women had specialized skills, such as those of hairdresser, cosmetician, lady-in-waiting, and the prestigious sole lady-in-waiting, and while these professions still did not require literacy, they would nevertheless have allowed a lower-class woman intimate contact with the elite. Industrial titles are attested as well, such as weaver, brewer, miller, page, and winnower of the estate.

As will be discussed at a later stage, women also actively participated in the domain of the temple. Priestesses of various deities (mostly but not exclusively female) are known in the Middle Kingdom, and there is no evidence to suggest that they held any less responsibility than the male priests. Women also held the title of adorer, "watcher of Min," and lady of Amun, as well as working as professional mourners for funerals. While this was not an exclusively female occupation, the preponderance of mourners depicted are women, including older women (marked by grey hair) and girls.[23] Singers, dancers, and musicians were often women, and while we think of these today as purely for purposes of entertainment, in Ancient Egypt they were integrated into religious rituals as well. These talented women could perform alongside men, and indeed both sexes seemed to work together in small groups who would be affiliated with various temples and palaces.[24]

While in the Old Kingdom women are attested in supervisory roles, this markedly decreases through the Middle Kingdom. For example, in the First Intermediate Period the title "overseer of the troupe of singers and dancers" was held by a number of women. By the Middle Kingdom, the title is attested only for men. Other supervisory roles held by women include overseer of a storehouse, steward (f.) of a storehouse, sealer, trustworthy sealer, chief of weavers, chief physician, and there is even one controversial case of a female vizier.

None of these professions required formal school education, except that of vizier, and, of course, that of the aforementioned scribe. How women attained reading and writing skills is unknown, but it is conceivable that a girl like Hedjerit would out of curiosity have watched her brother practice, and would perhaps even have asked him to show her the basics. Most girls would also likely have learned from their mothers and other women who played a major role in their lives. Because of the high maternal mortality rate, it is important to remember that many children would have been raised by their fathers' new wives, or female relatives, and some perhaps by their fathers alone. Girls may also have served as apprentices, as has already been discussed in reference to weavers and perhaps nurses. Even entertainers would have honed their innate talents through repetitive practice and drills, led by a trainer.

Some of the titles seem to be held only by married women, and seem to have been acquired on the basis of their husband's rank. The most common title, that of *nebet per* "lady of the estate," in the Middle Kingdom also seems to be associated with married women whose husbands held higher ranks. The term is sometimes translated as "housewife," but this glosses over the important managerial duties that would have been the responsibility of the *nebet per*. These would have included overseeing staff, servants, deliveries, organizing workshops (such as those of weavers), ordering supplies, and even tending animals. Evidence from documents such as the *Hekanakhte Letters* indicate that while the male head of the estate was gone, the wife could be left in full control. Along with their professional work, virtually all women would have held busy but untitled positions as child-minders, caregivers, and food preparers – work that men could also have helped with.

## Non-literate Professions

While the beginning of this chapter focused on professions that required literacy, there were many more that did not. The ones that were common for women have just been discussed, while boys in Lahun had a range of occupations open to them such as those of potters, metal-workers, carpenters, flint-knappers, laundry-men, confectioners, farmers, fishermen, fowlers, hunters, delivery-men, mat-makers, bakers, bricklayers, builders, butchers, brewers, and bodyguards. Part-time work was also possible, especially in the priesthood or the military. The Egyptians used a calendar broken up into 10-day weeks, and evidence from the New Kingdom suggests that workers employed by the state would work eight days, and then have two days off. Whatever work the individual was engaged in, whether as the main worker himself (such as a carpenter, bricklayer, or weaver) or as a supervisor of workers, the status of work had to be accounted for. Either letters could be written to the superior, or the progress would be reported as part of a detailed account.[25]

Workers of all time periods were paid in grain – some of which would have been used to make food for the home (bread and beer), while any left over could be used to trade for other goods. Aside from basic provisions, documents from Lahun and from Deir el-Medina demonstrate that differential wages were paid out according to profession.[26] Often a part-time job could be used to supplement the basic wage, which is likely to have been goods equaling the value of eight or ten loaves of bread and two jars of beer per day.[27] Some posts offered additional benefits – some in the form of higher wages, while men and women who worked in the priesthood, which was part-time in the Middle Kingdom, would have had greater access to otherwise scarce commodities such as meat and baked goods, as well as portions of the offerings that were left for the gods or the dead.

Not all professions were ones that boys would necessarily aspire to, but they were needed nevertheless. The labor force required for major state building projects, for example, seems to have been gathered through conscription. Indeed, the large quantity of name lists and attendance records from Lahun may be based on the need to organize and distribute these corvée laborers. For example, one register from the forty-fifth year of the reign of Amenemhat III provides a monthly "roll-call of the enlisted workers who are stone haulers who are for the section of month 4 of flood and month 1 of winter."[28] Another document provides a detailed listing of work crews in four columns on one side (recto) and another on the reverse side (verso).[29] Its most recent editors describe and interpret it thus:

> the recto list has name and filiation, then second name in red, then profession or reference to an official or authority (person for whom the worker answered the

call?), and preceded by checkmark including red or black dash (for presence or absence?) and hieroglyphs for placenames (domicile?) Ankh-amenemhat, Sekhem-Senusret and Kha-(senusret), the default perhaps being Hetep-Senusret.

If the above interpretation is correct, this provides us with the identity of the individual for whom service is provided, as well as either the place where the workers live or the location in which their duty is to be carried out. Generally, the roll-calls list the individuals by filiation (that is, by their father or mother's name) and by first and second name. Some of them specify their ethnic identity, with Asiatics being especially common. We find, for example, the "Asiatic Yey's son [. . .]."[30] We know that many of the conscripts were taken from the population at Lahun, as they are listed specifically as being from Hetep-Senusret, which is probably the ancient name for the town of Lahun, thus from the town itself. In particular, conscripts and stone-haulers are mentioned frequently late in the reign of Amenemhat III, suggesting that a labor force was being organized to work on his pyramid complex at nearby Hawara.[31] This is indicated in a roll-call where the name of a monument (probably the king's pyramid itself), Ankh-Amenemhat-living-forever-and-for-eternity, appears.[32]

Name list of enlisted given as stipulated Hetep-Senusret [. . .] work on Ankh-Amenemhat-living-forever-and-for eternity section of regnal year 43 month 2 and month 3 of winter

- Director Senusret's son Khety A[. . .]
- Secretary Senet's son Senbef Senbef[. . .]
- Commander Sat-[. . .]'s son Senusretankh Senbef[. . .]

The conscripts secretary and accountant of people seem to have been important individuals listed in many documents, whose responsibility would have been to track the workers and their attendance. The absence of six stone-haulers on winter day 11 (year unknown) was carefully noted on one surviving fragment,[33] while other Middle Kingdom documents reveal that unexplained absences were treated as criminal offenses and the perpetrators could suffer serious consequences.[34] They could even be treated as deserters, with their dependents being required to fulfill their labor obligations.[35] If an individual knew in advance that he could not fulfill a required duty, he could offer a surrogate to work in his stead, particularly if he were wealthy enough to pay for one. When the initial substitution was made and the precise duties had not yet been assigned, the gender of the substitute seems to have been irrelevant.[36] But because jobs were gendered in Ancient Egypt, once the conscript had been assigned a specific task the replacement worker would then be of the same gender, appropriate for that task. Letters show that when children were called upon to work in lieu of their parent (or a parent in lieu of his or her offspring), they were always of the same gender.[37] Documents such as these reveal a darker side to life in the Late Middle Kingdom. Not only men but women and even children could be removed from their homes and called into temporary service when needed.[38] Indeed, some of the Lahun name lists and work groups that include women and their children may be registers for allocating people to manual service, including agricultural. These were not slaves in the Roman sense of being personal property, but were laborers conscripted for a specified time and task.

New research suggests that once individuals had been selected and checked off on the name lists, they would be assembled in a place the Egyptians called an "enclosure" or *khenerut*.[39] While this word has often been translated as "prison," this meaning may not be completely accurate, and the term likely refers to a compound with a more complex connotation.[40] Up to early Dynasty 12, the term was associated with the military, as well as with the production of cloth. Specifically, it was also an area to which women were conscripted from the town for state works. By the Late Middle Kingdom, the *khenerut* was no longer associated with the military.[41] Instead, it probably referred to an actual physical area located near Lahun, but very much outside the town itself, where conscripts would be temporarily quartered prior to being consigned to their required labor duty by the "secretary of the main enclosure." They would probably have been housed and fed there while they waited to continue on their journey away from home.

We do not know how an Egyptian would have felt upon being called into service in this way, but in a culture where the pharaoh rules as divine, it is likely that unquestioning service would have been expected. Indeed individuals called upon at higher levels of service (other than for manual labor) considered it a privilege and were proud to be singled out for their ability, and immortalized their successful accomplishments on behalf of the king by erecting autobiographical stelae.[42] The highly regulated nature of the conscription, and the harsh consequences for attempted avoidance, however, suggest that for laborers and menial workers it was not always a task accepted without question.[43] In any event, at the very least being called into manual labor service must have been a potential disruption to any household in Lahun in the Late Middle Kingdom.

# Leisure

On the brighter side, life was also enjoyed in Ancient Egypt, and not only by children. In general, the Egyptians had an eye for beauty and symmetry that is apparent in all of their art, and a love of eloquent speech, which apparently included both oral and written elocution. In one sense it is difficult to differentiate work and leisure activities, and even in today's society there are many examples of overlap. The potter who enjoys the process of forming his creations and integrates his own individuality into them, the singer whose voice is a source of pleasure both for her and her listeners, and the scribe who delights in his multi-layered use of rhetoric and wordplay are just a few of the many possible examples. Certainly, "entertainers" in Egypt played a multi-faceted role. Singers,

**Figure 6.3**  Musicians from the Middle Kingdom tomb of Senbi (courtesy of Ken Griffin).

dancers, and musicians are included in attendance lists tracking their work in temples, but they are also integral characters in tomb paintings depicting banquets, feasts, and major events such as installations of monuments (Fig. 6.3).[44]

It is likely that dancers in particular had an important ritual role at burials, but they were also appreciated by the living as entertainers for both public and private functions. Judging from the representations, however, dancing was primarily a spectator event with strict separation between performers and viewers. With rare exceptions, men and women danced separately, often to the accompaniment of musicians and clappers. The dance steps themselves are unknown, although scholars have attempted to structure categories based on dance style. Some of the movements depicted are indistinguishable from what we would classify as acrobatics, and are treated separately by scholars, emphasizing again the difficulty in determining native categories.[45] Aside from the representations of movement, the clothing worn by dancers invariably sets them apart from the other Egyptians in the representations.[46]

The lack of musical notation means that the styles of music must also remain elusive, but tomb paintings do offer insights into the instruments and their players. Most instruments were played by both men and women, though through the Middle Kingdom women began to predominate, at least for festive events. In the Middle Kingdom rhythm was supplied by percussive instruments including drums, rattles, and the clapping of hands.[47] As is so often the case with Egyptian artifacts, some of the objects used to make music had other functions in other contexts. Clappers, for example, were also used to repel hostile demonic entities and were used in rituals associated with birth. *Menat* necklaces, which at one end consisted of strings of mostly faience beads, were not only worn but also shaken to create a percussive rustling sound. The sistrum was made of bronze, and

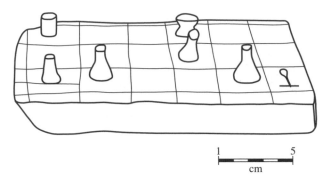

**Figure 6.4** Drawing of *senet* board EGY262 (h. 21.5 cm × w. 14.6) (courtesy of JJ Shirley).

resembled a loop which acted as a frame for a rows of disks or miniature cymbals. Shaking it by the handle would create a high tinkling or rattling sound. In scenes related to religious rituals, these three were mostly played by women and were associated with the goddess Hathor, whose distinctive face often adorned these instruments. However, they are also often found in funerary contexts, both as objects included in burials (some seem to have been too fragile for daily use and may have been produced solely for funerary use) and in scenes depicting the funeral itself. Wind instruments such as flutes and pipes are depicted from the Predynastic Period onward, and harps appear in the Old Kingdom. Other stringed instruments such as lutes and lyres also appear, some having been introduced from the New East, while others may have been native. Interestingly, few musical instruments were excavated at Lahun, and those that were, such as ivory clappers, have a distinct religious use.[48]

Other potential pastimes also cross the boundary between play and ritual. Board games have been found in Ancient Egypt, which initially would seem to have a purely secular use and to be associated with daily life, and yet they are often found in funerary contexts. The most famous perhaps are the four games of *senet* discovered in the tomb of Tutankhamun. *Senet* boards have been found in tombs from the Predynastic Period on, and beginning in the Old Kingdom the deceased could be represented as playing a solitary game of *senet* not for amusement, but as a representation of the link between this world and the sacred world beyond (Fig. 6.4).[49] By the New Kingdom, the design of the game had been revised to reflect its increasing role as a representation of the Egyptian *duat*, the afterlife. Thus the player (whether living or dead) would ritually re-enact the (hopefully) successful hazardous journey through the afterlife. Over 120 exemplars of *senet* have been found in cultures of the Ancient Near East and Egypt, created of a range of materials including simple clay, more complex faience, and even spectacularly ornate ones carved in wood with ivory decorations, suggesting that they were used by a wide range of classes as well.

**Figure 6.5** Mud game UC7222 (l. 6.3 cm) (courtesy of the Petrie Museum of Egyptian Archaeology).

The board itself is arranged in three columns of ten squares each, some marked as hazardous spaces, and some providing directions for the further movement of the piece. Movement was also randomly determined by the use of throwsticks and "knucklebones," in a way similar to the use of dice today. While the exact rules are not known, the basic movements are thought to have been similar to those of backgammon. The game of *senet* is attested at Lahun in the form of two of the boards:[50] a complete one on the inside of a wooden lid of a box that when excavated contained a baby burial and a vase,[51] and a partial example incised on limestone.[52] One of the squares on the latter is marked with the *nefer* sign meaning "good." Apparently this was a good square on which to land!

The standard pieces in the precise forms that are shown in depictions and are found in actual games found in other sites have not survived from Lahun. Another game board that survived was made of unfired clay with little indentations around the perimeter and in two columns down the center, with some of the depressions linked with incised lines. The overall shape and pattern are so similar to other examples of an Ancient Egyptian game now known as "hounds and jackals" that we can reasonably infer that this game was also played at Lahun. We know that pegs in the shape of hounds and jackals would have been placed in the indentations, but the rules of this game were not recorded either. Mud objects that strikingly resemble game-boards have also been found at Lahun (Fig. 6.5). These may have been played with sticks or reeds as pegs, but they concurrently could have been used to teach a child counting skills.

Some pastimes leave behind no material evidence, and our knowledge of them is based solely on representations. Consistently, the images featuring older children engaged in these physical activities reveal that there was segregation based on gender. The only exception is found in the Middle Kingdom illustration of a game where two boys stand upright while they twirl two girls around them so fast that they nearly defy gravity. Other than whirling, young men and women are not shown playing together, and the types of activities performed are also differentiated by gender.

The Middle Kingdom tombs of Beni Hassan show young men engaged in a number of physical activities that could be interpreted as training for battle and sport.[53] The fact that they occur in registers just above military scenes suggests that these depictions show training for hand-to-hand combat, rather than as a sport. This does not preclude the possibility of boys or young men performing them on the streets of Lahun as a pastime as well. The theme of wrestling seems to have been particularly popular, with a wide variety of positions and holds depicted step by step. The combatants are differentiated by skin color, thus clarifying the movements. Other games involved shoving, pulling, tug-of-wars, throwing sticks, lifting weights, sticks and hoops, guessing games, and grabbing each other's feet. Boys are also shown performing gymnastic feats such as flipping and doing handstands.

Just as wrestling was an activity associated with young men, ball games were usually played by young women. In the Beni Hassan tombs, girls are shown expertly juggling balls, and playing games of catch either in pairs or as a mounted team sport. In the latter, one girl carries on her back another girl who tosses a ball to another team. These same registers show women weaving and spinning, emphasizing that these activities were associated with females.[54] They also show girls performing solo backflips and being flipped by a partner, perhaps part of an acrobatic display or as an element of a dance. Altogether far fewer games for girls were depicted than there were for boys.

While I have used the term "girl" and "boy" here, it is important to note that the males and females engaged in these activities in Middle Kingdom tombs are represented as being of ambiguous age. Many of the games that have counterparts in Old Kingdom tombs clearly depict boys with sidelocks. In the Middle Kingdom tombs, however, the sidelock one would expect to find is not present, nor are the males wearing wigs characteristic of adult officials – instead their hair seems to be shorn very short. Likewise, the female acrobats shown in the Beni Hassan tomb have their hair plaited, not in the manner of a sidelock, but decorated with balls at the end. Unlike the naked wrestling boys, the girls wear strappy gowns, anklets, and bracelets, suggesting that they are older. All of the activities, whether female or male, required balance, strength, agility, and dexterity,[55] and possibly these images were meant to depict a show of proficiency of these skills. This would support a suggestion that these were not depictions of children at all, but of professionals.

Other activities such as swimming are infrequently mentioned or are depicted outside of specialized contexts. In one unique statement, a nomarch stresses in his tomb biography that he was allowed to have swimming lessons with the children of the king himself.[56] Men are rarely shown swimming, and when they are it seem to be a necessary part of their working activity, such as the Middle

116

Kingdom example of a man diving deep into the water to clear fishing weights that have become entangled.[57] Particularly in the New Kingdom, women are depicted as swimming among fish, birds, and lilies. In general, however, the presence of crocodiles and hippopotami would have made swimming in the Nile or even the lake of the Fayum a dangerous venture.

A safer pastime may have consisted of listening to stories and tales. The oral recounting of memorized tales is a common practice in virtually all literate and illiterate cultures, whether it be to an audience consisting of a young child unwilling to go to sleep or of an entire village. Storytelling is a dynamic event, relying on the involvement of the audience for feedback. The feedback may be minimal, depending on the culture, consisting only of visual cues of interest such as a widening of the eyes, a gasp, a peel of laughter, or it can involve the audience joining in on a well-known chorus or song. The telling of tales is an art, a performance, that changes with every telling. In discussing the rich tradition of African storytellers, Margaret Read describes how

> at night the people gather round the flickering fire, within the dark circle of the house, to hear the grandmother, as she leans against the house pole, telling how the animals live and talk. Her imagination and her personality illuminate the ancient stories with her own turns and phrases. The story is the same, but its telling is ever changing, for the long grass whispers its secrets anew to each hearer.[58]

Facial expression, hand gestures, voice modulation, choice of words, imitation of characters all combine to create a different story every time. Unfortunately, once the tales are written down, they are frozen, and lose the variable dynamic tension that would have existed between the storyteller and the audience. Equally unfortunate is the fact that aside from recording the tale in print or by digital means, the entire practice of storytelling leaves little to no direct tangible evidence. For Ancient Egypt, we cannot expect to find any material evidence of this practice. What we do find in relative abundance in the Middle Kingdom is literature written on both papyrus and ostraka. As discussed above, these texts were composed and copied by elite well-trained scribes, skilled in the art of formal composition. Sections of some stories are structured in a way that is evocative of tales that were conducive to oral recitation. The *Story of the Shipwrecked Sailor* is one example of a written tale that contains elements typical of folklore, such as being framed as a series of nested stories, using the theme of a talking fabulous beast, and employing certain repetitive and possibly onomatopoeic segments that would be conducive to oral transmission. The question of whether this story was originally an oral or a written composition is, however, highly debatable and unlikely to ever be resolved satisfactorily. A more important point to stress is that regardless of its origin, it could easily be memorized and then recited and repeated in an oral performance.[59]

The question of whether written works would have been performed or recited orally for the benefit of a wider audience is also complex, but is perhaps one that stands a slightly better chance of being answered on the basis of complementary evidence. A single image of a princess listening to the recital of a scribe, tomb paintings that show the act of recitation by the use of specific hand and arm gestures, as well as a few ambiguous references within literary texts may be interpreted as vague signs of the reading aloud of texts as public performance.[60] When an audience is mentioned in texts – as is the case with the didactic or teaching texts – it is usually the children of the elite. The settings are also usually those of the elite or the courts, and the content itself presents a worldview more consistent with that of the upper classes, rather than that of peasants or manual laborers. It is at least conceivable that some literary works were read aloud to a courtly or elite audience, although when this might occur and in what context remains unclear. Some texts may have been recited to a larger audience as well, but again, the evidence is ambiguous. If listening to the public telling of tales or the recitation of literary works was a common pastime, this is not reflected in the material record at all.

That literary texts were enjoyed in the daily life of at least a select few is highly likely, and a number of literary texts have survived from the village of Lahun. Included among these is a fragment of what has already been mentioned as perhaps the most popular Ancient Egyptian tale: the *Tale of Sinuhe*.[61] This story features an Egyptian who, for some mysterious reason, flees Egypt after hearing about the death of the pharaoh Amenemhat I, settles in Syria, and even raises a family there, but always longs to return to his native home of Egypt. Eventually, after writing to the new king of Egypt and explaining his eccentric behavior, he is welcomed back home to the court and invited to live out the rest of his life in his beloved land. The themes of this tale are ones that resonated strongly with the populace (particularly the elite): loyalty to the king, divine intervention and control, the constant desire to return home on the part of the hero, the familiar geography and practices of Egypt contrasted with the strangeness of the foreign land, and finally, pride in being an Egyptian.

Another fragment records part of a story of the murder and subsequent burial of a man named Hay,[62] while mentioning a man named Khenemsu. The latter appears in another fragment, which may or may not be related to the story featuring Hay.[63] Another papyrus starts with the common literary formula "there once was a man called . . . ," and in this case the protagonist is called "Neferpesdjet."[64] Other tantalizing scraps of what are likely tales have been found,[65] some revealing their likely genre only by handwriting style and language, others by the scant remains of the content. The process of composition or copying may be visible in some, like the story of Neferpesdjet, which seems to have been started but left unfinished.[66] The reverse sides of other papyri were reused for accounting, and others contained other literary texts. The fragment containing part of the story of Hay, for example, has on its reverse a magnificent hymn to the pharaoh Senusret III. Tales featuring the popular gods and the divine world were found as well. One of the longest features parts of the *Tale of Horus and Seth*,[67] while other manuscript fragments feature Anubis, Geb, and Nephthys. A number of these texts, as well as letters, reveal the sense of humor of the Egyptians, who enjoyed witty speech as well as bawdy tales.

Many of these texts, along with letters and administrative, medical, and accounting texts, were found in a single group in one of the middle-ranking homes in Lahun, but we cannot tell if this was the original area of deposition or a later transference. If this was indeed the archive of an individual, then it provides us with an interesting insight into the textual tastes of what was likely one of the elite literati in Lahun. Whether or not this individual read aloud to his family or to the public any of the texts he collected is unknown, but from the evidence it seems unlikely.

While a child such as Hedjerit could have attained a low level of literacy, it is doubtful that she would have had the opportunity to become as skilled at reading the complex literary texts as her brother could. Nor is it probable that she would have had access to these restricted documents, even if she could read them. As a young girl in the village of Lahun, her pastimes would more likely have consisted of playing with objects that could be used as toys, enjoying games with other children, many of which would mimic roles that she would soon play as an adult Egyptian, and curiously exploring her environment.

## Notes

1   For the Late Middle Kingdom see Quirke 1990; 2004b.
2   Baines 1983; Baines and Eyre 1983.
3   Bryan 1985; Lesko 1990.
4   For discussions of genre in Egyptian literature see Loprieno 1996.
5   Lichtheim 1973, 185–6.
6   A convenient overview can be found in R. Janssen and Janssen 1990, 67–89.
7   A. McDowell 1996.
8   UC32196 in Collier and Quirke 2004, 48–9.
9   See EGY71.
10  UC7091.
11  A. McDowell 2000.
12  This may apply to the Lahun model letters as well. For a discussion on the validity of using these sources as evidence for the early stages of education see A. McDowell 1996.
13  Eyre and Baines 1989.
14  A. McDowell 2000, 218.
15  P. Anastasi III, 3/13, in Caminos and Gardiner 1954, 83.
16  Ward 1986, 16–17.
17  A. McDowell 2000, 230.
18  A. McDowell 2000, 230.
19  Parkinson 1991, 150.
20  See Collier and Quirke 2002, 201; 2004, 158; 2006, 320–1.
21  Ward 1986.
22  Quirke 2004b, 73.

23  Werbrouk 1938.
24  Ward 1986, 73–8.
25  Ezzamel 2004.
26  Ezzamel 2004; A. McDowell 1999; Eyre 1999.
27  Ezzamel 2004, 523–9.
28  UC32168 in Collier and Quirke 2006, 156–7.
29  UC32170 Collier and Quirke 2006, 44–7; discussed also in Ezzamel 2004, 508–9.
30  UC32269 in Collier and Quirke 2006, 56–7.
31  Quirke 2004b, 13.
32  UC32182 in Collier and Quirk 2006, 48–9.
33  UC32275 in Collier and Quirke 2006, 272–3.
34  Ezzamel 2004, 514–15.
35  Quirke 2004b, 94.
36  Quirke 1988a, 88–9.
37  P. Berlin 10023 A and P. Berlin 10067 in Scharff 1924, 27–8, 44, cited in Quirke 1990, 163.
38  Quirke 1990, 162–3.
39  For the following see in particular Quirke 2004b, 13, 94–5; 1990, 163; 1988a. See the discussion in Ward 1986, 75–80, on *khenerut* with reference to singers and dancers.
40  For a detailed discussion of the term see Quirke 1988a.
41  Quirke 1988a, 101–2.
42  See for example the *Autobiography of Ikhernofret*, who was commissioned by Senusret III to make a monument on his behalf for the Abydos festival of Osiris, or the *Stela of Horemkhauf*, who was privileged to collect cult statues for the king (Lichtheim 1973, 123–5, 129–30).
43  A number of documents attest to conscripts fleeing the *khenerut* and deserting their duties (Quirke 1988a, 90–2).
44  Anderson 1995.
45  Decker 1992, 136–46.
46  Brunner-Traut 1958; Lexová 2000 (1935).
47  Lawergren 2001; Anderson 1995.
48  See EGY124.
49  Piccione 1980; Pusch 1979.
50  Quirke 2006, 104–5; David 1986, 163–4; Petrie et al. 1890, 30.
51  EGY73.
52  EGY262.
53  The following is best summarized in Decker 1992.
54  Decker 1992, 113.
55  Decker 1992, 117.
56  Decker 1992, 91.
57  Decker 1992, 89–95.
58  Margaret Read in Elliot 1938, vii, cited in Scheub 1990, 61.
59  See in particular Eyre and Baines, 1989, 109–14.
60  For a discussion and bibliography of the following see Parkinson 2002, 78–81.

61 UC32106C in Collier and Quirke 2004, 34–5. Its popularity is indicated by the large number of copies that have survived from a wide time range, with Parkinson 2002, 297–8, citing five Middle Kingdom and over twenty New Kingdom manuscripts on both papyrus and ostraka.

62 UC32157 in Collier and Quirke 2004, 44–7.

63 UC32105B in Collier and Quirke 2004, 32–3.

64 UC32156A in Collier and Quirke 2004, 42–3.

65 UC32105A, UC32106C, UC32107A, E+H in Collier and Quirke 2004, 32–7.

66 Quirke 2006, 105–6.

67 Parkinson 2002, 294.

# 7

# Religion

*In the cool of the morning I could hear the clatter of pottery as my mother prepared loaves of bread for today's meals, and being momentarily unobserved I took the opportunity to investigate the sweet acrid smell and wisps of dark smoke that were emanating from the courtyard. When I peeked into the room, I saw it came from the top of what looked like a small dwarf, with knees bent, and hands held above his head. Then I moved closer and saw that he was standing back to back with another, and the figure was carved of stone in its entirety. Its size, it only reached my knee. Then I bent to touch it, but it was hot! It fell with a loud noise, and then my mother rushed in and picked it up, and then while she was holding me she said: "See, it is the incense that satisfies God."*

## Religion and *Heka*

The divine, the supernatural world, was an ever-present reality in the earthly lives of the Egyptians. As we saw in the first chapter, the fact that Hedjerit was successfully born was attributed to a combination of the benign influence of the gods and the repulsion of hostile entities through the use of magic, or what the Egyptians called *heka*. In the modern western world the word "magic" is often assigned as a derogatory term to practices that run counter to or outside of the prevailing religion. At one extreme, magic is dismissed as trivial and in the same category as tricks, illusions, and entertainment. At the other extreme, magic is reviled and feared as the illegitimate counterpart to sanctioned religion.

The Egyptian concept of *heka*, although it is translated with the word "magic," had none of these negative connotations and was an integral aspect of religious practice. However, a comprehensive discussion is beyond the scope of this book, so for our purposes we might use the following simple working definition of *heka* as "the Egyptian conviction that a knowledge of words and actions of power can confer the capacity to alter radically the world of normal experience, whether it

122

be the normal experience of gods or men."[1] It was a power that was available and accessible to all Egyptians, as described in the *Instructions of Merikare*. One section of this Middle Kingdom text is devoted to the gifts that god provided mankind with, and along with elements such as the air, daylight, plants, and cattle, it is said that "He has made for them magic as a weapon to ward off the blow of events." While it was a gift from the god to mankind, the gods themselves were imbued with innate *heka*. Priests were magic-users as well, and some who were particularly skilled at using *heka* bore the title "master of *Heka*." While *heka* itself was a neutral power – there was no concept of black or white magic, or witches and warlocks – it could be used for both positive and negative purposes. In either case, it functioned in both the private and public spheres, and at both an individual and state level, within the context of religion.

Religion also was integrated into all facets of life – there was no artificial division between the secular and religious spheres. The king was also a god, while a temple functioned as a proclamation of his power, as a home for the god(s) associated with it, and as an economic institution. Even the space upon which a temple was built was sacred, while rituals provided further purification at every stage, including the burial of a foundation deposit. In the Middle Kingdom these may include food offerings, pottery and stone vessels, jewelry, mud-bricks formed around objects, building materials, and model tools (many of which also provide insights into everyday life). Homes had a practical use, of course, but their very construction also incorporated religious beliefs and elements that activated *heka*. Front doors, which act as barriers between the safe interior space and the unpredictable outside world, were often painted red – a powerful apotropaic color that was able to repel uninvited entities, whether they were earthly creatures such as humans or snakes, or demons crossing over from the other world. Even items of everyday life such as mirrors (as we have seen) and spoons were infused with religious aura.

The key to the use of *heka* and the practice of religion was knowledge. One had to know the proper words, gestures, and materials necessary to achieve the desired aims. This knowledge could be acquired through various means. Some of the more complex and state-related rituals were restricted to the use of selected priests and literate individuals who had access to texts stored probably in the scriptorium known as the House of Life. For everyday applications, such as those associated with successful childbirth or the curing of disease, the knowledge of proper practice would be transmitted orally, and by example. Unfortunately, these leave little trace in the archaeological record. Sometimes the only material manifestation that remains is an object whose use cannot be readily explained. As with so much of Ancient Egyptian life, we are left to interpret these as best we can. In particular, it is the everyday private religious practices that remain frustratingly intangible. Nevertheless, settlements such as Lahun do provide clues for our reconstruction, which in this chapter will focus on religious beliefs and practice, and on the application of *heka* in the life of the town's inhabitants and the local temples. Although Egyptian religion is often by default relegated to funerary customs, in fact these were but a part of the belief system, and those practices will be discussed at a later point.

## Divinities

References to deities abound in most genres of texts including literary, medical, and letters. Business letters that have survived from Lahun are all ones that a scribe would write on behalf of the "servant of the personal estate" of an individual, and like business letters today, they follow a standard template of sorts. They begin with an address by the servant to his lord, then proceed to discuss the concerns of the communication (which are often related to commodities such as seed or grain), and end with a "hearing clause" such as "may your hearing be good" to encourage the careful reading of the letter by the recipient. Often, a blessing on behalf of the recipient is also included in the form of a statement declaring the beneficiary to be in the favor of a specific god, sometimes of a specific area. For example: "The servant of the personal estate Horwerra [name of servant] says to Iaib l.p.h. [estate owner and recipient] in the favor of Hathor [goddess] mistress of Byblos as your humble servant wishes."[2] With the exception of "Sheret," the deities mentioned in the model letters are all popular ones: Sokary, Anubis, Sekhmet, Sobek (twice), Hathor, and the pharaoh himself (twice). Some seem to be aspects associated with a specific location, such as the aforementioned Hathor mistress of Byblos and Anubis lord of Miu, while most are deities that would have been known in any area of Egypt (which is precisely why they appeared in formulaic model letters).

Analyses of other documents, including accounting, legal, and temple documents as well as letters, offer insights into the deities that were venerated locally.[3] Sobek in particular was worshiped in the area, and a reference in a letter to Sobek lord of the town probably does refer to a neighboring temple. Nearby in the Fayum, Amenemhet III built a large temple to Sobek, and in the pharaoh's mortuary temple Petrie discovered a colossal statue of Sobek and one of Hathor. The goddess Hathor was arguably the most popular goddess for most of Egypt's history. Most often represented as a cow, as a woman with a cow's head, as a woman wearing a crown with a sun disk between cow horns, or simply as a full-frontal woman's face with cow ears, she represented beauty, love, femininity, motherly care, and joy. A single Egyptian deity could appear in different aspects, and one of her most popular was that of Sekhmet, a lioness-headed deity associated with destruction and vengeance but also healing.

Sopdu, another deity mentioned in the texts, was a god of the east, with an Asiatic pointed beard and a crown of two tall feathers. His temple was likely in another settlement, *Ges-jaby* ("the left/eastern side"), somewhere in the larger Illahun region.[4] Anubis was the jackal-headed god of embalming and funerary rites, and possibly had a cultic space at the town itself that will be discussed below. The god Sokar was a deity whose function, like that of so many Egyptian deities, was complex and fluid. Often represented with the head of a falcon, his primary role was within the funerary realm, and in the Memphite region in particular he was the main deity of the necropolis. He was also, however, associated with crafts such as metal-work and jewelry-making. The pharaoh, as living embodiment of the god Horus, was also divine and bestowed divine favors. It is not surprising to find any of these deities mentioned, as they were all popular at that time.

The reference in the letter to the aspect of Hathor associated with Byblos is particularly interesting for our understanding of Egyptian life in the Middle Kingdom. Byblos was a major sea port on the Phoenician coast that had enjoyed trading relations with Egypt from the Predynastic Period onward. The main deity of Byblos was the goddess Baalat (which simply means "the Lady"), who was identified with Astarte (of Canaanite origin) and Ishtar (of Mesopotamian origin). At her Phoenician temple, Egyptians identified "the Lady" with their own goddess Hathor, and thereafter Hathor lady of Byblos became one of the most venerated aspects of the goddess in Egypt as well. The fact that she is mentioned in the very templates for Egyptian letters is therefore no surprise. We have already come across numerous indications that there was cultural exchange between the inhabitants of Lahun and those of the Levant, and this manifestation of Hathor of Byblos in the model letters reinforces our impression of Lahun as a cosmopolitan town. However, they offer scant insight into religious practice and the impact of the divine at a practical everyday level. For glimpses of private religiosity we turn to archaeological evidence.

## Divinities in the Home

As discussed earlier, Bes and Taweret were two of the most common household deities at all levels of society. They protected vulnerable individuals, such as pregnant women and young children. Their help could be tapped through the use of amulets, as well as specialized instruments such as the birth tusks and bricks already discussed. In addition, figurines were created to help focus prayers and to channel requests to the deities. One limestone statuette of the standing hippopotamus goddess Taweret was found in Lahun, and was about 31 cm high.[5] At this height, it could easily have been placed on a shrine or a cultic installation. Although these shrines were not found in Lahun, they have been uncovered in New Kingdom settlements such as Amarna and Deir el-Medina. However, the statuette was attached to a solid base (now broken off), and could just as easily have been placed directly on the ground. Another statuette that was never finished is more ambiguous, (it has been called an ape), but the tripartite wig and large belly do suggest it was Taweret, especially as the limestone bears traces of red paint.[6] It is likely that the use of red paint was to enhance the apotropaic power of the figures, indicating again that ordinary Egyptians had access to at least some levels of *heka* to transmit their prayers to the goddess, and conversely to channel her powers to protect people from harm.

**Figure 7.1**  Mud hippo UC7210 (l. 6.3 cm) (courtesy of the Petrie Museum of Egyptian Archaeology).

Bands of red were painted on another limestone hippo, this time shaped as a pure animal, but in this case the purpose may have been quite different. In Ancient Egypt, the nature of the hippo was ambivalent, for as well as representing Taweret, the hippo in pure animal form also represented Seth, the Egyptian deity associated with chaos and rebellion. This identification was prevalent in the late Middle Kingdom, and in this case the red paint could have been used to emphasize the Sethian link.[7] The painted bands could even have acted as ropes or tethers to restrain the hippo from harming the individual, while concurrently representing the symbolic victory of order over chaos.[8]

Other figurines found at Lahun that may have had a similar ritual function include those in the form of crocodiles, birds, pigs (this identification is often debatable), lizards (?), quadrupeds that cannot be easily identified as a specific animal, a startling black mud ape (?) with beaded eyes, and humans, both male and female.[9] Many of these are made of mud (Fig. 7.1) and were originally interpreted as toys, but the context in which comparable objects are found at other Middle Kingdom sites, such as the forts of Uronarti and Buhen, cemeteries (tombs of adults), and shrines dedicated to Hathor, suggest that at least their use was multivalent, and that some are unlikely to have been toys at all.[10]

The female figurines have already been discussed to some extent, and will be again when we discuss the issue of fertility both in this life and in the afterlife. At the moment, it is important to note that rather than being a single homogeneous group, the female figurines come in a variety of shapes, sizes, and materials, and the different types conceivably had different uses. For example, in Lahun alone, the following types of humanoid figures are attested (gender has here been assigned only when obvious primary sexual characteristics are represented or other Middle Kingdom markers of gender are present, such as hairstyle):[11]

1   Female:
   a   faience figurines decorated with black marks (often interpreted as tattoos) and girdles or belts;

b wooden "paddle dolls";
  i hair with mud pellets that was probably meant to be placed on female "paddle dolls";
c clay figurines decorated with deep incised dots.
2 Male:
  a limestone figures of two boys wrestling or embracing, with traces of red paint;[12]
  b mud mummy in a sarcophagus.[13]
3 Gender uncertain:
  a wooden figure with movable limbs (wearing what appears to be a long skirt and therefore possibly female, possibly Asiatic);
  b rag "doll";[14]
  c clay human with head painted red;[15]
  d mud figures with elongated head;
  e the previously mentioned mud "ape."

In much of the literature and many catalogs, ambiguous figures are labeled by default as male. However, unless there is a corresponding type with manifest female characteristics, that assumption is here avoided. When the Egyptians wanted to emphasize the masculinity of a representation, whether two- or three-dimensional, they had recourse to as many gender-related markers as for femininity. In some cases the ambiguity may be the result of the creator assuming the default is male, or of being specifically ambiguous because the gender was unimportant for the function, or simply of the piece being unfinished.

The question we need to ask is how these objects might have been used, and what role they could have played, in the daily life of the inhabitants of Lahun. The relatively large quantity of mud artifacts suggests that they were popular, and from the crudeness of their shapes we can infer that they were not created by specialists. Made of mud and left unfired, they could nevertheless have served as humble votive offerings (dedications) to the local deities in return for blessings received, or have been offered along with prayers in the hopes of receiving favors. Because they were so ubiquitous, they could have been used by any member of society, of any age. As discussed before, they could also have been used as toys, and functioned as teaching tools for instilling piety in children. It is also possible that some, such as the one shaped like a human with the head painted red, could have been used for execration rituals.

These are rituals designed to render ineffectual any hostile individuals, groups, or malignant forces that could potentially harm an individual Egyptian, or the state itself. The best known of these rituals incorporate the use of text, object, and gesture. Through the writing of lists of the enemies or forces to be defeated (usually in red ink) on an object such as a pottery bowl or figurine, usually shaped as a foreigner or prisoner, and then the smashing or burying of the object, the potential power of the adversary was sympathetically broken and neutralized as well. A large number of these bowls or figurines have been discovered from the

Middle Kingdom, and include the following categories (only a few examples are given here so the reader can get a flavor of the texts, as the lists range from the very brief to rather protracted and repetitive catalogs):[16]

- *Nubia:*
  - the ruler of Kush, Auau, born of [. . .], and all the stricken ones who are with him;
  - the ruler of Saï, Steqtenkekh, and all the stricken ones who are with him;
  - every Nubian of Kush, of Muger, of Saï, of Irs [. . .], of Nasem, of Rida, . . . ;
  - their strong men, their messengers, their confederates, their allies, who will rebel, who will plot, who will fight, who will say that they will fight, who will say the they will rebel, in this entire land;
- lists of *Asiatics* and *Libyans* following the same formula.
- *Egyptians:*
  - all people, all patricians, all commoners, all men, all eunuchs, all women, all nobles, who will rebel, who will plot, who will fight, who will say that they will fight, who will say that they will fight, who will say that they will rebel, every rebel who will say that he will rebel, in this entire land;
  - the deceased Ameni, tutor of Sit-Bastet, who raised Sit-Hathor, daughter of Neferu. . . .
- *Evil things:*
  - every evil word, every evil speech, every evil slander, every evil intent, every evil plot, every evil fight, every evil disturbance, every evil plan, every evil thing, every evil dream in every evil sleep.

These texts reveal the power that the spoken word had in Ancient Egypt. The danger was not only from those who fought and rebelled, but also those who *said* that they would fight or rebel. Threats from the living as well as the dead were treated just as seriously as the actions themselves. The very thought of any hostile act, whether verbalized or not, whether consciously considered while awake or dreamed about while asleep, that could disrupt order in Egypt was enough to warrant a pre-emptive magical strike. While complex lists such as these were necessary for the protection of the state and its inhabitants, a resident of Lahun could have perhaps fashioned his or her own figurine, then painted it or parts of it red, and later performed whatever ritual was necessary in order to insure that the power of the adversary was nullified. Thus, rather than being a toy, the humanoid figure listed above as (3c) with the red-painted head may have been a powerful magical conduit through which a poor resident could access the same *heka* that a priest would use for the protection of Egypt.

A curious type of figure that was found in other Middle Kingdom sites is that of (2a) above, the limestone figures of two boys wrestling or embracing, with traces of red paint still visible. These have been variously interpreted as toys representing apes or young wrestlers (especially in light of the prevalence of tomb paintings depicting wrestlers).[17] However, these may also have a religious significance. A similar figure found in a tomb in Abydos has been interpreted as representing two males emphasizing the "eternal struggle between opposing forces" by engaging in combat.[18] The theme of the recurring victory of order over chaos was one of the key motifs in Ancient Egyptian myths, including the fundamental Horus and Seth cycle that provides the model for kingship in Ancient Egypt, as well as the nightly struggle of the sun god Ra against Apep, the serpent of chaos. These themes are played out in Middle Kingdom tombs in the form of scenes of wrestling, as well as hunting in the desert and fishing in the marshes where order (*maat*) is continually maintained by the virtual subjugation of the wild. The Lahun "wrestling" figurines may have fulfilled the same function on a domestic level.

Many of the other figurines mentioned above were used in the process of activating *heka* through spells. From the Middle Kingdom these spells have survived on scraps of papyri as well as being embedded within the funerary corpus of texts known by Egyptologists as "the Coffin Texts."[19] The spells themselves were generally organized like a prescription: they often stated the goal of the spell or the problem it was meant to solve and specified the correct words to be spoken, along with any gestures and objects that needed to be used. As in other documents, most of the text was written in black ink, with important sections emphasized by the use of red ink. But the crux of their effectiveness was that the predicament and the cure were set within a religious context through the use of myth. Deities were called upon for aid and both the healer and the patient were identified with gods. Isis and Horus are the most frequently attested, with the healer often playing the role of Isis, and the patient Horus, thus re-enacting their divine drama and allowing the participants to embody their power.

An example of a spell (dating from the New Kingdom) is:

> The crew stood still, saying: "Ra is suffering from his belly! Let there be called to the great ones who are in Heliopolis: 'Please write: "Ra is suffering from his belly. If he spends a time suffering from it, will then the god live on underneath?"'"

> "Let an appeal be made to the opening of the West Region through the soil. As soon as he has placed his hand on his belly, his suffering will begin to be healed!"

> Words to be said over a woman's statue of clay. As for anything he suffers from in his belly – the affliction will be sent down from him into the Isis-statue, until he is healed.[20]

In this case, the magical paraphernalia consisted of one simple item – a clay figurine in the shape of a woman's figure of Isis, thus a female figure.[21] Because most spells refer to myths, they are one of our richest sources for Egyptian stories about their gods. A very few episodes are related as longer narratives, but they are the exception rather than the rule. Spells such as this also conveniently provide clues to the use of artifacts which would otherwise remain enigmatic. Some of the objects initially described by archaeologists as children's toys may very well have had an important ritual function as integral components of spells such as this one. That spells were used in Lahun is confirmed by a fragment of a papyrus roll that contains the remains of a spell for protection:[22]

> I pluck [. . .] me against anything. A man should say this formula making his protection while passing around. Item: I am the one who is in the blinded wedjat-eye, I am its protection. A man should say this formula, writing an eye on his hand in red ocher when he has added his name in its pupil in writing; then he [. . .] it. This is to save him from pain . . .

While many if not most of the inhabitants were illiterate, the spells could easily have been memorized and transmitted orally. For the more exotic and unconventional afflictions, such as the plague that seems to have affected Egypt in the New Kingdom, people would have had to rely on priests who had access to the scriptorium for uncommon spells. Because the priesthood was a part-time occupation in the Middle Kingdom, some remedies would have been provided by local lector priests well versed in the use of magic. Indeed, the tools of the trade of just such a literate individual, who was skilled in both magic and healing, were found during an excavation of a Dynasty 12 tomb in a storehouse behind the Ramesseum far south in western Thebes. The excavators discovered a wooden box with a jackal painted on its lid that contained: magico-medical papyri, literary texts and fictional tales, a hymn to Sobek, an onomasticon (a listing by categories of various animals, plants, and towns), a ritual for the statue of Senusret II, part of a religious drama, copies of dispatches to the fortress of Semna, and administrative texts.[23] Nearby were found fragments of hippopotamus birth tusks; reed pens; "an ivory clapper"; "a segment of magic rod"; various amulets and beads; figurines including ones of women, a lion, a baboon, an ivory herdsman with a calf, and a wooden figure of Beset wielding two snake wands; and a large snake staff made of bronze, which was originally found entwined with hair.[24] The box itself was labeled as the property of an "overseer of secrets" – one of the titles that could be earned by a priest.[25]

Because artifacts of this type are attested in other contexts, including Lahun, it is probable that that town as well had its magical and medical needs served by one of the part-time priests who would use artifacts and texts such as these, perhaps proclaiming his proficiency by wielding a similar serpent staff of bronze. But when in a hurry, other methods of combating mundane problems could also have been common knowledge in Middle Kingdom Lahun. We can easily imagine Hedjerit watching her older brother taking some red ocher, mixing it with water, and carefully drawing a wedjat eye on his hand while reciting the correct formula.

Spells have survived for an immense range of predicaments ranging from scorpion and snake bites, headaches, burns, bellyaches, colds, fevers, nightmares, and disorders of various limbs and organs to the dreaded Asiatic disease, the influence of demons,[26] and the generic protection of the house. As the types of problems for which magic was used shows, the line between magic and medicine was blurred, if it existed at all, and magical rituals would have been practiced on a daily basis. The materials proscribed for the creation of magical objects and ingredients were varied, though certain materials appear more frequently than others. Many would have been readily accessible to any Egyptian – one remedy for pain required only spit,[27] while another was more complicated and required stalks of reeds twisted with mucus into four knots. Reeds, knots, milk, feces, honey, and beer appear frequently, while more exotic ingredients such as gold pellets[28] or the phallus of an ass[29] would have been available only to a select few. Spells or magically charged items could also be enclosed within a cylindrical case and then worn about the neck as constant protection.[30] One such case was found in a Middle Kingdom tomb at the nearby cemetery of Haraga.[31] Made of a copper alloy coated with incised gold, it contained three copper wire balls and the decayed remnants of some organic material – probably the remains of a spell written on papyrus. But objects specifically made of clay or mud were some of the most commonly prescribed ingredients of spells, and these objects – unlike those made of more perishable materials such as clumps of grass, papyrus, or milk – are more likely to have survived to the present.

Clay was not simply used as a cheap substitute for more expensive materials, but was itself a magically potent substance. The fact that the very formation of clay is a creative process is reflected on the mythical level as well. The god Khnum uses clay to create each individual's *ka* or double. It can also be a powerful weapon in the hands of a god. In order to trick the god Ra into revealing his name, the great magician goddess Isis mixes the spittle of the aged god Ra with earth, and uses this clay or mud to make a "noble serpent" with which to bite and poison the sun god. The divine association of clay is confirmed in a much later ritual of the "four clay balls." There, it is specified that they are "balls which came into existence for Ra, the issue of Geb, the issue of Osiris, you who are solid on earth, you who are alive in Nun."[32] While that ritual was restricted to the high priesthood, and other balls that were placed in tombs were meant to protect Osiris, clay and mud balls have also been found in non-royal contexts such as at military fortresses, administrative centers, and settlements such as Amarna. Early researchers sliced one of those balls in half to reveal locks of hair inside.[33] The use of clay is clear, but the reason for putting hair into a ball and preserving it is not immediately apparent. Here, modern ethnographic evidence may provide clues. In the 1920s a British doctor named Winifred Blackman went to live with the villagers of Upper Egypt, who at that time still retained many old customs.[34] Being a woman herself, she had access to a layer of traditions and beliefs that would have been inaccessible to males. There, many of the boys in both Muslim and Coptic families had their heads shaved, except for tufts. At a certain point that seemed unrelated to his age (though Blackman notes that it usually occurred well before the boy had reached puberty), the boy's tufts would be cut off. The hair was then either buried loose just outside the location where the haircutting took place (usually a tomb or a mosque), or was first placed in a ball of clay. The hair was then dedicated to an intermediary to the divine, either a sheikh (if Muslim) or a saint (if Coptic).

It is possible that a similar practice existed in Ancient Egypt, although the more equal emphasis on boys and girls would perhaps point to the hair belonging to that of either gender. However, this is one possible reconstruction only. The hair may have belonged to adults, or to the aged, and have been placed in the clay to symbolically protect the individual. Or conversely, holding a ball of clay with someone's hair may have proffered control over that individual to the keeper of the hair. Whatever the purpose of the clay balls in Ancient Egypt, these objects and others made of clay, mud, and even stone were simple to fashion yet rich in magical power, and thus must have been popular in the everyday lives of the Egyptians.

In contrast, faience objects had to be made by specialists. Although faience is a ceramic material, it is not made of clay. Instead, it is composed of ground quartz or sand (the primary ingredient of which is silica), to which lime, natron, or plant ash have been added. This dry material would be mixed with water, then shaped by hand or in a mold, or modeled over a core, glazed, and then fired. Copper in the glaze would create the trademark bright blue-green color, though in the New Kingdom the Egyptians experimented with adding pigments to the glaze to produce a wide range of color. The color of Egyptian faience is similar to that of lapis-lazuli, , the exotic stone from Afghanistan, and the word for both materials was the same: *tjehenet*, meaning "glittery-bright," indicating that this characteristic, rather than just the flat color itself, was the distinguishing feature of both materials. At times, faience seems to have acquired a value of its own, perhaps because of its "glittery" nature, which was associated with the wings of the falcon, or perhaps because its color could be similar to that of lapis. Thus, on a wealth index that is based on the effort that had to be expended for a raw material, faience is given a value of 11 (the highest is given 19) and thus ranks ninth from the top. But on an index that is based on internal Egyptian criteria, which would include its symbolic value, it rates a 7 (the highest is given 14) and thus ranks seventh from the top – higher than we might expect, though still about midway.[35]

These inconsistencies remind us that the value that we would place on a particular material is not necessarily the same as that of the Ancient Egyptians. As a further example, on an effort-expenditure index lapis and bronze rank the highest, with gold ranked much lower. But according to Egyptian documentary evidence, silver, electrum (a mixture of gold and silver), and gold are at the top, followed by lapis. Religious beliefs play an important role in this, as silver was not only a rare substance but was believed to represent the bones of the gods, electrum the rays of the sun, gold divine flesh, and lapis the color of the hair of the gods.

Faience was a difficult material to work with, and required specialists. Objects of faience were therefore not always destined for the same use as ones of clay or mud. For example, female figurines of faience similar to the one found in Lahun are usually found in tombs and in shrines, especially those devoted to Hathor. In the Middle Kingdom these figurines were particularly common and were likely placed in tombs to protect the deceased (both males and females), and at shrines to encourage the goddess to ensure a woman's fertility and successful birthing of a child by people who could afford such objects. These figurines' ultimate destination and the expertise required to work with this material is a possible explanation for their scarcity in Lahun relative to figures of clay.

While clay balls and animal figurines would be used when needed, other religiously charged objects would have been a constant everyday presence in the home. Cult installations, offering stands, lamps, and incense burners can be considered as semi-permanent features of the homes in which they were found. While some of the artifacts here may have been destined for use only in temples, the fact that the probable findspot of many of them was the homes allows for their interpretation as objects of domestic use as well, and they will be discussed here within that context. The offering stands that have been found in Lahun are unique to that settlement, and remind us again of the danger of overgeneralizing from one site to another that may be distant in time or place. Although made of different materials (two are of limestone, a smaller one is of fired clay), the ones that have survived mostly intact feature two bow-legged humans standing back to back. The largest intact pair hold an offering tray on their heads,[36] while the smallest intact pair have their hands down, and the small offering tray is placed on the top of a rectangular columned structure (perhaps meant to represent a shrine) that surrounds them.[37]

We are not sure what would have been placed in the containers – bread or dough have been suggested, which were apparently found in situ on some stands,[38] but the specific offering could also have been variable depending on the ritual context. A limestone stand found in the mayor's house[39] is shaped in the form of two pudgy figures holding a deep bowl, which might have held incense for burning or oil for use as a lamp (Fig. 7.2).[40] Fragments of what might have been similar stands have been found made of limestone and pottery – all that remains of these is the chubby bodies or the heads with attached bowls (Fig. 7.3).[41]

Initially, and still in most literature, these stands are described as being in the shape of dwarfs. Their bowed legs, forward-facing heads, and pot bellies are interpreted as representing those characteristics associated with the god Bes, or his affiliate, the apotropaic demon-fighting god Aha, or his feminine counterpart Ahat, who was particularly popular in the Late Middle Kingdom.[42] In his discussion on a similar figure now in the Leiden museum, Maarten Raven has noted that these features are ambiguous, and that the sexless facial features, stubby legs, slack breasts, and rotund belly are also characteristic of a specific corpus of female figured vessels from the New Kingdom.[43] The latter have been interpreted as

**Figure 7.2** Dwarf lamp/tray UC16520 (h. 30+ cm) (courtesy of the Petrie Museum of Egyptian Archaeology).

**Figure 7.3** Dwarf lamp/tray head UC16525 (h. 10.0 cm) (courtesy of the Petrie Museum of Egyptian Archaeology).

vessels shaped in the form of pregnant women that would have contained a substance to help a pregnant woman bring her child successfully to term. The genitals in both the stands and the vessels were either unmarked or ambiguously marked – the protuberance on the genitals of some of the vessels is interpreted as a tampon – and this is unlikely to have been accidental. Egyptian deities and categories were not strictly bounded, and the Middle Kingdom stands could embody within them at the same time the concept of successful female pregnancy and fertility, along with the apotropaic functions of Bes or Aha or Ahat. As Raven explains:[44]

> In other words, the iconography of this family or class of deities is best regarded as a polythetic set of attributes: each depiction possesses a large number of the attributes constituting the set, each attribute is shared by large numbers of depictions, but no single attribute is both sufficient and necessary to define the class membership. This explains why one cannot designate these figures as Bes, Aha, Ptah, Pataekos, or even "The Dwarf." It is impossible to equate these terms with strict iconographical types, implying that the presence or absence of one attribute would be characteristic of one of these deities only.

However we choose to label them, on the basis of their iconography and context it is probable that these stands were used in household cults associated with birth, rebirth, and fertility. These rituals may have been focused not only specifically on the women in the household, but on the general concept of insuring the protection of the household as a whole, and the continued fruitfulness and productivity of each of its members.

Other stands with similarly shaped bowls but different forms have also been found in the Lahun region, and these also are unique to the area. In the town, at least three fragments of limestone burners and one complete one were found that were shaped like miniature columns on square bases (Fig. 7.4).[45] The shafts of the columns were round, and the capital of the complete one was carved to resemble closed white lotus buds (actually a water lily) bound with rope. On top of the capital was a square abacus on which sat a small cup with a hollow depression to hold either incense, oil, or a bit of dough. Judging from complete ones, the burners likely stood almost 42 cm tall – approximately the same height as the larger of the anthropoid offering stands. Two of the limestone columns were found in the corridor of one of the tombs in the Lahun cemetery. The one shown in Fig. 7.1 still contained within it the charred remains of a wick, indicating that this one was used as a lamp.[46] The shape of this lamp is not lotiform, but rather smooth and unadorned. There are not enough lamps remaining for us to infer that the different shapes correlate to different functions – for example, domestic versus funerary. The fact that these were found in the tomb should not lead us to imagine that their sole use was as funerary artifacts. Others were found in the town itself, and it is possible that the lamps/burners could be used wherever they were needed. Lamps also had a multivalent purpose: they provided illumination, but filled with scented oil they would also offer the gift of sweet aroma.

The use of an offering stand in any environment, whether it be outdoors or in a temple, tomb, or home, would demarcate that area as a sacred space. While religion permeates so much of Ancient Egyptian life, this sanctified zone was a specifically liminal area within which the boundaries that separate the divine world and the profane were more permeable. The stands were visual, tactile, and

**Figure 7.4** Column lamp UC16794
(h. 43.0 cm) (courtesy of the Petrie Museum
of Egyptian Archaeology).

functional markers, scent could also be used to evoke a particular state of mind while stimulating memory and recognition. In Ancient Egyptian myths, the presence of a god was often heralded by his or her divine aroma. As an offering to the gods and to sanctify a space, the Egyptians therefore burned incense to create an atmosphere that was both suitable for reverence and inviting to the gods. Indeed, the Egyptian word for incense is *senetjer*, which means "to cause to be divine." As one might expect, incense is well attested in inventory lists and supplies that were destined for temple use, but incense pellets are also attested in two removal papyri from Lahun that seem to have had a more domestic function.[47] The offering stands or lamps mentioned above also could have held incense. One that is currently housed in the Petrie museum and is likely to be from Lahun has the remains of a dark deposit that has yet to be analyzed, but which could possibly be incense.[48] We can imagine that a specific area of the home, a room, or even a part of a room, would have been reserved for prayer and offerings to the gods – a sacred space the boundaries of which were demarcated visually and through scent. In Lahun, the heady aroma of incense would have wafted through homes as well as temples, a continual reminder of the numinous presence of the divine.

In a room in one of the medium houses, Petrie found another unique artifact (Fig. 7.5) in the shape "of an arm supporting a cup, evidently intended to be

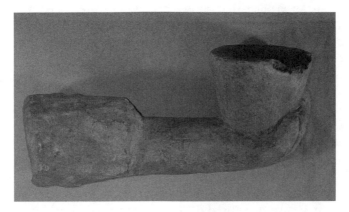

**Figure 7.5** Hand incense holder/lamp UC16521
(l. 24.0 cm × h. 10.7 cm) (courtesy of the Petrie Museum
of Egyptian Archaeology).

built in to a wall so as to project."[49] The cup would likely either have held incense
or been filled with oil and a wick for use as a source of illumination.[50] The hand
itself had religious significance, as the hand of god was a familiar concept to
Middle Kingdom Egyptians. Although it was not until the New Kingdom that
the idea of a man's destiny being entirely in the hand of god was expressed, we
find other religiously charged artifacts shaped as hands. For example, clappers
that were used in dancing rituals (particularly those associated with Hathor) and
to frighten away demonic entities were often shaped in the form of an arm and
hand.[51] One ivory hand with the emblem of Hathor on the wrist, found in the
New Kingdom settlement of Deir el-Ballas, is thought to have been used as part
of a dance to Hathor, during which the hand would be held aloft and reflected
in a mirror. New Kingdom elite women could hold the title "hand of god,"
which reflects the role of the hand as a feminine construct in the main creation
myth.[52] Because this particular artifact is without parallel in Egypt, it is difficult
to assign meaning to it, and it could very well have been simply a clever invention
on the part of a craftsman.

The recipient of the offerings, whether these consisted of foods, libations,
illumination, or scent, is, however, unclear. On some of the stands, the figures
are dwarf-like, and could represent the god Bes. In this case, the offerings could
have been presented in return for or to encourage the god's help in household
matters. But they could also have been seen as intermediary figures, present on
the stand to aid in the delivery of the offering to its final destination – which may
or may not have been a deity. New Kingdom settlements such as Deir el-Medina
and Amarna provide strong evidence for the presence of cults dedicated to dead
relatives and practiced in the home. Busts of both male and female deceased
ancestors (probably going back no more than two generations) were found in

homes, as well as an artifact that shows how they were used. An ostrakon was found with a drawing on it of a woman pouring libations before one of these busts. This is a rare case where contemporary explanatory evidence for private religious practice has been found in Ancient Egypt.

The same settlements have also yielded stelae depicting the deceased holding a water lily, often seated before a table of offerings. The deceased is described on the stelae as an *akh iqer ni Ra*, that is an "effective spirit for Ra," and it is thought these may have been used in ancestor cults as well.[53] Unfortunately, there have been no busts or stelae of this type found in the Middle Kingdom. Possibly some of the figurines shaped like humans may have been used in ancestor cults, but there is no evidence for this. At most we can say that it is possible that the stands could have been used in an ancestor-related ritual, but no more. They may have been used daily, or when needed, as a means to provide offerings to Bes, or to other deities. What is more certain is that these intriguing artifacts are witness to the desire of the Egyptians to provide offerings to the divine world directly, without requiring the presence of an intermediary such as a priest.

## Temples and Priests

Temples and priests did, however, play a role in the life of the townspeople of Lahun, particularly in terms of economy, but to some extent in those of religion as well. As mentioned above, the main deities attested in the immediate region were those of Hathor lady of Atfih (goddess of beauty, pleasure, and fertility), Sobek of Shedyet (the crocodile god), Anubis (the god of embalming), and the pharaoh Senusret II, who was considered divine.[54] There are, however, few remains of temples in the settlement itself. The most obvious and prominent one is the valley temple of Senusret II, located just south-west of the town walls. Aside from the king himself, the only other god associated in documents specifically with the pyramid complex was the funerary god Anubis.[55] It is likely that Senusret II's valley temple also provided a location of the worship of the jackal god as a secondary cult.

It is important to remember that temples in Ancient Egypt were not like most modern temples and churches: places designed for worship by the general public. Instead, the temple functioned as an economic institution and as a home for the god(s), with access restricted to the priests (who worked on a part-time basis at this period and in shifts) and the other temple staff. As a child, Hedjerit may have peeked through the temple doors to try to see inside, but it is unlikely that she would have made it very far within them. Like tombs and homes, the temples were designed to become increasingly more restricted and private the deeper inside one got. Only the high priest had direct access to the deepest recess where the cult statue that embodied the deity was housed. What occurred there was meant to remain secret and hidden from uninitiated eyes, and indeed, we are able to grasp only the framework of the rituals that were performed there, and even that evidence is mainly from later texts.

One of the most important responsibilities of a high priest was that of maintaining the cult statues on a daily basis. The god was believed to inhabit the image of the god, and thus the statue was treated as if it were divine as well. Often made of stone or metal (such as gold or silver) to emphasize its permanency, each small statue could also be adorned with additional jewelry and precious stones, especially before being brought out for procession. Because we do not have any surviving intact cult statues from the Middle Kingdom, we must rely on textual evidence such as the *Stela of Ikhernofret* for details. The treasurer recounts: "I decked the body of the lord of Abydos with lazuli and malachite, electrum, and every costly stone, among the ornaments of the limbs of a god. I dressed the god in his regalia by virtue of my office as master of secret things, and of my duty as pure priest." In the morning it was necessary to awaken the god within the shrine by reciting prayers, chanting hymns to the accompaniment of music, purifying him with the aroma of incense, bathing, oiling, and clothing him, and feeding him offerings. Again on the basis of later texts, it is likely that a similar ritual took place at mid-day, and at sunset. These transitional times were also liminal zones when the boundaries between the divine and the mundane worlds were at their weakest, allowing for easier access between gods and humans.

Knowing full well that the gods needed to absorb only the nutritional essence of the food, after allowing time for this to take place the priests and temple staff would actually share the physical food. This "reversion of offerings" was one way that the rituals deep within the temple affected the lives of at least some of the townspeople. For at this time, in the Middle Kingdom, the priesthood was not yet a professional institution, but was rather a part-time assignment. Priests were divided into four *phyles* or watches, and each worked for one lunar month. This means that the most an individual priest would expect to work at the temple was for three months of the year. The priest would likely have looked forward to this month of service, as he would not only be blessed by proximity to the divine, but also be able to share in the benefits that the god received, which included eating food such as meat that would be rare in the priest's everyday world. After one *phyle* left the temple, they would document in writing that everything was left in order when they finished their watch, stating that "all items belonging to the temple are intact and sound . . . handed over by the retiring temple-watch to. . . ."[56] During the months when he was not in service to the temple, the priest would be able to apply his knowledge to recite the proper spells or to provide appropriate treatments and remedies for his neighbors in the town.

As mentioned above, the closest physical proximity to the god was restricted to the high priest. His assistants would participate in the rituals, but the ultimate responsibility for the well-being of the god lay with the Egyptian high priest, or *hem-netjer* ("servant of god"). In theory, the king was the sole high priest of the god, but in practice this duty had to be delegated to others. Other ranks of priest that would have been present in the temples have been mentioned earlier and include the pure priest (*wab*) and the literate ritual priest (*khery kheb*). All of these individuals could also be hired out to maintain the mortuary cult of a high-ranking official after he died. One extensive contract has been found, written by a Twelfth Dynasty nomarch named Djefai-Hapy, that describes in great detail the specific payments to the priests he hired from the local temple along with the precise rituals that the hired priests were to carry out on his behalf. Priests could also be called upon to serve outside their local temple during the erection of important monuments and buildings. One famous illustration of the colossal statue of a nomarch of Middle Egypt named Djehutyhotep shows rows of soldiers, nobles, and priests engaged in the pulling of ropes attached to the statue to move it.

Nor was the priesthood exclusively male. During the Old Kingdom, the title "priestess of Hathor" was prominent on statues and stelae of women. During the Middle Kingdom, we find the titles of *wabet* (priestess), *wabet nit Khonsu* (priestess of Khonsu), and *wabet nit Ges-jaby* (priestess of *Ges-Jaby*).[57] The title *hem-netjer* (high priestess) was also given to women. Because the title itself is gender neutral, the only way to tell the gender of the bearer is by the name and the determinative. The attested deities served by a female *hem-netjer* include Amun,[58] Khonsu,[59] Pakhet,[60] Neith,[61] and Hathor. The priestesses of Hathor were particularly prominent in the Middle Kingdom and were usually married, while priests of the goddess were rare. A high priestess of Abydos[62] and a female version of a *hem-ka* (funerary priest) are also known.[63] There is no reason to think these were "honorific" titles, that is ones that were given as a mark of status rather than accurately reflecting a profession that a girl such as Hedjerit could look forward to.

Temples employed not only priests, but numerous other workers as well, such as doorkeepers, guards, scribes, cooks, administrators, and overseers. Many temples also had their own areas devoted to animal husbandry, though accounting evidence suggests that the cattle that were donated to the temple in Lahun came from the town rather than from temple herds. Prominent among temple staff were singers and dancers. These were not mere entertainers for the pleasure of the public, but were essential to the proper running of the temple and to maintaining the balance of *maat*. An attendance list from Lahun gives us an idea of the organization and identities of those working at the local temple.[64] Like priests, the dancers and singers were divided into four watches with anywhere between two and four dancers listed and two singers per watch. However, these watches could not have been organized as monthly shifts but were perhaps divided by time of day, or some other criteria, as more than one watch is often listed per day. For example, dancers from groups one, three, and four, and singers from groups three and four, are listed as having been present during the "opening of the year" festival. Not all dancers and singers were expected to attend every festival – indeed, the individual with the most consistent attendance is the Asiatic

Khakhperra, who out of a possible 17 festivals is marked as having been present for eight, and absent for one. Surprisingly, even though other evidence reveals that women were also dancers and singers, the ones named in this papyrus were all men – the singers were native Egyptians while most of the dancers were specifically listed as Asiatics or Nubians. Other foreign dancers are listed in hymns, in particular those devoted to the goddess Hathor, and it may be that foreigners were thought to have special skill.

Obviously, singers and dancers must have supplemented their incomes from other sources as well. Their talent and skill were acknowledged in representations, where in tomb decorations these artists are depicted in close proximity to the deceased and appear to have been afforded a measure of respect; on stelae, where they could be privileged by inclusion in image and by name; and in texts. We do not have enough data on individuals to formulate an accurate picture of the working habits of these singers and dancers – like priests, they may have held other responsibilities as well. For example, a singer may have also worked as a weaver, mother, and estate manager *nebet-per*. She may have used her talent at the temple, been hired for funerals, and been engaged to entertain high-ranking guests of the mayor at a banquet.

While singers need no equipment other than talent and thus leave behind less physical residue of their craft, dancers often used instruments that survive. Clappers made of ivory or wood, already mentioned in connection with rituals designed to repulse demons, were also used as percussive instruments while dancing. They would have been attached to the wrist by a thong passing through a hole at one end, and played much like castanets. The ends of one ivory pair found in Lahun were carved with the head of a cow, probably representing the goddess Hathor (Fig. 7.6).[65] They could also be shaped like hands, complete with painted fingernails and bracelets. Dancers are represented on tomb walls using clappers as well as a sistrum (as described earlier).

In many cultures, dancers use masks to capture the essence of an animal or god. While funerary masks abound from Ancient Egypt, few masks have been found that were designed for the use of the living. One mask that seems to have been designed for just this use was found in Lahun in the same house as a pair of ivory clappers. The face is black and red, and there is a trace of what might be a small ear. Holes have been cut through the painted cartonnage[66] for eyes to see and nostrils to breathe through. Once again though, little remains to affirm its original use. It could have been worn by a man or a woman, as the mask itself has no overt gender characteristics. The features suggest that it was meant to represent one of the Bes-images, including the female Beset, or Aha ("the fighter," whose image appears on many of the birth tusks as well as headrests), or Bes himself, but even this is uncertain. This mask could have been worn by a healer to aid a successful childbirth or to heal an ailing individual, or by a dancer in a religious procession. Both of these interpretations are certainly possible, and one could imagine a dancer performing at a temple wearing the mask and keeping time with clappers.

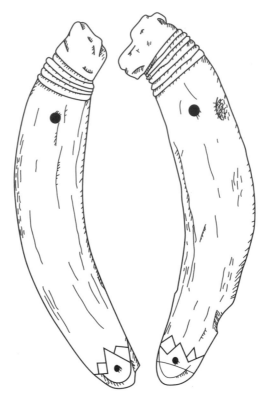

**Figure 7.6** Drawing of ivory clappers after
The Manchester Museum, The University of
Manchester, EGY124 (l. 18.4 cm × h. 3.8 cm)
(courtesy of Sam Channer).

Although we know that many of the dancers were male, it continues to be a
profession that tends to be associated with women. Indeed, some scholars have
claimed that there was a link between female dancers and prostitution, even
though there exists no evidence for this in the archaeological or textual record.
This may be another instance where western sensibilities have colored the interpretations, with the idealized freedom of women "entertainers" being linked to
capricious sexuality.[67] On the contrary, in many religions dance and song help to
create an atmosphere of religious ecstasy among the faithful while the dancers
themselves reach an alternative state that brings them closer to the divine. This
can still be seen today during the religious festivals of numerous faiths, including
traditional religions of East Africa, such as that of the Bantu of Somalia, as well
as more recent religions such as that of the Sufi whirling dervishes.

The attendance list from Lahun also provides us with some of the names and dates of some of the festivals that were scheduled in year 35 of the reign of Amenemhat III. The list is incomplete, but nevertheless it is revealing.

- Month 1 Flood:
  - "opening of the year";
  - "front of the year";
  - "jubilation";
  - names of perhaps four other festivals lost in the gaps between fragments.
- Month 2 Flood:
  - "pouring the sand";
  - "cloth of Khakheperra (Senusret II)."
- Month 3 Flood:
  - "evening offering in taking the river";
  - "taking the river";
  - "month";
  - (reading and translation uncertain).
- Month 4 Flood:
  - "sailing of Hathor";
  - "festival of Sokar."
- Month 1 Winter
  - Nehebkau;
  - "raising the field."
- At least two months between Month 1 Flood and Month 2 Winter:
  - "half-month";
  - "month";
  - "day of butchery for the god";
  - "anointing of the gods";
  - "day of butchery for the god";
  - "half-month";
  - "month";
  - "sailing of Hathor lady of Hutnennesut";
  - probably two other festivals.
- Month 2 Winter:
  - "festival of Sokar – dragging Sokar" (over two consecutive days);
  - "month";
  - "half-month";
  - "year."
- Month 3 Winter:
  - "sailing of the land."
- Month 4 Winter:
  - no festivals recorded.

- Month 1 Summer:
  - "half-month."
- Month 2 Summer:
  - "festival of the ruler may he live, be healthy and well."
- Month 3 Summer:
  - no entries preserved.
- Month 4 Summer:
  - no entries preserved.

Some of the festivals appear only once, others are repeated. Other texts mention festivals associated with the new moon, full moon, "*wag*" (a festival associated with Osiris and the dead), Thoth, Sobek, and Anubis.[68] Many of these could be considered as national festivals that were celebrated all over Egypt (such as those of the gods Sokar and Nehebkau);[69] others were regional ones, such as the "sailing of Hathor lady of Hutnennesut," during which the cult image of the goddess may have been ferried between Hutnennesut (Herakleopolis) and Lahun, or the festival of Sobek. Some of the celebrations seem to have been local to Lahun. An example of a festival that would have had less relevance for the rest of Egypt was the "cloth of Khakheperra" (Senusret II), who was the founder of the town and the pharaoh to whom the main temple was dedicated. Festivals to Anubis could have been local as well, as his cult may have been celebrated in the valley temple of Senusret II.[70] Others were not related to a specific deity, but were rather seasonal or timely, such as the month, half-month, and year.

Supplies and deliveries to the local temples were carefully recorded by scribes, and give us an idea of the amounts of comestibles that had to be provided for them. The lists include beer, cattle, barley, emmer, cakes, and an astonishing variety of breads. These include *bit*-loaves, *pat*-loaves, *pesen*-loaves, *bekhsw*-loaves, *seshet*-loaves, *t*-loaves (this is a standard type of bread), and cones of white bread (a type of bread reserved for religious use). One papyrus lists deliveries to three separate temples devoted to Sobek, the crocodile god: Sobek lord of Djedu, lord of Geregbaf, and lord of Resehwy. The verso of this papyrus includes a record of "12 Asiatic women" and "12 labor-women" who perhaps also were directed to work in the temples.[71]

Certainly the temple staff would have been varied. The supplies that came into the temple had to be handed over, recorded, distributed, and stored, raw products would need to be processed, and the process would have included not only the men and women who did the work, but also their overseers (who in the Middle Kingdom seem to have been nearly exclusively male). However, the numbers of personnel of the temples, whether of the Lahun valley temple or temples that may have been in the region, were not overly large – certainly fewer than 50 individuals were needed to maintain one of the larger ones. Accounts of supplies and records of attendance on the part of temple staff indicate that most of the religious festivities were processions that occurred within the environs of the temple itself – celebrations rather than festivals that for the most part would not necessarily have played a major role in the daily lives of most of the townsfolk of Lahun.

This reminds us that Middle Kingdom temples were not the vast institutional complexes that we are familiar with from the New Kingdom. Their impact on the local population would also have been proportionally less. The picture of the extensive temple of Amun at Karnak bustling with priests and attracting crowds of thousands at noisy hectic festivals lasting for days cannot simply be transplanted into the Middle Kingdom scenario. In the New Kingdom festivals were also an opportunity for individuals to consult the god as an oracle. Pottery shards with oracular questions, many designed to have a yes or no response, have been found in Deir el-Medina. However, there is no evidence for this practice in the Middle Kingdom, or from Lahun. The only text that remains from Lahun that was associated with divination was a hieratic papyrus that features a neat vertical column consisting of the word "day," followed by either the word "good" (*nefer*) in black, or the word "bad" (*dju*) in red.[72] Three of the days are listed as both good and bad. It is an unfinished papyrus, and even the other side remains blank. However, the large spaces left on either side of the column indicate that it would have been filled in with more details. Later versions inform us that the formulas would have read something like: "Day 1: Favorable today, till the coming forth of the moon. Day 4: Bad. Do not offer to your god today."[73]

The question remains of who would use these. They are mostly found in temple contexts, suggesting that their use was restricted to that of priests. We cannot simply assume that these "calendars of lucky and unlucky days" or "horoscopes" (as they are sometimes erroneously called) were generally consulted by the general populace, or that they affected the course of their daily lives.

## Pilgrimages

Archaeological and textual evidence provides a clue that some of the inhabitants of Lahun could have traveled south to the town of Abydos to participate in the annual festival dedicated to the god Osiris-KhentyAmentiu there. Abydos was a sacred site for much of Egypt's history, and it was the location where the first kings of Egypt were buried. The tomb of a First Dynasty pharaoh called "Djer" became known as the tomb of the god Osiris. The god originally associated with this site was the jackal-form KhentyAmentiu, "Foremost of the Westerners," but by the end of the Old Kingdom the god Osiris had absorbed this role, and was worshiped in the local temple. Along with cemeteries, there developed in the area private chapels, an area for the votive dedications, and a town, possibly in part as a response to the growing cult of the god. The temple was built on the uppermost of a series of natural stone terraces that arose from a depression just north of the old cemetery and the tomb of Djer. The Egyptians therefore called that district "the Terrace of the Great God" and the temple that of "Osiris, Foremost of the Westerners."

An autobiography of the treasurer Ikhernofret provides us with details of his role in organizing the annual event. He helped to decorate the shrine that housed the statue of the god, and the barque upon which it sat. Rituals would be performed by priests within the temple, and then the barque and shrine would be carried out by priests for all the public to see. As the procession slowly made its way south down the terrace from the temple to the "tomb of Osiris" and back, scenes from the Osirian cycle of myths were re-enacted, probably with the active participation of the spectators. Mock battles were staged, a nightly vigil was held, and rituals were carried out until the deity emerged resurrected and victorious in his role as god of the afterlife. Participation in the festival guaranteed the participant a rare opportunity to witness the god, and people flocked from different areas of Egypt to attend the event. To commemorate their visit, in an area by the temple (the votive zone) Egyptians would erect stelae with an image of the participant (and selected other individuals), hymns or offering formulas, or prayers, as well as often the names of spouses, children, and other relatives, co-workers, and even the sculptor of the stela itself.

Having one's name forever marked in stone at the sacred site offered one permanent access to the event, and a brush with divinity. It even seems that physical presence at the event was not necessarily required, as one letter remains wherein the donor requests that his stela be dropped off and erected at the site, even though he could not visit in person.[74] Apparently a virtual visit was better than none at all. Most of the people who erected stelae were officials, administrators, temple staff, and musicians, but one votive marker was even donated by a washerman, showing that it was not a completely exclusive privilege but was accessible to a range of social classes.[75] Other individuals would bring votive offerings of different types, or perhaps ingratiate themselves with other people in the hopes of being mentioned on a stela.

If Hedjerit's father, Sasopedu, and his family ever had the opportunity to physically visit Abydos and take part in the rituals of Osiris, they would probably have wished to have a stela erected to commemorate that event. We will never know how many individuals took part in the festivities but were unable to leave behind any material testament to the event. Even if they did not take part in the Osiris festival, there were numerous other ways that a family would show their devotion to their deities. Although temples were not the focus of regular worship in the way they are in the Judeo-Christian tradition, communication between a deity and an individual could be generated in other ways. Myths, prayers, and rituals were a natural part of life for the villagers of Lahun. Their gods were not distant and aloof, but were immanent, and their presence was felt in many daily activities. Sometimes this was a positive experience, but as we shall see, the inhabitants of the divine world were not always beneficent and could also be actively malign. The artificial division between religious and secular practices and lifestyles that is promoted in many modern western cultures would have seemed alien to an Ancient Egyptian.

# Notes

1 Lloyd 2006, 71. For a thorough discussion of Egyptian magic see Ritner 1993; 1995.
2 UC32196 letter 8 in Collier and Quirke 2004, 49.
3 Quirke 1997.
4 Quirke 2004b, 124, notes the lack of certainty in assigning this title to the temple sphere, or a juridical status.
5 The statuette is EGY270a and the base is EGY270b.
6 See EGY133. Quirke 1998a, 143, describes it as an ape, although if it is not a hippopotamus the head suggests rather a baboon (though I am unaware of parallels of baboons with tripartite wigs).
7 Red was the special color of Seth, who in his negative aspects was presented as being a quick-tempered, passionate, moody, and violent god who had no control over his impulses. In the Ramesside *Dream Manual* a personality type known as a "follower of Seth" was described in detail with all these negative characteristics and even red hair.
8 Lacovara 1992.
9 Quirke 1998a.
10 Tooley 1991.
11 Note that this is an external typology, which is useful for our purposes but does not necessarily reflect the native Egyptian categories.
12 See EGY132 and EGY134.
13 UC7185.
14 UC30094.
15 See EGY126.
16 Excerpted from Ritner 1997, 50–2.
17 See EGY132, EGY134; Quirke 1998, 143; David 1986, 162–3.
18 Bourriau 1998, 121, cat. no. 113.
19 These were funerary texts written on coffins of the First Intermediate Period to Middle Kingdom, designed to help the deceased successfully enter and live in the afterlife.
20 Adapted from Borghouts 1978, 32.
21 A "woman's figure of Isis" is also mentioned in a spell to keep away scorpions (Borghouts 1978, #84).
22 UC32171B in Collier and Quirke 2004, 68–9.
23 Bourriau 1988, 110–11; Ritner 1993, 222–32.
24 Bourriau 1988, 110.
25 See Ritner 2006, 205–25, particularly 206.
26 For a convenient overview of the role of demons see Sweeney 2006a.
27 Borghouts 1978, #52.
28 Borghouts 1978, #68.
29 Borghouts 1978, #59.
30 R. Janssen and Janssen 1990, 23–4.
31 UC6482.

32  Aufrère 1991, 683. Ra is the sun god, Geb is the god of the earth, Osiris is god of the dead, and Nun is the originally watery chaos that is represented on earth as the Nile.

33  Number EGY686j.i, while the other ball, EGY696j.ii, remains intact. Some of the ones from Amarna have also been opened and have been found to contain hair (personal observation at the Bolton Museum). See also UC7237.

34  W. Blackman 1925.

35  Richards 2005, 111.

36  EGY279.

37  EGY280.

38  Petrie describes how "whenever they are found charged, [they] have a cake of dough stuck to the dish " (Petrie et al. 1891, 11); David 1986, 134.

39  Originally labeled as the "acropolis."

40  UC16520.

41  UC16523; UC16524; UC16525; UC16527; UC16521.

42  Altenmüller 1965, 39.

43  Raven 1987.

44  Raven 1987, 16.

45  EGY275; EGY276; EGY277a/b; UC17250.

46  UC16794.

47  UC32179 and UC32183 in Collier and Quirke 2006, 28–9, 32–3.

48  UC7006.

49  Petrie et al. 1890, 26; UC16521.

50  Jean Cocteau in his 1945 movie *La Belle et la Bête* made use of the imagery of dis-embodied human arms as candelabra to evoke a haunting, surreal atmosphere in the Beast's castle, emphasizing the ethereal nature of the events taking place therein.

51  UC30355–UC30358; UC7143 for Middle Kingdom examples.

52  The self-generated primeval god Atum masturbated with his hand to create the first pair of gods. Although Atum embodies both the female and male creative forces, the word for hand in Egyptian, *djeret*, is feminine and therefore the creative process engendered by his hand would be represented by a woman.

53  Demarée 1983.

54  Quirke 1997.

55  Quirke 1997.

56  See for example P. Berol 10003 A rt III (12–19) in Luft 1992a.

57  Ward 1986, 6.

58  Fischer 1985, 18.

59  Quirke 2004b, 124.

60  A deity represented with the head of a lioness. The titles of priestess of Pakhet, Neith, and Hathor are referred to in Ward 1986, 10–11.

61  A warrior goddess.

62  Fischer 1985, 18.

63  Ward 1986, 11.

64  UC32191 in Collier and Quirk 2006, 92–5. The following section and the festival list are adapted from this source.

65  See EGY124.

66  Cartonnage is made from plastered layers of linen or papyrus strips.

67 A similar phenomenon could be seen in 1950s America, where actresses were frowned upon as women of loose morals. Interestingly, scholars do not link male entertainers with prostitution. See also Gosline 1999, 119–21; Toivari 2001, 149.
68 Luft 1992b.
69 Nehebkau ("one who binds the *kas*") is a rare example of a male deity that takes the form of a human-headed snake, sometimes with human arms, legs, and a phallus.
70 Quirke 1997.
71 UC32147G in Collier and Quirke 2006, 258–9.
72 UC32192 in Collier and Quirke 2004, 26–7.
73 Troy 1989.
74 Leprohon 1978.
75 Franke 2003a.

# 8

# Sickness

*Hearing my beloved dog Kemy-Shery barking from upon the roof, I climbed the stairs and shouted "Come here my little Kemy!" With great joy she bounded toward me to be as close to me as a Sole Companion. Laughing I reached out my arms, but my foot, it slipped and I fell back down the stairs. When I reached the bottom I gave forth a loud cry of pain, for my arm, it was bent and I could not move it. When my brother found me, he asked my old grandmother to come. She probed my arm, and stated "This is a simple break in the bone — an ailment I will fight with" and placed my arm in a splint until it healed.[1]*

## Bones

Illnesses, injuries, and the debilitating affects of old age are part of the everyday problems that must be dealt with in every culture. Accidental trauma would have been commonplace in many environments such as the home and the workplace, especially for those who engaged in manual labor, while those in the military were also subject to intentional physical harm, indeed as were law-breakers (such as those who attempted to evade their state labor duty). Even an active little seven-year-old child like Hedjerit would have acquired a collection of cuts, bruises, and scrapes, and to those she would likely have paid little attention. Osteological analyses on human remains from the Old Kingdom onward show evidence of properly aligned and healed bone fractures, testifying to the use of a healer for this type of injury.[2] Unfortunately, in the case of some patients, their bone breaks were not properly set and these individuals may have found themselves with permanent mobility problems of varying degrees.

Thorough analysis of the types and locations of injuries by site, gender, age, ethnicity, and time can provide important information on the lifestyles of the individuals buried in the cemeteries under investigation. For example, the 1908 study by Wood Jones of approximately 6,000 individuals buried at Aswan, under-taken as part of the salvage project before the building of the dam flooded the entire area, revealed a striking proportion of certain types of fractures. Of the 200 fractures noted, nearly one-third, that is 31.25 percent, were of the forearm, while 13.75 percent had broken collar-bones, 12.50 percent had broken thighs, and 10 percent had broken legs. Other fractures were noted in smaller frequen-cies, but the strikingly high number of forearm and collar-bone fractures was suggestive to scholars of intentional trauma, such as beatings. However, because the bodies ranged in date from 6,000 BC to the first century BC, it is difficult to interpret this evidence. More work would need to be performed on these bones to determine if these fractures were more common for one gender, one time period, or even a restricted age range.

Unfortunately, Haraga – the cemetery that was probably associated with the middle and poor classes of Lahun – was hastily excavated in 1923 and the human remains are no longer available. We must thus rely on research being performed on contemporary cemeteries, with the understanding that there may have been differences, some minor, some major, in the health of geographically distinct populations. One important analysis is in progress on the skeletal remains of 53 individuals buried in Abydos, most dating to the Middle Kingdom. This site provides at least three examples of Egyptians who sustained fractures from inten-tional violence that subsequently healed.[3] One of these was a 17–18-year-old man who had apparently sustained a blow to his forehead with a blunt object while he was still a child. The fracture on the forearm of another man in his late twen-ties to early thirties was of the type that is typical of a defensive posture. The remains of another woman who lived to be 30–5, which was within the average range of age of death for an Ancient Egyptian woman, indicate that her death was anything but natural. Besides having suffered through multiple fractures of her ribcage, she also sustained a compound fracture on her right hand that sub-sequently became infected. The placement and kind of fracture suggest that it occurred when she stretched out her right arm to break a fall. While this could have occurred naturally, the knife wound that she sustained to her back, piercing right through to the ribs, could not have been, and it is this final injury that likely caused her death. Forensic analyses such as these remind us that violence between people was as much a feature of the ancient world as it is today.

Interpersonal violence is attested not only by the archaeological evidence, but also by medical texts that prescribe the proper treatments for dealing with the resulting physical damage. Papyrus Edwin Smith in particular provides graphic descriptions of some of these injuries and their treatments. After checking the patient, the physician had to decide whether the injury was treatable, or whether the wound was fatal, in which case the best treatment consisted of making the patient more comfortable. In some cases, the long-term prognosis was not imme-diately apparent. For example, one case described a fracture of the upper arm that was complicated by a wound (perhaps a compound fracture that had broken the skin):[4]

Title: Practices for a break in his upper arm with a wound on it.

Examination and Prognosis: If you treat a man for a break in his upper arm, fractured with a wound on it, and you find that break wiggling under your fingers, then you say about him: "One who has a break in his upper arm, fractured with a wound on it: an ailment I will fight with."

Treatment: Then you make him two strips of cloth. You have to bandage him with alum and treat him with an oil and honey dressing until you learn that he arrives at a turning point. But if you find that wound that is on the break with blood coming out of it and obstructed on the inside of his wound, then you say about him: "One who has a break in his upper arm with an obstructed wound on it: an ailment for which nothing is done."

The human remains at Abydos also reveal trauma caused not by violence, but by the accumulation of years of hard labor and repetitive motions. In the same study by Brenda Baker,[5] the anthropologist noted that the vertebrae of some of the adults, both younger and older, had depressions that could have been caused by lifting or carrying heavy loads. Some of the joints showed stress, indicating that these individuals were engaged in repetitive movements that caused early degradation of their joints. In some, the constant pressure led to osteoarthritis, particularly in the lower back and neck – again indicative of carrying or lifting heavy loads. While we might initially expect that these types of injuries would be more common in the lower classes, at Abydos they were also suffered by high-status individuals, indicating that manual labor was practiced by all types of people at that site. A more specialized type of repetitive stress is manifested in the recently analyzed bones of commoners at the New Kingdom city of Tell el-Amarna.[6] Here, the knees and toes of 2 percent of the adult remains show stress and degeneration that might have been caused by repetitive kneeling for long periods at a time.

At Abydos, the forensic evidence also showed levels of nutritional deficiencies that were probably the result of poor absorption of nutrients during childhood caused by inferior-quality food and prevalent parasites. In addition, all of the human remains showed evidence of infection, perhaps caused by fungal infections or tuberculosis (evidence for the latter condition was also found in Theban cemeteries of all time periods). Yet these conditions should not necessarily be considered as typical for all of the Middle Kingdom population – as the anthropologist notes, they are markedly high compared to other contemporary Egyptian and Nubian populations.[7] While the townspeople of Middle Kingdom Abydos were conspicuously unhealthy, this may have been a feature of living in this specific Middle Egyptian settlement. The environment of the Fayum created different conditions for the townspeople of Lahun, and it would be hasty to assume that they too suffered the same afflictions as their counterparts who lived far to the south. More data is required. Even within a single geographical region, the remains may reveal different lifestyle patterns depending on the time period. The remains of 211 Middle Kingdom individuals, compared with 273 dating from the New Kingdom to the Late Period buried in the Theban necropolis, showed interesting parallels and disparities. While evidence for tuberculosis was consistent for both time periods, other conditions were temporally dependent.[8] Bones can exhibit signs of certain metabolic conditions and nutritional deficiency, and paralleling the case of Middle Kingdom Abydos, the Theban cemeteries verified a greater prevalence of these in the Middle Kingdom than in the later periods. However, the degenerative bone and joint diseases (particularly in the back) as well as trauma (which were also seen in Middle Kingdom Abydos) in the Theban cemeteries were noticeably greater in the Late Period remains, "suggesting a higher mechanical load in the later populations."[9] How this "mechanical load" compares to that of the Abydos population cannot be determined without a direct comparison of the evidence.

## Disease

Paleopathological and now DNA testing of Middle Kingdom mummies has also confirmed the presence of major diseases such as tuberculosis in Ancient Egypt. Prior to these recent technological advances, the disease could be suspected in the remains of individuals with specific skeletal deformities that can be associated with forms of the debilitating disease, but ultimately the modern-day diagnosis was difficult to confirm. Now the new techniques of analyzing tissue at the molecular level have confirmed that tuberculosis was prevalent from the Predynastic through the Late Period. One study was recently performed on seven bodies from Abydos (Predynastic to Early Dynastic), 37 from a tomb in Western Thebes (Middle Kingdom to Second Intermediate Period), and 39 more from five other Theban tombs (New Kingdom to Late Period).[10] Traces of the ancient DNA of tuberculosis was found in 18 of the 83 specimens, that is nearly 22 percent, a figure that was consistent among all the time periods. More advanced testing has even allowed different sub-types of tuberculosis to be identified in Ancient Egyptian remains.[11] Contrary to the expectations of many scientists, the strain of tuberculosis found in cattle, *M. bovis*, was not detected in the samples. This marked lack of the bovid strain suggests that the long-standing theory that tuberculosis arose from the rise of agriculture and increasing contact between cattle and humans may need to be seriously revised. Thus, these studies are important not only for advancing our knowledge of the presence of this contagious disease in Ancient Egypt, but when applied to a wider range of remains, they will provide important information regarding the spread of the disease both within and between cultures, as well as for our understanding of the origins of the disease itself.

Tuberculosis was, therefore, a part of everyday life in Ancient Egypt, affecting just over one out of every five individuals. However, this is one case where our modern records are more revealing than the ancient ones. Although one-fifth of Egyptians may have been infected by the airborne disease, far fewer would have

153

shown any symptoms. Even then, the symptoms of tuberculosis in its later stages (few if any are manifest early on) are rather generic, and consist of fatigue, fever, weight loss, night sweats, and productive cough, which in the later stages may be painful and bloody. The disease is difficult to recognize even in the twenty-first century of the common era, and in Ancient Egypt, while there were treatments for each of these symptoms, there was no knowledge of the lethal disease itself and no awareness of its contagious nature.

Similarly, we know that a major scourge of Middle Kingdom Egypt, particularly for the inhabitants of Lahun, would have been schistosomiasis (also called bilharziasis).[12] This disease is carried not by a virus but by a tiny, slender parasitic worm whose life-cycle requires a human host and a specific species of fresh-water snail. These snails live on the banks of the Nile, where they play host to one stage of the schistosomes. They leave the body of the snail as virtually invisible swimming worms that are able to enter the skin of any human that happens to be in the water in their vicinity. From there, they enter the blood stream, breed, and deposit their eggs in the internal organs, particularly the bladder. When the infected individual urinates, the eggs are released and proceed to hatch when they hit fresh water. The main ailment associated with schistosomiasis is anemia. Thus the predominant symptoms – chronic fatigue, predisposition to illnesses, and urinary infections – are again those that are easily overlooked or blamed on another source. The only alarming and visible sign is blood in the urine.

As with tuberculosis, the only reason we know of the existence of this disease is from modern analyses of mummies and from its prevalence in the modern population of Egypt.[13] The latter, however, may be misleading. For the numbers of individuals infected by schistosomiasis has been increasing with advances in land reclamation combined with the building of dams that create the environmental conditions in which the snails flourish. While schistosomes have been found in mummies, they are not mentioned in textual sources and obviously we cannot expect to find any representations of them. Without our ability to perform scientific analysis on their physical remains, the presence of these diseases that were such a part of Egyptian life would have remained undetected. As for the Egyptians themselves, when afflicted with symptoms such as aches, fever, and blood in their urine, they would not have blamed an invisible virus or parasite, but instead would have held responsible demons and the dead from the beyond, as will be discussed below.

## Animal Assaults

While they were not aware of the perils of microscopic creatures, they were well aware of the danger of other earthly creatures such as worms, snakes, scorpions, and crocodiles. For all of Egyptian history, there were more spells written for the repulsion of these creatures than for any other harmful entity or ailment. Some of the spells were specific, and some lumped together all of these creatures that use burning poison as their weapon. "Oh any male snake, any female snake, any spiders who bite with their mouths, who sting with their tails, you will not bite him with your mouths, you will not sting him with your tails! Keep your distance from him! You will not use your heat against him . . ." reads part of one spell.[14] Those at risk included not only the poor, but all ranks, even the pharaoh, as is attested by the prevalence of spells designed to ward off snakes in the Pyramid Texts.[15] The gods themselves were not immune, and indeed Isis herself had to protect her young child Horus from the poison of scorpions and snakes. Because of this, many of the spells re-enact her actions, thus allowing the living, even though he be a humble herdsman, to temporarily embody Horus. Most of the spells are from the New Kingdom and later, including this one, but because incantations against scorpions and snakes are also found in the Coffin Texts (but meant to function to protect the deceased in the afterlife), we can safely assume that similar ones may have been known in the Middle Kingdom.

> Hi you scorpion who came forth from the tree with its sting erect, the one who has stung the herdsman in the night when he was lying down! Was no reciting done for him? Reciting was done for him over *hedeb*-drink and beer, as for any strong fighter. The seven children of Pre[16] stood lamenting; they made seven knots in their seven bands[17] and they hit the one who was bitten with them. May he stand up, healed for his mother, as Horus stood up, healed for his mother Isis in the night when he was bitten. The protection is a protection of Horus![18]

The "seven children of Ra" here probably refers to the seven scorpions who accompanied Isis on her journeys in the Delta with the baby Horus. In this instance, as in many others, like can be used to fight like – the divine scorpions will vanquish the poison caused by the earthly scorpion, and the herdsman will be healed as was Horus.

Herdsmen, often living out in the open, were particularly vulnerable to the dangers of both the desert and the Nile. Some, therefore, seem to have been equipped with enough powerful *heka*, magic, to ward off some of these dangers. Old Kingdom tombs in particular contain reliefs depicting the theme of herds of cattle traversing the many channels of the Nile in the marshes of the Delta under the watchful eye of their caretakers. The waters here brought life, but they also concealed the presence of lethal creatures such as the greedy crocodile. In one scene, two herdsmen are shown on a boat with one attempting to neutralize the power of the waiting crocodile by pointing with his index finger as a magical gesture (Fig. 8.1). An individual distinguished by his kilt, like the one in the figure (as opposed to the other herdsmen, who at most wear loincloths), and leaning on a staff, may have recited an incantation known as a "water song." A caption on another tomb provides us with the words that he would recite to repel the crocodile (called a "marsh-inhabitant") and to allow the cattle to safely cross. "Oh herdsman there! Let your face be watchful for this marsh-inhabitant who is

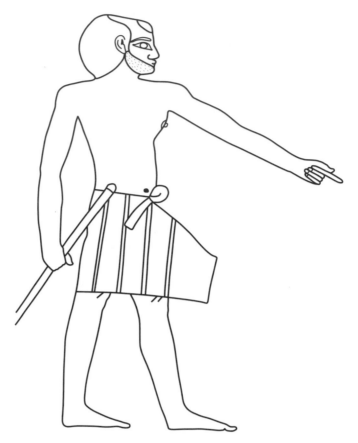

**Figure 8.1** Drawing of magical gesture (courtesy of JJ Shirley).

on the water, to prevent these here falling a victim to this marsh-inhabitant. May he come as a sightless one. Let your face be very watchful for him!"[19]

Knowledge of these spells and their recitation, however, was probably restricted to the literate priest, the *rekh-khut* or "knower of (ritual) things," which referred to one with access to the House of Life.[20] This is stated explicitly in another spell to ward off crocodiles and other underwater dangers, which began with the heading: "The first spell of all kinds of water-songs, about which the magician has said: 'Do not reveal it to the common man – it is a mystery of the House of Life.'"[21] Not surprisingly, it seems that specialists wished to retain control of some spells and practices. This does not, however, imply that we should imagine special priests waiting at river crossings like traffic wardens. In the Middle Kingdom, the priesthood was made up of members of the community who worked in shifts. Thus the "knower of things" was one who had acquired his knowledge at the House of Life and dutifully performed his stint at the temple. But the rest of the time he might have been occupied with his usual work, whether that would be as an official, a carpenter, or perhaps even a herdsman. Indeed, the fact that the spell specifically states it needs to be kept secret implies that this was a potential problem, and that some of these may have been known by people who were not priests. Another Middle Kingdom text (Coffin Text 836) clearly states that it is the herdsman himself who should recite the spell.[22] Whether this herdsman therefore had to also be a priest, or whether this was knowledge to which herdsmen were privy because of the dangerous nature of their occupation, is not clear.[23]

While spells such as these attempt to prevent an attack by crocodiles, if they did not work, a survivor would be in desperate need of swift treatment, either for having been nearly drowned by the crocodile, or for the aftermath of mangling by its razor-sharp teeth. The bite of a crocodile is specifically referred to in two papyri, and in each case the treatment was the same as that given for any major tearing wound in the flesh – bandaging with fresh meat.[24] In most cases, however, attacks by crocodiles were fatal, and the body was likely never found. Even though in this case the proper burial rites could not be performed, the deceased could nevertheless be granted access to the afterlife. New Kingdom Books of the Afterlife[25] graphically depict those who had been drowned being welcomed as the blessed dead by Horus himself.[26] He says to them: "Oh drowned ones, who are dark in Nun . . . You swim in the great Nile. You land on its bank. Your body does not decay. Your flesh does not go bad. You inhale what I have assigned to you. You are these who are in Nun, the drowned ones." Because the Nile was considered as the earthly manifestation of the primeval creative waters of Nun, those who died therein, whether by drowning through accident or the pull of the crocodile, had access to the afterlife.[27]

But the creature that embodied the biggest threat to the people and gods of Ancient Egypt was the snake. In Egyptian myth, the sun god had to battle chaos every single night, and this chaos manifested itself in the form of a giant snake called Apep.[28] Luckily the sun god Ra, sometimes with the help of the powerful god Seth as well as other gods, was able to fetter, contain, and vanquish (though not kill) the monstrous fiend. Thus, Ra is called upon for help in one Middle Kingdom treatment that is titled "Spell for descending into a thicket":[29]

> Backward, snake who is on his hillock, shuffler who is in his thicket! Your teeth are broken, your poisons are scattered. Ra has warded off the attack you hurled at me. Spit out snake who has come forth from the earth, black one who is in his hole! However, if you mean to direct an attack against mankind, the flaming eye of Horus will extinguish it and people will become silent!

Likewise, Horus when he was a child and left alone in the Delta was assailed by snakes. As was the case with the sting of the scorpion, therefore, the Egyptians concentrated on trying to expel the venom by the magical means of spells identifying the patient with Horus and setting the episode on the mythical plane. Isis is often the healer, calling upon the gods to help save her child: "Come to me, father of the earth, my mother Nut, Atum, who made the gods, who are in heaven, out of the eye of the living god. I am Isis, the daughter of your daughter. The son of your son has been bitten by the *khefty* (enemy) of the one who is in his mound."[30]

That the Egyptian healers had direct familiarity with snake bites is reflected in the descriptions contained in a New Kingdom papyrus devoted to incantations against snakes.[31] The symptoms as described in the papyrus seem to match the known symptoms of a non-fatal cobra bite, which include burning pain, an inability to stand followed by paralysis, difficulty in breathing, drooling, and a weakened heart, followed by a quick recovery. Sometimes the words of the spell were to be written on a substance and then ingested with a liquid, usually beer,[32] or for long-term protection they could be recited over prescribed items that would be wrapped in a pouch to be worn around the neck. The complexity of these spells again indicates that they were known to specialists, and by the time of the New Kingdom, healers who specialized in the treatment of poison (both scorpion and snake and probably spider as well) were known by the title *kherep* (Conjurer) of Serqet.[33] Because there are so few sources mentioning a Conjurer of Serqet in the Middle Kingdom,[34] it is likely that in a town such as Lahun, the victims of venomous creatures relied on general healers and their local off-duty priest for help.

## Alimentary, Ocular, and Dental Disorders

Other, more mundane, non-trauma-related ailments would also have plagued Egyptians of the Middle Kingdom, and these are well attested through ancient sources as well as modern scientific analyses. Many of these affected the stomach, the eyes, and the teeth. Because of the lack of refined sugar in their diet, the Egyptians did not suffer from cavities the way we do today. Nevertheless, other dental disorders such as abscesses, tartar build-up, periodontal disease, and severe attrition of the enamel (likely caused by sand and grit, which would inevitably make their way into the food) were common in all sites where forensic analysis has been performed, including Abydos.[35] These must have been quite painful and troublesome and could sometimes lead to serious infection and death. Although dental problems were common, there is little evidence of specialists in dentistry. Our main source for healers is official titles, and in one study of these only one practitioner was named as both a doctor and dentist in the Third Intermediate Period and Late Period, and three in the Old Kingdom and First Intermediate Period while in that earlier time period we also have evidence for two individuals who were dentists only.[36] Unfortunately, we have no titles associated with dentistry from the Middle Kingdom (indeed individuals with the title of "physician" are exceedingly rare at this time and limited to those assigned to treat the king), but we may expect that at the very least physicians of that time would treat some of the secondary difficulties associated with dental problems. As it is still the case in many parts of the world today, often the solution would be to simply extract the offending tooth – a task that does not necessarily require the services of a professional.

The desert winds blow sand not only into food, but also into eyes, causing discomfort and potential damage. In poor sanitary conditions and high heat, flies and other insects are attracted to the moist region of the eyes, and numerous ocular ailments are mentioned in texts. Because the eye is a soft-tissue organ, little remains in the archaeological record, and we must rely on our understanding of visual representations and textual sources. The eyes of harpists in particular, and sometimes singers, are often represented without pupils, or with apparently closed lids, and while this is usually interpreted as representing blindness it could also simply represent the closed eye of one who is engrossed in his performance. The evidence is inconsistent, and in one tomb where two harpers in near-identical positions are portrayed, the eye of the female is clearly open, while the eye of the male is unfortunately missing because of a chip in the wall.[37] In another tomb the same individual is show as singing with an open eye, but closed or blind while playing the harp.[38] Because Egyptian art was conceptual and symbolic instead of representational, rather than physical blindness, the idiosyncratic depiction of the harper's eye could be a metaphor, a way of encoding the concept that the musician was caught up in the emotions of his art. In any event, physical blindness, whether temporary, permanent, or night blindness, was certainly known and attested in numerous texts with the word *shep*.[39]

Most eye diseases and their associated treatments are, however, known from the Ebers Medical Papyrus. Although this papyrus dates to the early New Kingdom, it is likely that the ailments described therein and their remedies would have been familiar to healers of the Middle Kingdom as well. References to cloudy eyes and a darkness in them may refer to cataracts, while chronic conjunctivitis was likely the disease known as *nehat* in Egyptian, and even ingrown eyelashes are mentioned as hair that grows in the eye. Blood and yellow or pink spots in the eye were considered treatable, as were generic inflammations.[40] However, many of the eye problems listed in the papyrus are referred to by words whose translations are yet unknown. The treatments for diseases often consisted of the application of a specified mixture of materials to the eye or the surrounding area. Eye-paint, whether made from black galena or green malachite, was, not surprisingly, common in the prescriptions, as were fats, balms, minerals, honey, and milk – ingredients commonly advocated for the treatment of a variety of ailments (discussed below). While usually the mixtures were to be applied to the eye and then left undisturbed, a more complicated one was recommended for a traumatic injury to the eye that required monitoring over a period of days:[41]

Another made for the *tekhen*-injury of the eye.
Day one: marsh water.
Day two: honey, 1; black eye-paint, 1; on one day.
If it bleeds: honey, 1; black eye-paint, 1; bandaged with it for two days.

If, however, much liquid flows down from it, you should prepare for it a remedy *aafs* (? wrung out): *iau*, 1: green eye-paint, 1; incense (*senetjer*), 1; top of *heden*-plant; cooked.

A passage from the Middle Kingdom Lahun Gynecological Papyrus describes the treatment for a woman who aches in her limbs and her eyes. The appearance of eye pain connected with gynecological matters may seem unusual to us, but the Ancient Egyptians understood human anatomy differently than we do. Air and fluids – including those that brought life, such as blood and semen, as well as those that brought illness and disease – were believed to be transported through the body via various channels called *metu*. Today, these would be differentiated into sinews, tendons, veins, arteries, and ducts that connect very different parts of the body than those linked by the Egyptian *metu*. A generic term for the foul source which caused disease and illnesses was *wekhedu*, which was associated with wrongness, and was thought to be carried to various parts of the body via the *metu*. Thus we can find an interconnection between pain in limbs and the eyes and their believed source, which was pain in the uterus, as in the following passage from the Gynecological Papyrus:[42]

Examination of a woman aching in all her limbs and the sockets of her eyes . . .
You should say of it "it is pains of the uterus."
You should treat it with a measure of oil, [. . .] *ished*-fruit, grapes, notched sycamore fruit, beans, *peret-sheny* [. . .]
Grind and refine, boil and drink for three days.

The sheer number of these ocular ailments and their treatments – a total of 95 are listed in the Ebers Papyrus – stresses the serious impact that a loss of vision would have had on the life of an Egyptian, as indeed it does on any individual of any time.

## Assault by the Demons and the Dead

The body in general, and especially the head and the gastro-intestinal systems, were also susceptible to aches and pains and were just as difficult to treat. Again, our source for the existence of and specific treatments for headaches, stomach-aches, fevers, weakness, and fatigue comes from texts. For the most part, these consist of spells and prescriptions used to repel the invisible entities that were believed to be attacking the living. From at least the First Intermediate Period through the Late Period, these were identified as invading denizens of the land of the dead. The texts specifically named the male and the female *akhu* (that is, those that we usually think of as the transfigured and justified dead – those people who had carried out the correct rituals and had the requisite knowledge to successfully live forever in the farworld), the male and female *mut* (the unjustified dead or the damned), and the male and female *djay* (adversaries or generic enemies of the gods). These hostile dead, adversaries, and generic enemies were blamed for a host of problems in lists from the Coffin Texts, execration texts (lists of malignant forces written on clay pots or figurines that were presumably then broken to neutralize their power), oracular amuletic decrees (Third Intermediate Period vows by deities to protect children, which were rolled up, placed in a container, and worn as a charm to ward away all the listed dangers), as well as the magico-medical texts.

These entities seemed to be particularly blamed for problems related to possession or invasion of individuals and of spaces and are attested in a number of spells whose purpose was to thwart them. One spell was designed to prevent any adversaries or dead who might be within the body of the victim from killing him,[43] while another was meant to protect a house from any of these enemies who might attack in the day or the night.[44] Other incantations were designed to ward off these beings that were also deemed responsible for the "plague of the year,"[45] fevers or cold,[46] eye disorders[47] including night blindness,[48] and bleeding possibly associated with miscarriage,[49] or ones whose influence had entered specific parts of the victim's body such as the belly,[50] the head,[51] or the breasts.[52]

While all of these potential invaders mentioned in these spells resided in the farworld,[53] their roles and attributes varied. The ones that were labeled as enemies (*kheftju*) or adversaries (*djay*), or simply as the host of dead (*mut*), were those who had threatened or transgressed against the gods, and for whom the proper rituals were not carried out. They were therefore doomed to eternal punishment and unrest – predisposed to intimidate the living in whatever way they could. But these spells also mention the *akhw*, the "transfigured dead." The irony is that a so-called demon could include an Egyptian who had worked very hard to become an *akh*, one of the blessed dead who were allowed not only unrestrained travel throughout the many regions of the farworld, but also free passage into the land of the living. A number of spells in the Book of the Dead insured that this ability would be granted to the *akh*. It seems that these *akhu* or justified dead, who could appear as benevolent ghosts,[54] also had the power and the will to potentially harm the living in the same manner as the generic enemies and unjustified dead. These pugnacious beings, who inhabited the farworld, like the gods, were able to step through the permeable membrane between the worlds and attack the living. Their presence could manifest itself in the form of bodily pains and illnesses, or even mental anguish such as nightmares. This is the flip side of a belief in the numinous, of living in constant potential contact with the divine. While one could petition the gods and plead for their attention and intervention, the hostile dead and malignant entities were equally close at hand.

That these demons who were a part of the daily life of the Egyptians were the same fiends who were vile enemies in the farworld is also made clear by reference to their being reversed. This portrayal of enemies facing in the wrong direction abounds at the royal level, where the stereotypical adversaries of the pharaoh are twisted with their head facing backward, unable to see forward.[55] In similar fashion, the unjustified dead and the enemies of the gods could be forced to live a reversed life in the farworld. Those who were not instantly relegated to the second and final death were condemned to a variety of indignities, tortures that might include living a life incompatible with *maat*, eating their own feces and drinking their own urine.[56]

This reversed posture is also described in one of the previously discussed "spells for a mother and child"[57] that were designed to protect the vulnerable individual (in this case a child) against demons that attack in the dark. Here, the invading demon is described as creeping stealthily under the cloak of darkness but facing backward:

> May you be spat out, one who came in the utter darkness, who entered creeping – his nose is behind him, his face turned back – having failed in that which he came to do.

> May you be spat out, one who came in the utter darkness, who entered creeping – her nose behind her, her face turned backward – having failed in what she came for.

> > Have you come in order to kiss this child?
> > I will not let you kiss him!
> > Have you come in order to silence (him)?
> > I will not let you silence him!
> > Have you come in order to harm him?
> > I will not let you harm him!
> > Have you come in order to take him away?
> > I will not let you take him away from me!

> > I have made his protection against you,
> > with sweet clover – this means the use of force,
> > with onions – which harm you,
> > with honey – sweetness for people, bitterness for those yonder
> > with the tail of an *Abdju*-fish,
> > with the jawbone of a bull
> > with the back of a Nile-perch.

Even the concoction that is used to repel the intruder works precisely because its affect on him or her is the opposite to the one it would have had on the living. Onions, which the Egyptians recognized as being beneficial to the living, were harmful to the damned, while honey, sweet and healing for the righteous, was bitter for the demons. This again reflects the core Egyptian belief in the concept of *maat*: that there was a fundamental and correct order in the world that needed to be properly maintained. But *isfet* "wrongness," the antithesis of *maat*, was also a constant threat and had to be kept at bay, often by applying the theory that what was good for the upright citizen would be harmful to those who were "un-*maat*."

While the extant copy of the Berlin papyrus with the "spells for a mother and child" dates from the early New Kingdom, it is likely that they originated in the Middle Kingdom,[58] and these incantations, or ones like them, may have been known to the priests of Lahun. Other texts call upon the beneficent gods for aid in the battle against the invisible enemy. In the beginning of the following spell, the sufferer identifies himself with Horus and Thoth[59] and calls upon the goddesses Isis and Nephthys to relieve his suffering by exchanging their heads for his: "'My head!' said Horus. 'The side of my head!' said Thoth. 'Come to me, mother Isis and aunt Nephthys, that you may give me your head in exchange for my head, or rather the side of my head!'"[60] The spell relies on familiarity with other myths, in this case one in which Isis literally loses her head. As with other myths, no narrative version of this discombobulating event has survived, but it is referred to in texts as early as the Coffin Texts. As is the case with most spells, it ends with an instruction to recite the spell over a specific item, in this case over knotted threads that are to be placed on the left foot of the patient.

Stomach-aches were also blamed on intruders, as is obvious in this excerpt from a spell designed to dispel *akhu* from a belly:[61]

"Come to me mother Isis and sister Nephthys! See, I am suffering inside my body, or rather, the members there!"

"Do worms interfere? Does it look like worms?" so said the goddess Isis. . . .

After drawing the requisite images onto an unspecified material which is laid on the belly of the sufferer, the pain-causing demon is quite realistically said to "leave as a wind from your behind."

Along with asking the gods for aid, in the Old Kingdom and through the Second Intermediate Period letters were written to dead relatives and friends, asking for help from the beyond.[62] They have been found in sites throughout Egypt, and date from the Old to the New Kingdom, with most clustering around the First Intermediate Period.[63] They were written by non-royal individuals, and were addressed to the authors' deceased relatives or acquaintances requesting favors in this world or the next. Although the letters could be written on papyrus, and rarely on stelae, they were also written on pottery vessels and left in or near the tombs. Some of these letters, particularly the earliest ones, were written on bowls that may have originally been filled with offerings for the deceased, both out of respect and as further encouragement for the dead to help the living.

The content of the letters consisted of requests to the dead either for personal favors in this world – such as healing, settling household quarrels and property disputes, or even the birth of a healthy child – or for direct intercessions on behalf of the living within the farworld itself. The letters often began with a greeting from the writer, and an expression of hope that the gods were taking good care of the dead in the afterlife. The problem would then be detailed, with what the living expected from the dead. In one of these, a man begs a deceased relative

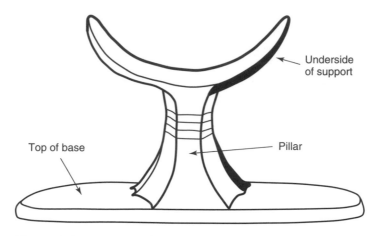

**Figure 8.2**  Drawing of headrest (courtesy of JJ Shirley).

to save his sick maidservant: "Watch over her! Rescue her from whoever, male or female, is acting against her."[64] In another, a man implores his dead wife to fight on his behalf in the afterlife and to "expel the pain of my body!"[65]

It is not only textual evidence that reflects the concept of battling with disease or pain-bearing agents. As mentioned earlier, objects such as the hippopotamus birth tusks were inscribed with weapon-bearing divine and supernatural creatures designed to repulse any harm. These same entities appear on the tiny faience spouted cup found in the elite cemetery of Lisht, which was probably used as a feeding cup, or as part of the rituals associated with the birthing process. These are not only artifacts that might have been used to keep away harmful entities. In the hot Egyptian climate, headrests were used to support the head of a sleeper, keeping it cool as well as keeping it out of easy reach of spiders, scorpions, and other creeping bugs (Fig. 8.2).[66]

Made of wood and often supplemented with a soft pad or pillow, these head-rests could be plain (as is most common in the Middle Kingdom), but they could also be decorated with protective spells and apotropaic figures.[67] These depictions can be found on the top of the base of the headrest, on the supporting pillar, and on the underside of the curved portion that actually supports the individual's head. The images included those of Bes, Beset, Aha (see Fig. 2.3), griffins, hip-popotamus goddesses, or fantastic creatures containing the most recognizable portions of powerful animals, such as the crocodile. Along with their frightening appearance, these deities guarded and defended their vulnerable wards with an assortment of weapons such as spears, daggers, and hand-held snakes and rearing, striking cobras. In some cases the cobras can be seen in the mouth of the deity, their power in the process of being consumed and absorbed by the deity. The rearing cobra, with its ability to spit burning poison from a distance, was also believed to be the ultimate weapon against the chaotic forces, incinerating them with fire and flames.

Similar figures are described in the Coffin Texts, and can be occasionally seen in the Middle Egyptian coffins that feature the Book of the Two Ways. Within this context, their function was to guard the passageways within the farworld, thus restricting access to those who had proved themselves worthy by correctly identifying their names and epithets, or by speaking the correct spell. These composite beings are often termed "demons," but this is a misnomer, for they were not harmful to those who legitimately belonged, only to intruders. In a similar vein, the guardian images protected the sleeper from nightmares, which were often blamed on the same malignant entities that were responsible for many illnesses.[68]

Thus incised or painted figures acted in a similar apotropaic capacity whether they appeared on wands or cups or headrests.[69] They were used to protect vulnerable individuals, including children, pregnant and birthing women, sleepers, the sick, and perhaps even the very old, from the onslaught of demonic forces by creating a sacred space within which the individual – or the substance in the case of the cups – would be kept safe. Their usefulness continued even after death, as indicated by their inclusion among burial goods.

The idea of illness as invader and of healer as fighter was prevalent in the Middle Kingdom, and a number of other spells have survived that reflect the belief that the source of many of the ailments that are in the western world ascribed to an internal physical or psychological source, or to bacteria or viruses, were mostly blamed on the malicious entities who crossed over from the afterlife.[70] This is not surprising as even today the precise causes of ailments such as headaches are difficult to discern, and to the sufferer it can feel as though one is being pummeled, assaulted, and tortured by an alien within.

## Burns, Splinters, Cuts, Scrapes, Bruises, General Aches and Pains

Every member of Hedjerit's family would also have been susceptible to the same everyday injuries that beset people today. Burns would have been a frequent problem for the many craftsmen who worked with metals such as copper, bronze, gold, silver, and electrum, in terms of both the manufacture and preparation of the raw material, and the production of objects. The production of faience and pottery also required the use of heat, open fires, and kilns. Though no smelting ovens, furnaces, or kilns have yet been recognized within the town of Lahun, it has not been fully excavated. As discussed earlier, the survival of molds and the tools which were made by the molds hint at nearby production of these types of artifact.[71] Bakers were also susceptible to burns, and even household baking, which often took place on open hearths, would lead to injuries. In a town like Lahun, curious children in particular would have found themselves easily burned either on these open stoves, or by accidental contact with torches and incense burners.

165

It should come as no surprise by now that the main remedy for burns was to recite a spell over a poultice of various mixed ingredients (often including the milk of a mother who has borne a male child) that was placed over the burn. The patient is identified with the young Horus, who has wandered off and been burned by a flame in the desert, and is eventually found and saved by his mother Isis. The Ebers Papyrus also includes remedies that consist of various poultices, with a different one to be applied daily during consecutive stages of the burn. One sequence included black mud on the first day, cattle feces and another unidentified substance on the second day, acacia resin, dough, carob, and oil on the third day, and so on.[72]

For the treatment of everyday injuries such as splinters, scrapes, cuts, and bruises, there is little evidence. These fall into the realm of injuries that either heal on their own, or are easily treated at home, and do not therefore require written instructions or obvious tools. The removal of splinters, for example, could easily be done with the aid of tweezers. As previously discussed, these are multi-purpose utensils that were found in the town of Lahun, but there is no way to tell if any particular pair was used to pluck stray hairs or to remove a splinter. Bandages could be made of strips of linen, while honey, an ingredient that actually does have anti-bacterial properties, appeared in many of the remedies and may have been used as a salve. One mundane yet potentially fatal accident that is attested in a Middle Kingdom text is emergency care for getting a fish bone stuck in the throat:[73]

"The Unique One belongs to me, as my servant! The Unique One belongs to me! My bread is in the town, my portion of meals is in the field – bone, get right!

A man will say this spell over a cake. To be swallowed by a man in whose throat a fish bone is stuck."

This is an example of a remedy that can be found in other parts of the world as well – not through diffusion, but because the method is reputed to work.[74] The use of a cake or piece of bread is supposed to soften the small bones so that they can be swallowed. A second Ancient Egyptian spell is also to be said over a cake that must be swallowed, so the remedy was at least popular, if not completely efficacious.

# Old Age

In many parts of the modern world, the great improvements in health care and preventive maintenance have led to an ever-increasing population of people who those societies consider to be the aged. This has in turn changed the way that the aging process is viewed, and medical schools are now beginning to include treating the elderly as part of the training of physicians.[75] As visible as the elderly are in modern western society, they have left little trace from Ancient Egypt. In part that is because there were few people who lived to what we might consider old age (over the age of 65), but it is also likely that the effects of old age were considered a natural if not always attractive part of life. As a person ages, organs begin to fail and the immune system weakens, leaving the individual more susceptible to diseases and prone to complications after injuries. There are also social side-effects of age, which vary according to the culture. In some, particularly those cultures where the attainment of old age is a rare occurrence, the very old retain an active role in society and are revered for their accumulated wisdom, while in others there is a withdrawal from the more mundane activities associated with the material world.[76]

Determining when and who was considered elderly in an ancient culture is as difficult a process as establishing the transitions between infancy, childhood, and adulthood. Old age in the modern world is usually based on chronological age and set at the same as the age at which an individual is expected to retire. It is unlikely that chronological age was a factor for the Egyptians in thinking of an individual as old – birthdays and chronological age are rarely mentioned in texts, even in autobiographies. These presentations of an individual's life focus on their career and social achievements, and transitions are marked by promotions with only general references to the life-stage at which they occurred. An exception can be found in a number of literary texts from the pharaonic period where the ideal lifetime is noted as 110 years.[77] A magician in the *Tales of Wonder* from the Middle Kingdom is described as "a man of 110 years," while in a number of New Kingdom texts the hope is expressed that the reader might "complete 110 years upon earth." The reality was that few individuals would reach anywhere near that age, and many of the characteristics of old age would have appeared decades earlier.

Material evidence pertaining to the elderly in Ancient Egypt is, however, rare. For the most part we must rely on texts and representations on tomb paintings that focus on presenting an idealized world. In *The Teaching of Ptahhotep*, a wisdom text written to provide a model of good conduct for elite males, the physical debilitation of old age is emphasized:

> My Sovereign Lord:
> Old age has arrived, infirmity has descended,
> Misery has drawn nigh, and weakness increases.
> One must take a nap like a child every day,
> The eyes are blurred, the ears are deaf,
> And vigor wanes because of weariness.
> The mouth is silent and no longer speaks;
> The memory is gone and cannot recall even yesterday.
> The bones ache through frailty,
> Pleasure has become repulsive, and all taste has vanished.
> What old age does to men is totally despicable.

> The nose becomes plugged and cannot breathe;
> Even standing and sitting are a bother.[78]

The speaker here petitions the king to allow him to appoint an individual to help him to fulfill the duties that he is no longer capable of performing on his own: "Permit your humble servant to appoint a staff of old age. Let my son be allowed to succeed to my position." The image of the son as a "staff of old age" emphasizes the role of the son as a physical and tangible asset to his father. For officials, this was seen as the duty of the eldest son, who would be expected to assist his father to fulfill the responsibilities of his office and eventually take them over. It does not seem to have been an automatic process, as the older man has to request authorization to formalize this transfer of power. From Lahun a deed of conveyance has survived wherein a man named Mery transfers his office to his son, who is named Intef (but nicknamed Iuseneb), in return for the son acting as his support: "I am giving my position of controller of the watch to Mery's son Intef called Iuseneb in exchange for being a staff of old age, because I am now grown old. Let him be appointed at once."[79]

Once again, these texts offer glimpses into the norms of the life of officials. Nevertheless, there are signs that at other levels of society it was also expected (or at least hoped) that children would help to care for an older person, whether that person was a man or a woman. One census that has survived from Lahun reveals that older family members, particularly women, did at times move into and become part of the household of their children. These documents, called in Egyptian *weput*, provide insights into the size of households in the town of Lahun. One set (previously mentioned) is particularly revealing, as it tracks the changing household of a soldier (Hori) and his family over time. During the first stage of the household, Hori is listed with his wife Shepset and their infant son Sneferu. At the next stage, his mother (presumably a widow at this point) and five sisters (two of whom are specified as children) are included in his household. When Hori dies, his son Sneferu is left with a household that contains his mother (Shepset), his grandmother, and three of his father's sisters. It is unclear whether all these individuals lived within the same home as the main householder, which would suggest that the physical size of homes could change,[80] or whether these lists include individuals who were dependent on the householder, but who did not necessarily live in the same physical building. In either case, the older woman was able to find a place in the household of her son and later her grandson.

While these documents provide us with clues as to living arrangements in Lahun, they do not reveal how family members regarded their senior kin. The census presents a bald list, and does not disclose whether or not Hori's mother had an occupation outside the household, or whether she took over household duties, nor does it specify the level of dependency. Whether an elder woman such as Hori's mother was respected for her wisdom or was considered a burden also remains completely invisible.[81]

In contrast, the physical manifestations of aging are more manifest in artistic representations. While they are not frequently represented, individuals who were considered older are nevertheless recognizable. The main characteristics include leaning on a staff (especially for those of higher rank than those around them), a marked pot belly, rounded back and shoulders, and pronounced wrinkles. These characteristics do not necessarily reflect a negative attitude toward age. Fat rolls, for example, are used to represent wealth as well as age – they mark the individual as one who is able to eat well. But the most obvious signs of age in Egyptian paintings are graying hair and baldness. These are also one of the few manifestations of age for which we have treatments in medical texts. Papyrus Ebers lists 24 treatments for hair including preventing hairs from turning gray, removing them altogether, and encouraging the growth of hair in balding men.[82] These ranged from applications of boiled black lizard to complex combinations of animal fats or hedgehog spikes that would also be boiled and rubbed into the head.

That growing old was sometimes actively avoided is suggested by a remarkable formula on the back of a text that is otherwise concerned with treating injuries and trauma. Following two prescriptions for rejuvenating skin, a new section is introduced with the title: "Beginning of the scroll of making an old man into a youth."[83] The main ingredient consists of pulverized bitter almonds, which are made into a dough that is soaked and kneaded until it exudes an oil. This oil is then to be carefully collected and one must "anoint a man with it. It is something that repels a cold from the head. If the body is wiped with it, what results is rejuvenation of the skin and repelling of wrinkles, any age spots, any sign of old age, and any fever that may be in body. (Proved) good a million times." Remedies such as this one might sound remarkably familiar from many modern advertisements for treatment of wrinkles and signs of age.

## Medical Substances

Aside from almonds, cakes, and lizards, the Ancient Egyptians availed themselves of an entire range of plant, animal, and mineral products to treat injuries, illnesses, and disease. Although the majority of the substances have not yet been identified by scholars, it is clear that the choice of ingredient to prescribe was eclectic and was determined by any number of factors.[84] As mentioned previously, certain foods, such as honey and onions, that were pleasant for humans were deemed to be distasteful to invading demons. Other substances were selected on the theory of similarity, that like will either repel or promote like. Thus, for the encouragement of hair growth one prescription recommended that a black lizard be crushed and boiled in oil and then applied to the head. Most Egyptians had black hair, so the use of a black reptile was prescribed. In addition, the hieroglyphic sign for "lizard" was also used for "many," therefore the remedy relied on wordplay: one placed an ointment of lots of black on the head, to encourage the growth of lots of black hair.[85] Some products of animals are specified because of their association with deities. For example, the urine of an ass might be prescribed for a woman who has a terrible toothache (considered as a sign of a uterine disorder because of the perceived direct link between the uterus and the mouth). The ass was associated with the god Seth, the same deity who was blamed for a number of disorders, but who could also be called upon as a powerful combatant against malignant forces.

Certain ingredients were strikingly popular. Honey was used in many combinations, and is an example of an ancient substance that is still used today for its medicinal properties. For example, because honey has anti-bacterial properties, smearing it onto a wound would have helped to stave off infection. This does not suggest that the Ancient Egyptians were aware of bacteria, but they may have observed that injuries treated with honey healed faster than those that were not, and perhaps this confirmed to them that the sweetness of honey was successful in warding off demons who were doomed to live a reversed life in the farworld. Other ingredients were popular because of their obvious and established beneficial effect in one context, which could hopefully be transferred to another. Thus, the milk of a mother that had successfully given birth to a child, in particular a son, was included in many treatments. Some of the less savory ingredients included urine (as mentioned above) and feces, both of which were usually applied externally to the troubled part of the body. Finally, oils and fats were often prescribed especially for applying salves. The fat could be derived from vegetables, fruits, and nuts, or from a number of different animals including asses, geese, pigs, cattle, crocodiles, snakes, hippos, and even lions.

The recommended substances could be mixed together, pounded, crushed, ground, cooked, boiled, soaked, steeped, strained, and even knotted. The most common vehicles for prescriptions that needed to be drunk were water, beer, wine, honey, oil, and milk[86] – vehicles that are still popular today. The resulting concoction could be swallowed, inserted into the rectum as a suppository, or applied to the problematic part of the body either externally or internally (often mixed with a fat or oil). Some mixtures were burned, with the resulting fumes directed toward the afflicted part of the body to heal it or to drive out offending demons.

## Medical Texts

Much of our knowledge of Ancient Egyptian medicine for the whole of Egyptian history derives from the survival of manuscripts. It is generally acknowledged now that in pharaonic Egypt magic and medicine were intertwined. A strict demarcation between "empirico-rational medicine," which relies on observation, diagnosis, and treatment with no reference to the divine world, and "magico-religious medicine," which relies on help from the gods, simply cannot be maintained.[87] Indeed, even in the modern world aid from the divine world is often requested through private (or even public) prayer at the same time that "conventional" medicine is applied. What we call "spells" in ancient Egypt were used to treat ailments and disease, and usually required a prescription of physical substances to be applied or ingested in order to be efficacious as well. Likewise, the texts that are usually recognized as being closer to the western idea of medicine include supplications to deities, and the treatments are often set against a mythical background, which may or may not be overtly expressed. Ideally, the treatment for each ailment is structured as a discrete unit consisting of the title, description of the symptoms, diagnosis and prognosis, prescription, and incantation. Not all the documents are arranged according to this precise structure, nor are these sections always clearly delineated. Nevertheless, this is the most consistent pattern of treatments in these types of texts.

As with other evidence from Ancient Egypt, it is important to be aware of the complexities of dating the various manuscripts. This book deals with life in Egypt's Late Middle Kingdom, and the contents of some of the papyri may not have been familiar to those Egyptians. In the case of some manuscripts, there is a consensus among scholars that although the surviving copy is later the contents were known in the Middle Kingdom, and in some cases even earlier. In the following list those compositions that are believed by the majority of modern scholars to date to that earlier time are indicated. Most of the texts were not excavated and have no clear findspot, and therefore their dating must rely on philological, linguistic, and textual analyses.

Aside from the corpus of major papyri dealing with medical issues, there are numerous papyrus fragments and ostraka upon which were written medical treatments. These are more difficult to date, and are used as evidence only when their content finds parallels in the material that has more certainly been dated to the Middle Kingdom. This category includes the numerous spells that rely on placing the patient, healer, problem, and cure within mythological frameworks that were popular in the Middle Kingdom, particularly that of Isis healing her son Horus, as well as those that do not name deities who were popular only from the New Kingdom onward.

The following is not comprehensive, but is a listing of the main texts that are cited in discussions of issues related to medicine and sickness in Ancient Egypt.[88] The purpose of this list is both to show the range of ailments that were known and treated in the Middle Kingdom, and also to note ones that are sometimes cited but that should be treated with more caution when discussing treatments in the Middle Kingdom. The first group below consists of papyri that are generally considered to date from the Middle Kingdom on the basis of either context or style and parallels.

### *Lahun Gynecological papyrus* (UC 32057)

This papyrus was excavated in Lahun and features treatments designed for the female reproductive system in terms of both disorders and prognoses for birth.

These include problems related to excessive bleeding, discharge, and pain, methods for determining whether or not a woman is capable of giving birth, and methods for preventing conception.

### Papyrus Turin 54003

This Middle Kingdom text is the source for the remedy for choking on a fish bone discussed above, as well as for remedies for snakebite and eye disease.

### Papyrus Ramesseum III, IV, and V

These papyri were found in a wooden box along with other ritual items that likely belonged to the "overseer of secrets," the magic-user and healer previously discussed in chapter 7.[89] Ramesseum III includes general internal medicine, gynecology, children's diseases, and eye problems. Ramesseum IV focuses on contraception and infant's and women's diseases, while V focuses on stiffness in joints, muscles, and tendons. As discussed earlier, the archaeological evidence suggests that joint problems were a serious difficulty in at least some areas of Egypt during the Middle Kingdom, so it is not surprising to find treatments being recorded.

### Papyrus Berlin 2027

Although this manuscript is from the New Kingdom, scholars generally agree that it and the following two papyri originated in the Middle Kingdom. This papyrus consists of a series of incantations to help new mothers during childbirth, insure their ability to feed their infants, and protect them while they are in a vulnerable state.

### Edwin Smith Papyrus

This well-known papyrus features detailed treatments for the types of trauma that are common in battle and on work-sites, but that can be also be the result of any interpersonal trauma (that is, trauma caused by an act of violence of one person against another). Not only is it the most familiar of the medical papyri to people interested in the subject today, but it was apparently popular in the New Kingdom as well. Called an "instruction book" in Egyptian, nearly all of the cases are annotated with notes (called "glosses") where the healers were trying to clarify the problems and treatments. Apparently these physicians sometimes had trouble in understanding terminology that was no longer commonly used during the New Kingdom. The entire text is strikingly organized by parts of the body, from the top of the head to the vertebra. Each case is subdivided into a title, an examination, a diagnosis and prognosis, and the treatment. In some cases, the problem was deemed untreatable, and the patient would either heal on his own, or not. The back of this papyrus consisted of prescriptions (in different handwriting) including other medical issues related to gynecology, troubled complexions, aging, and the anus.

### Papyrus Ebers

This extensive papyrus deals with a host of general medical problems including those of the stomach, skin, anus, head, eye, blood vessels, teeth, ears, nose, throat, and hair, as well as worms, pests, urine, burns, flesh wounds, ulcers, tumors, gynecology, and the bites of animals including humans and crocodiles. Other texts from the New Kingdom that are not generally attributed to an earlier source include the Papyrus Hearst, which repeats in a smaller, more portable format some of the cases in Papyrus Ebers, as well as remedies for snakebites; Papyrus British Museum 10059 (also called the London Medical Papyrus), which contains a section on burns and gynecology as well as many incantations; Papyrus Carlsberg VIII, which mainly deals with pregnancy and conception on one side, and on the other repeats many of the eye treatments found in Papyrus Ebers; Papyrus Chester Beatty V (headaches), VI (rectal diseases), VII (scorpion stings), VIII (some of the problems here are not identifiable while others are glossed over by scholars as "magical"), and XV (prescriptions for thirst); and Papyrus Berlin 3038, which contains pregnancy tests and repeats some of the cases in other papyri. In some of these papyri, the treatments are the same as those found in earlier texts, but some are not attested earlier. In the case of the new treatments, while we cannot definitively know if they were known in the Middle Kingdom, it is perhaps safest not to assume that they reflect knowledge and practices that were prevalent prior to the New Kingdom.

Finally, a number of papyri are often cited that date to the Ptolemaic and Roman periods. These include the Brooklyn Snake Papyrus, which contains an extensive list of snakes, their bites, and treatments, and Papyrus London-Leiden, which offers help for a range of earthly and supernatural problems.

## The Healers

Every town in Egypt must have had healers, whether official or unofficial. The presence of titles in the Middle Kingdom such as "doctor" (*sunu*), "overseer of doctors" (*jmy-ra sunu*), "chief of doctors" (*wer sunu*), "chief of palace doctors" (*wer sunu per aa*), and "chief doctor of the king" (*wer sunu ni nesu*) indicates that there was a hierarchy of physicians. Some of these were privileged to treat the pharaoh and his court, some were sent out to treat the inevitable industrial accidents that would occur on quarrying and mining expeditions,[90] while others may have had a more general role. As was often the case in Ancient Egypt, officials usually held multiple titles, and many of these individuals also carried titles associated with ranks of the priesthood, such as the lector priest (*khery-heb*) or "knower of things" (*rekh khut*) discussed above. In general, the *sunu* likely dealt with injuries from trauma and surgeries. Some of these doctors were also competent in other sub-specialties, including dentistry. One talented individual is listed in his First Intermediate Period stela as a doctor, gastroenterologist, and ophthalmologist of the court as well as a proctologist (literally "herdsman of the anus") and indeed an inspector of doctors of the court.

In contrast, the poisonous bites of serpents and scorpions were probably referred to a specialist, the "conjurer of Serket" (*kherep Serket*), if one was available, while contagious diseases were the domain of the "pure priest of Sekhmet" (*wab ni Sekhmet*).[91] That individuals could concurrently bear titles marking them as physicians, priests, and specialists in magic reflects the melding of magic and medicine that was a hallmark of Egyptian treatments. It also emphasizes the requirement for literacy in order to be able to provide certain treatments. Not only were some individual incantations specified as inaccessible to commoners, but some of the major compositions (such as Papyrus Edwin Smith and Papyrus Ebers) were introduced by "beginning of the secret knowledge of a physician," to emphasize the restricted nature of the knowledge contained therein. Only those who were literate and who had sanctioned access to copies of the papyri, likely housed in the House of Life, were in theory able to successfully treat the ailments and injuries that they cataloged.

In reality, however, many more individuals must have practiced the art and science of medicine. As we saw earlier, wet nurses are attested in the Middle Kingdom texts, including those of Lahun, and must have played a significant role at the least in the recognition of pediatric ailments. Although gynecological issues appear in numerous documents, the actual process of giving birth was likely considered a natural event – part of the ordered world as opposed to the ailments and diseases that stemmed from the chaotic realm. It was not necessary, therefore, to record any instructions. Unless there were serious complications, it is unlikely that doctors were needed, and experienced midwives may have been equipped to deal with many of the unforeseen problems.

Other remedies would have required swift and immediate implementation if they were to be effective at all. For example, a person choking on a fish bone would not have had time to find a sanctioned doctor or priest for help. In such cases there was likely a remedy that can be considered a part of that nebulous assortment of lore that we refer to as folk medicine. This kind of knowledge derives from a variety of sources and the patterns of transmission are often impossible to detect. In Ancient Egypt, with the exception of certain incantations that were specifically described as being classified information, there are few indications that physicians treated their patients in utmost secrecy. In most cases there would have been others who would have seen and heard the process, and possibly kept it in mind for the future. At the very least, if the patient were conscious, he may have remembered the gist of the treatment. In other cases, simple trial and error would have been the source. In all of these cases, the information would have been transmitted orally and would thus be invisible in the material record.

Sickness

The townspeople of Lahun suffered many of the same irritating ailments that plague us today – anemia, arthritis, dental problems, gastro-intestinal disorders, headaches, and vision conditions. Accidents led to fractures, wounds, bruises, and burns. Some afflictions that were prevalent in Ancient Egypt, such as schistosomiasis, are thankfully rare in most of the modern world. The practical assessment and evaluation of the ailments were logical, even if the attributed cause and the method of treatment at times seem peculiar to us. But from within the Ancient Egyptian frame of reference, they made sense, and were based on both the beliefs and the practical experience of the people. Certain individuals had access to medical knowledge that was restricted in nature, and these became more specialized healers. For common injuries or complaints, however, most people would have relied on self-treatment or help from relatives and those in the close community. When Hedjerit fractured her arm, her family would likely have turned to someone they knew was experienced, perhaps an older individual such as her grandmother, to confirm the prognosis and set the bone. But for some ailments, there was no cure and the result would be death – the topic of the next chapter.

## Notes

1   Fractures of the distal radius (often specifically of the radius bone), known as "colles fractures," are the most common injury suffered by active children.
2   Nunn 1996, 174–8.
3   Baker 1997.
4   J. Allen 2005, 95.
5   Baker 1997.
6   Rose 2006.
7   Baker 2001, 47; 1997.
8   Nerlich et al. 2002.
9   Nerlich et al. 2002, 380.
10  Zink et al. 2003a.
11  Zink et al. 2003b.
12  Nunn 1996, 68–9.
13  Kloos and David 2002.
14  Borghouts 1978, 94, spell #143.
15  Pyramid Texts are funerary texts written on the inside of Old Kingdom pyramids from the end of the Fifth Dynasty to the Middle Kingdom. Their function was to help the king reach the afterlife successfully.
16  "Pre" is a variant of the name of the sun god "Re."
17  For the importance of knotting in magic, see Wendrich 2006.
18  Borghouts 1978, 77–8, spell #108.
19  Borghouts 1978, 83, spell #122.
20  Ritner 1993, 207, 225–31.
21  Borghouts 1978, 87, spell #126.
22  Sweeney 2006a, 157, citing Gilula 1978.
23  Pinch 1994, 59–60.

24  Nunn 1996, 190.
25  These were religious texts initially restricted exclusively to the pharaoh that depicted the afterlife in text and image. Their focus was the voyage of the sun god at night (and in some cases in the day), with detailed representations of the topography and what would happen in each of the various regions.
26  See for example Book of AmDuat hour 10, and Book of Gates hour 9.
27  Zandee 1977, 237.
28  The Greeks called him Apophis.
29  After #136 in Borghouts 1978, 91.
30  Leitz 1999, 9 (P. BM EA 9997 Incantation 3, III, 14–15).
31  P. BM EA 9997 published in Leitz 1999. For the following see particularly p. 5.
32  Alcohol helps dissolve many ingredients and is still used as a base for many medicines, the most obvious being cough syrup.
33  Serqet (also known as "Selket") was the goddess associated with scorpions. She is easily identified in images by the scorpion she wears on her head. For a discussion of this type of healer see Nunn 1996, 135.
34  Quirke 2004b, 37–8.
35  Baker 1997. Grit in food has also been confirmed by analysis of ancient bread (Samuel 2000, 565.)
36  Nunn 1996, 118–19.
37  In the tomb of Rekhmire, TT100.
38  Anderson 1995, 2561.
39  *Wb* IV, 444.
40  Nunn 1996, 200–2.
41  Ebers 337 in Nunn 1996, 201.
42  UC 32057, 2, 22, in Collier and Quirke 2004, 61.
43  P. Chester Beatty VI, vs. 2, 5–9 (Borghouts 1978, #8 ).
44  P. Chester Beatty VIII [8] VS. 1, 1–2, 4 (Borghouts 1978, #11).
45  P. Edwin Smith [53] 19, 2–14 (Borghouts 1978, #18).
46  Borghouts 1978, #55.
47  Leitz 1999, 79 (BM EA 10059 Section XIII Incantation 57 [Wreszinski Incantation 22]).
48  Leitz 1999, 64 (BM EA 10059 Section VIII Incantation 22 [Wreszinski Incantation 34]).
49  Leitz 1999, 69 (BM EA 10059 Section IX Incantation 28 [Wreszinski Incantation 40]) and 70 (BM EA 10059 Section IX Incantation 30 [Wreszinski Incantation 42]).
50  Borghouts 1978, #27, P. Leiden I 348 [22] RT. 12, 7–11 (Borghouts 1971); Borghouts 1978, #47, 76
51  Borghouts 1978, #39, 40, 41.
52  Borghouts 1978, #64.
53  This is the afterlife, inhabited by the gods and the dead, that the Egyptians called *duat*. A translation of "underworld" or "netherworld" implies that this zone was below or under the land of the living, and indeed in some Egyptian texts it is described as "below," but in others it was "above" in the sky, and in others simply "over there." I have thus chosen to use the word "farworld" as it is the closest to the Ancient Egyptian conception.

54 A levitating ghost is described in P. Chassinat II (Posener 1960), while the story of Khonsuemhab and the Ghost tells the tale of a ghost who is unhappy with the state of his tomb (for the publication see von Beckerath 1992 and for an English translation see Simpson 2003, 112–15).

55 Ritner 1990.

56 Kadish 1979.

57 P. Berlin 2027 C1, 9/2–6, in Erman 1901, 11–12.

58 Parkinson 1991, 129–30.

59 Thoth was a god associated with justice, scribes, and writing.

60 After #45 in Borghouts 1978, 31.

61 After #26 in Borghouts 1978, 22.

62 Accessible translations of the letters can be found in Wente 1990. The main publications are Wente 1975/6; Simpson 1970 and 1966; Gardiner 1930; Gardiner and Sethe 1928.

63 Two examples have been found from the New Kingdom.

64 Wente 1990, #350215–16.

65 Szpakowska 2003, 24.

66 Dewey 1993.

67 UC16065; UC16113; Petrie 1927, Gurob #40; Schott 1958, Heidelberg #290; Seipel and Schlossmuseum Linz 1989, Louvre N3736a and British Museum 35807; Perraud 1998, Louvre E4321 + E4293.

68 Szpakowska 2003, 171–4.

69 This is confirmed by Perraud 2002, noting two Middle Kingdom headrests upon which are inscribed spells for protection. These spells included formulaic expressions that are virtually identical to those found on a number of inscribed apotropaic wands also dated to the Middle Kingdom: "to be said by" + the name of the protective entity, followed by an expression such as "we come," and finally the term "protection" often with the preposition "concerning" + "the object." The similarity in formulas is not coincidental, and confirms that the wands and headrests could function in a similar manner.

70 Sweeney 2006a.

71 Only recently, a faience factory has been identified in the not-too-distant site of Lisht. Nicholson and Peltenburg 2,000, 181–2.

72 Nunn 1996, 182.

73 After #28 in Borghouts 1978, 23.

74 My thanks to my students Lee Turley, Ceri de Lloyd, and Lana Gonzalez, who when the spell was mentioned concurrently confirmed that the remedy is known in northwest England, south-west Wales, Georgia, and Tennessee.

75 See for example the University of California, Los Angeles, Medical School.

76 R. Janssen and Janssen 1996, 2–3.

77 R. Janssen and Janssen 1996, 60–9.

78 Simpson 2003, 130.

79 UC32037 in Collier and Quirke 2004, 100–1.

80 Kemp 2005, 217–19.

81 One of the few serious studies on the life of aging women is Sweeney 2006b.

82 Papyrus Ebers 451–73, 476.

83 J. Allen 2005, 113–14.

84  Nunn 1996, 136–62.
85  P. Ebers 469.
86  Nunn 1996, 140.
87  Weeks 1995, 1787; Sweeney 2006a. See as well the discussion in Nunn 1996, 96–7, who nevertheless maintains this distinction as it is useful for the purposes of his monograph.
88  Compiled after Weeks 1995, 1793–4, and Nunn 1996, 24–41.
89  Ritner 1993, 222–32.
90  For Middle Kingdom examples see Renefseneb and Heryshefnakht (Nunn 1996, 128–9.)
91  Quirke 2004b, 37.

# 9

# Death

*It was when I was a young girl, still tying the fillet,[1] that my revered mother Dedet, maa-kheru,[2] bore my brother in my presence. As he emerged from between her thighs, and his cord was cut with the pesesh-blade, he wailed with a great cry of "ny!"[3] But the blood that emerged with him — it did not stop. It pooled like the inundation that satiated Sekhmet in the midst of her fury.[4] The healer had used the ivory tusk and had placed the threads of the border of a knotted jaa.t-fabric in my mother's vagina, and over it recited: "Anubis has come forth to keep the inundation from treading on what is pure — the land of Tait.[5] Beware of what is in it!"[6] But the gods did not hear, and when day had dawned my mother had reached her final mooring.[7]*

Death was as much a part of daily life in Ancient Egypt as it is today, if not more so. For Egyptians did not live as long as most people do today, and death would have touched the lives of many more youngsters, and would have been familiar to adults and the old. The cemeteries of western Thebes that span the Middle Kingdom through the Late Period consistently show that of those who survived childhood, most died in their twenties and thirties.[8] While this may seem young to us today, it was the norm for Ancient Egypt, and lives were still lived to the fullest within that shorter lifespan. Due to the vagaries of the survival of archaeological remains, with deterioration occurring more rapidly in the inhabited regions of the Nile valley than in the desert regions of cemeteries, combined with the past desire on the part of early explorers for acquisition of wealth from tombs, Ancient Egypt has been portrayed as a culture whose people were obsessed with death. As we have already seen throughout this book, nothing could be further from reality. While a good deal of energy certainly was expended on insuring that loved ones were provided with the proper burial rituals, this was partly in order to insure that they would be reborn and then continue to live happily in the afterlife (through maintenance rituals), and partly to help the living cope with their loss. Death and dying were themselves never portrayed or mentioned in any detail.

In death, even more than with everyday life, much of what we know of the rituals, practices, and beliefs derives from the small body of evidence that has been left to us mainly from the world of the elite. Beliefs in particular, attitudes toward death, hopes and fears regarding the afterlife, are expressed mainly through texts. Recent discussions of the subject have, therefore, relied on this evidence to try to uncover the conceptions and perceptions of death in Ancient Egypt. Only a few authors acknowledge that this may be an extremely biased picture, one that reflects only a tiny segment of the population, and even fewer openly raise and attempt to answer the question.[9] A passage from the popular *Tale of Sinuhe*,[10] a fictional tale composed in the Middle Kingdom and recopied for centuries, is often cited for what it reveals regarding funerary practices and beliefs. The following is the response of the king to Sinuhe's letter requesting return to the land of Egypt from the foreign land where he dwelled.[11]

A night vigil will be assigned to you, with holy oils and wrappings from the hands of Tayet.

A funeral procession will be made for you on the day of joining the earth, with a mummy case of gold, a mask of lapis lazuli, a heaven over you, and you placed in a hearse, with oxen dragging you, and singers going before you.

The dance of the Oblivious ones will be done at the mouth of your tomb-chamber, and the offering-invocation recited for you; sacrifices will be made at the mouth of your offering-chapel, and your pillars will be built of white stone in the midst of the royal children's.

Your death will not happen in a foreign country; Asiatics will not lay you to rest; you will not be put in a ram's skin when your coffin is made.

This is too long to be roaming the earth! Think of your corpse – and return!

The passage provides us with insights into sanctioned burial practice at the elite level. Although this text dates to the Middle Kingdom, the traditions seem to have survived, and many of these scenes are reproduced in vivid color in tombs of the New Kingdom, and verified by the remains of elite mummies. An outline of this process according to the *Tale of Sinuhe* is given here, and will be expanded below in more detail within the context of the rituals that might have been performed for Hedjerit's mother. At the outset, the passage above refers to a nocturnal vigil during which the body is oiled and purified, while the mention of Tayet or Tait, the goddess of weaving, alludes to the body being wrapped in linen. This is followed by the funeral procession once the body has been placed in a coffin. The coffin is described as being of gold while the lappets of the mummy mask are of lapis-lazuli, which are the colors of the skin and hair of the gods respectively. The top of the inside of the coffin was, in the Middle Kingdom, painted with star-clocks or with a vertical text invoking the sky goddess Nut,[12] described by the pharaoh in the Sinuhe tale as "a heaven over you."

The coffin is placed on a catafalque, which will be drawn by oxen. Singers mourn and precede the advancement of the coffin, and at the entrance of the tomb chamber, *muu*-dancers (translated in the text above as "the Oblivious ones") will perform a dance the precise function of which is still debated.[13] At that point, a series of funerary rituals is performed in the accessible area of the tomb. It begins with the recitation of the standard offering formula that will insure provisions for the deceased for eternity, and sacrifices, both physical and virtual. Sinuhe will be treated as a member of the elite, and will be provided with statuary and stelae of the finest stone and even a pyramid, and will be buried in the cemetery surrounding the tomb of the pharaoh himself.[14] Burial at home was important for the Egyptians, for they could only be insured an eternal after-life if the correct Egyptian rituals were carried out. Sinuhe is thus assured that his rites will not be carried out by foreigners, and he will be buried as an Egyptian in a proper coffin, rather than according to foreign custom in the skin of an animal.

Although this description and process were clearly meant for Egypt's elite, they can be used as a general framework, with appropriate modifications, for a reconstruction of funerary practices associated with a member of the middle class such as Hedjerit's mother. The concept that the eldest son is responsible for arranging the deceased's burial is prevalent throughout Egyptian literature. The tradition has its source in the Osirian cycle of myths, where the well-being of the resurrected god Osiris was maintained by his son Horus. While no full narrative of the myth exists in the surviving Egyptian literature, for our purposes it is useful to pull together the various threads that are found in disparate sources and weave them together as a cohesive story. Our concern here is with those elements that deal with the myth as a model for mummification and rebirth. After Osiris has been murdered and dismembered by his brother Seth in a bid for the rule of Egypt, his various body parts are gathered together by Isis, his sister and wife, and their sister Nephthys.[15] To find all the parts, they take flight as kites, and in tomb paintings and on coffins they are often depicted in their bird form at the head and foot of the mummy. Isis, who is a great magician in her own right, is able to put all the parts together to magically bring Osiris back to life. She revivifies him completely, and is able to conceive a child by him.

Successfully reanimated, the god is allotted the afterlife as his realm. After avenging his father's death and battling with Seth, their child, Horus, goes on to be allocated the rule of the realm of the living. Egyptian myth does not follow a linear timeline, but is rather set against a backdrop of both eternal sameness (*djet*) and eternal recurrence (*neheh*). In religious texts, therefore, even though according to a rigid linear timeline it would seem that he had not yet even been conceived, Horus was the one responsible for the final and most important funerary rituals for his father Osiris. In the same way, in the land of the living the eldest son was presented as being responsible for the most important funerary rituals of the deceased. In the Middle Kingdom and indeed right through the Roman Period, it made no difference whether the deceased was male or female

181

– every individual who went through the stage of death was referred to as the "Osiris." Likewise, should the deceased not have a son of his or her own, a daughter, adopted child, or even hired priest could perform the role of Horus.

In certain circumstances, women were placed in the position of being responsible for the funeral as the surviving daughter, wife, or other relative of the deceased, but in general the accountable party was the eldest son.[16] This tradition was one that was likely practiced by most if not all classes of Egyptians, and we can expect that Hedjerit's older brother, Senbubu, would have arranged the proper procedures for his mother. Indeed, the right to an inheritance was at least partially dependent on taking care of the burial for the deceased – thus encouraging children to take responsibility for insuring a proper burial for their parents.[17] Because of the singular lack of remains from the Late Middle Kingdom, particularly of the non-elite, the following scenario must be considered as provisional.

## The Body

An immediate concern would be preparation of the body. In the hot climate putrefaction would set in early, and the corpse would need to be moved out of the house to a location where it could be wrapped. This location was on the west bank of the Nile, and since most settlements were on the east bank, the funeral process would have begun by crossing the river. The town of Lahun, however, was on the west bank of the Nile and so no river crossing would have been required for Dedet and her family. If Dedet had been a member of the royal family or of the elite, her corpse would then have been mummified. This complex process developed over the centuries from its beginnings in the Predynastic Period. Archaeologists excavating in Hierakonpolis discovered that the heads and hands of many of the females (and only females) had been wrapped and padded with linen.[18] The mummies have been dated to approximately 3600 BC, at least a half-millennium before the next examples of mummification are known. It is not known why only females were mummified, and it is important to note that as far as we know, unlike the later mummies, these were not royal, but seemed to be from the working-class levels of society.

By the time of the Middle Kingdom, the process of mummification had become both greatly expanded and concurrently restricted in terms of access. The full process began with removing the corpse to a special temporary structure (called a "divine booth" or *seh netjer* for the pharaoh, and a "purification tent" or *ibu ni wab* for the elite), where it would be washed and purified with oils. The Egyptians recognized that soft tissue such as the brain and internal organs were subject to rapid decomposition. Since it served no obvious function, the brain tissue was removed by either making a hole in the nasal cavity, or through the eye socket, or via a hole in the base of the skull which would then be packed.

**Figure 9.1** Human-headed canopic jar from Hawara UC16027 (jar = h. 21.0 cm; lid = h. 9.0 cm) (courtesy of the Petrie Museum of Egyptian Archaeology).

The internal organs were removed by a priest by incising the left side of the corpse with a knife of flint. Even after the Egyptians had learnt to use metal, flint was still used not only because it is a very sharp stone, but also because the implement itself had acquired a religious significance. The lungs, liver, intestines, and stomach would be removed and placed in stone (usually limestone) containers called canopic jars. In the Middle Kingdom, these were usually inscribed and had lids in the form of human heads (Fig. 9.1). The four jars could then be placed in a specially designed chest.

Once the soft tissue had been removed, the longest stage of the process could begin – drying the body. The main desiccating agent was natron, which is a form of salt. Once dry, the body would be transported to the "house of purification" or *per wabet* for further packing, stuffing, and washing. At the "house of beauty" or *per nefer* the corpse would be further prepared for its eventual reanimation by the application of ointments, perfumes, and oils to make it smell good. Hair might be added in the form of wigs or extensions, missing limbs replaced, and in the New Kingdom even artificial eyes could be inserted.[19] Once the appearance had been recreated to the point where it would be fully functioning and recognizable in the afterlife, the body would be wrapped in linen. The quality of cloth varied depending on rank, with new, unused linen of a high thread-count being used for royalty, while others would be wrapped in fabric that had been used in life. Some members of the elite would also have an extra garment included, one that had been used in life, then was washed, re-pleated, and deliberately turned inside out, perhaps as a mark of respect.[20] A mummy mask might be added with gold-colored skin and blue-black hair (like lapis-lazuli) to symbolize the transfiguration that would take place. The final stage was the disposal, probably by burial, of the materials that had been in contact with the corpse.

## The Cemetery

The actual mortuary evidence from the Late Middle Kingdom, as limited as it is, suggests that for the non-elite members of society, mummification was not generally an option.[21] The dead in the lower-class Lower Egyptian cemeteries near the Fayum were rarely mummified and were instead wrapped in linen or even matting.[22] It is likely, therefore, that Dedet's body would have been brought from her house, and transported through the village of Lahun to one of the locations for wrapping. Because there are no depictions or descriptions of the body being brought from the place of death, we do not know how her corpse would have been transported across the desert sands, but it was likely carried or carted. As previously mentioned, there would be no need for a river journey, as Dedet was already on the west bank. It is possible that the first stop was made at the house of purification for washing. Her corpse would then have been transported to the house of beauty, where she would have received minimal beautification treatments and been wrapped in reused linen.

Her wrapped body would then have been carried by her relatives and servants, or mounted on a cart or sledge drawn by oxen or more likely donkeys,[23] in a funeral procession to the place of burial. Judging from New Kingdom tomb paintings and the rare textual descriptions, along with priests, mourners played an important role in the cortège. The wealthy could even hire professional mourners to wail for them, while the poorer likely relied on family and friends. Most, though not all, of the mourners were women, and the paintings depict them in highly stylized poses that, along with the lyrics of the laments, were more emotional than those of men.[24] Scenes from the New Kingdom tombs of Ramose (Fig. 9.2) and of Roy (Fig. 4.7 above) provide typical examples.

The mourners' long hair could be flung over their faces, their arms were upraised to their foreheads, their breasts sometimes were exposed; some mourners were shown kneeling with their heads to their knees, and virtually all were shown with exaggerated tears. These signs of deep sorrow and grief are clear enough to be instantly recognized as such by anyone of any culture, even the very young. But the role of mourners of every funeral, whether it was one that was royal or of the poor, was to re-create the laments of the goddesses Isis and Nepthys at the side of Osiris, thereby contextualizing the funeral procession back into the mythical realm. This was a critically important component of the funerary ritual that would ultimately lead to the deceased's revival in the afterlife as an Osiris herself. Dedet would probably have been mourned by her sisters, her husband, her in-laws, her aunts, her daughters, perhaps her sons, and of course

**Figure 9.2** Mourners from the New Kingdom tomb of Ramose (courtesy of Ken Griffin).

her eldest daughter, Hedjerit. While hoping that the deceased would live a happy and eternal life in the realm of the gods, Dedet's family would still miss her.

Just five miles east of the town of Lahun in an area known as Haraga (or el-Harageh) is a series of cemeteries with tombs that date to the Predynastic, Late Old Kingdom, First Intermediate, Late Middle Kingdom, New Kingdom, and Coptic Periods. The cemeteries were excavated in 1923 by Engelbach,[25] who identified at least 804 tombs (all plundered)[26] in five of the cemeteries as being of Late Middle Kingdom date. Between three of the cemeteries are two wadis[27] that contain the poorest graves, which are also of Late Middle Kingdom date. Although we cannot be certain, it is probable that this was the cemetery in which many of the inhabitants of Lahun, including Dedet, would have been buried.[28] Most of the tombs in the cemeteries proper were shaft tombs of the type that were found in low-lying desert regions during the Middle Kingdom. There was a range in the depth of each shaft, and most had more than one horizontal chamber dug facing north and south off the vertical shaft itself (Fig. 9.3).

In this case, as was usual in ancient Egypt, north and south were aligned parallel with the course of the river Nile, and do not therefore necessarily align with "true" directions according to a magnetic compass, or to the north star. Each chamber would have held a coffin, allowing for families to be buried in the same tomb.

While these chambers were inaccessible once they had been filled with a coffin and any goods, we know from other cemeteries that most of the elite tombs of the time also had chapels on the surface to allow the living to interface with the

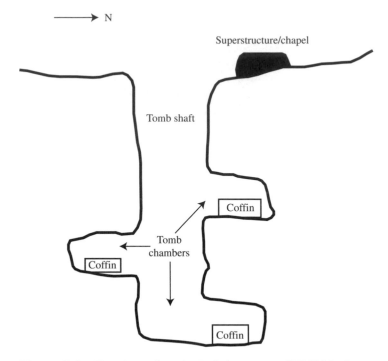

**Figure 9.3** Drawing of tomb shaft (courtesy of JJ Shirley).

dead. These *mastabas*, as they are now called, were roughly rectangular in shape and made of mud-brick. The interior of the walls might have been decorated and they usually contained stelae with offering prayers and an autobiography of the deceased. The autobiographies were not necessarily physically written by the deceased who could have dictated to a scribe. Although they make extensive use of stock phraseology and common formulas, the texts were nevertheless meant to be unique, highlighting that individual's achievements over any other's. The importance of these texts for our understanding of Ancient Egypt cannot be overestimated.[29] They provide us with a wealth of titles and, because their authors stress their relationship and service to the pharaoh, they contain important clues as to social structure, bureaucracy, and historical events. Because they were the privilege of wealthy officials, however, we would not expect to find long auto-biographies in the superstructures of most middle-class tombs.

In the poorer cemeteries at Haraga, any surface structures that may have been built did not survive, but the remains of stelae found in the shaft debris suggest that originally they were present. Although these would have been much smaller versions of the sometimes massive elite *mastabas*, nevertheless they reveal that the same practices were carried out by the poor as the rich – they differed in scale but not in function.

The poorest tombs in Haraga were found in two wadis that are today probably inaccessible or completely destroyed by cultivation.[30] In this area no shafts were dug, but the dead were instead densely packed into surface graves – simple depressions or shallow pits in the sand in which a lightly wrapped body would be placed, often without a coffin. As poor as these graves were, even they contained simpler versions of the same goods that have usually been associated with elite graves. Although we shall deal with grave goods below, it should be noted at this point that some of these graves contained materials that we usually consider as indicators of "material wealth: gold, copper, amethyst, and carnelian."[31] Although little detailed analysis was recorded for individual tombs in this area, researchers have been able to draw important conclusions based on Engelbach's records of the wadi tombs and those on higher ground, and by comparing this necropolis with other contemporary sites.[32] The first conclusion was that of the bodies that could be still be sexed, there were generally equal numbers of men and women. Small children were predominantly missing, but as discussed earlier, this can be explained by their separate burial locations. Just as both men and women of the Middle Kingdom had equal opportunities to be reborn as an Osiris, there were no restrictions on space based on gender. Particularly in the Twelfth Dynasty, however, there was a marked segregation based on socio-economic status, restricting access to the shaft tombs on higher ground to those families of higher standing,[33] while the poorest were relegated to the surface graves.[34] One of the indicators of status was position on the hill, with the higher levels on higher ground, but this was by no means the only marker of social and economic standing in Haraga, as we shall see below.

## Coffins and Coffin Texts

If we go back to the funeral of Dedet, it is likely that her beautified and wrapped body would have been carried to the cemetery, where perhaps the funeral procession would have been met by *muu* dancers like the ones who greeted Sinuhe's procession at his elite tomb in the royal cemetery. As a weaver and a priestess, Dedet was not of the lowest status, and she would have been granted access to a shaft tomb at Haraga.[35] Her mummy would also have been provided with a coffin. Anthropoid coffins (shaped in the form of a human) were first used in the mid Twelfth Dynasty, but they seem to have been reserved for use by the upper classes until they became more common at the end of the Thirteenth Dynasty, when they were often placed within the more common rectangular coffins.[36]

By the Late Middle Kingdom, few coffins were decorated on the inside. In the cemetery of Haraga, only a single such coffin remained, and it was one that had been reused for the body of a child who was much smaller than the coffin.[37] The outside was decorated with a palace frieze, and a false door with eyes so the deceased could look out. All four inner sides were painted with images of objects that would have been used in funerary rituals, or buried with the body. These include broad collars, a mirror, a headrest, fans, bags, ritual vessels, and food. This coffin also included a depiction of a harp, scepters, and royal headdresses, indicating that it was a coffin made for an individual of high status. Another coffin found in the cemetery was more typical, having vertical and horizontal texts on the outside. These consisted of the offering formula, wishes for a good burial, and protection for the body of the deceased.

Other First Intermediate Period and Middle Kingdom elite coffins were also decorated with a series of funerary texts that had their roots in the royal Pyramid Texts. Because these were found mostly on the insides of coffins (and sometimes even tombs), these are known as Coffin Texts.[38] Many survive and were later rewritten as New Kingdom Book of the Dead spells. The approximately 1,200 utterances consist of funerary rituals and offerings, identifications with a god (especially the creator god), transformation spells (where the deceased metamorphoses into the form of an animal such as a lion, falcon, or grasshopper), incantations to ward off both earthly and supernatural enemies, spells for entering the beautiful west (the farworld, filled with cool breezes and gardens), and aides for traversing the unpredictable and heavily guarded paths that were constantly at risk from the angry demons and the unjustified dead. In one example we find a graphic description of the flaming portal through which the deceased must pass, and the monstrous yet divine guardian who allows access only to those who can demonstrate that they deserve to proceed by reciting the correct words:[39]

> The first portal, of which it is said: vigil of fire.
> It is its flame which repels from it.
> Fifty cubits along its side is its fire,
> and the front of its flame traverses the earth from this sky.
> The gods said of it – it is charwood.
> It came from the arms of Sekhmet.
> . . .
> Open to me. Make way for me. See, I am come.
> O Atum[40] who is in the great sanctuary, O seizer of the gods.
> Rescue me from that god who lives on meat-sacrifice, dog-faced, human-skinned,
> keeper of the bend of the waterway of fire,
> who swallows shadows, who snatches hearts, who throws the lasso and yet is not seen.

Throughout the Coffin Texts, the key message is that the deceased has the proper knowledge, and knows the correct words to prove that he not only belongs in the same realm as the gods, but is now a god. This is explicit in spell 949, where the deceased recites, "I know you, I know your names, I live as you, I come into being as you, I will leap up and I will run to you. As for you older gods who would oppose me, I will be conducted on the path of my warrant."[41]

In many of the texts the deceased identifies himself or herself (these texts were used by both men and women) with the most powerful deity – the primordial creator god. In the excerpts presented here of one hymn, the individual is equated with Shu, the god of the air, who here plays the role of the creator god.[42]

The Chapter of the *ba* of Shu,[43] assuming the shape of Shu:

I am the *ba* of Shu, a god who comes into being by himself.[44]
I came into being in the form of "the-god-who-came-into-existence-by-himself."
I am the *ba* of Shu, the god whose shapes are unknowable, as I came into existence in the form of the god who created himself, hidden of forms.
. . .

He created me in his heart, he made me from his knowledge, he exhaled me from his nostrils.[45]
. . .

I grew from his legs; I came into being from his arms; I ascended from his limbs; he created me in his heart; he made me from his knowledge.
It is not by a regular birth that I was born![46]

These eloquent texts provide an unparalleled view of Egyptian conceptions of the afterlife, the nature of the gods, and funerary rituals. One series of coffins from Middle Egypt even contains detailed descriptions and maps of the various ways through the afterlife – a cosmography that Egyptologists call "the Book of Two Ways." Although the Coffin Texts were written and revised by priests and theologians, it is possible that many of the basic principles and ideas that are expressed in them filtered through to the different strata of Middle Kingdom society. At the very least, the idea of rebirth in the afterlife and the continuity of life was certainly prevalent even among the poor, as is reflected by the importance laid on the position of the corpse and on the inclusion of grave goods.

But coffins inscribed with these texts were nevertheless accessible only to those who could afford them, and were increasingly rare even for the wealthy in the Late Middle Kingdom. Dedet's wooden coffin was probably plain, uninscribed, and rectangular in shape, unlike Sinuhe's more decorated version. Her body would have been carefully placed on its back, with arms extended to the side, while her head would have either remained supine so that she faced upward, or been turned to the side so she could face the rising sun in the east. Dedet was now prepared for the final ritual that would need to be performed on the body itself: the "opening of the mouth."

## The "Opening of the Mouth" Ritual

Performed at the entrance to the small mud-brick superstructure that represented the cult chapel for this tomb, the "opening of the mouth" ritual was one of the most fundamental funerary procedures. Until it was completed, the deceased had no hope of passing through death to become reborn in the afterlife. Perhaps because of its critical importance, this ritual is one of the few for which we have details, although the complete text is known only from New Kingdom sources and later.[47] This is the only ritual that is presented as a series of discrete actions depicted in the form of vignettes, and accompanied by brief descriptions – much like stage directions and recitations.[48] This funerary rite had a long history, and it is mentioned as early as the Fourth Dynasty, in the tomb of Meten, and then reappears in the Pyramid Texts.[49] Middle Kingdom references to the ritual are rare and brief, as are its appearances in the Coffin Texts and in the later Book of the Dead. The ritual does not seem to have been limited to pharaohs and royalty, and scenes of the ritual make their appearance on tombs, coffins, and stelae of individuals from all strata of society.[50]

The entire elaborate ceremony seems to have been comprised of 75 discrete episodes that focus on the statue of the deceased, opening the mouth, purification, burial, slaughter, nourishment, and temple rites.[51] The depictions show sacred activities such as purification, censing, anointing, clothing, feeding, and using special tools to touch various body parts of an avatar of the deceased, whether that be a statue, anthropoid coffin, a representation of the deceased dressed in festival attire, or even a royal cartouche.[52] By the New Kingdom it did not seem to matter which model represented the deceased, for the purpose of the ritual was not to revivify the object itself with life, but to reawaken the senses, mobility, and animation of the actual dead individual. As is the case with the Pyramid Texts, Coffin Texts, and Book of the Dead, not every episode appears in every tomb, and indeed no location includes all the possible episodes. However, two of the activities are always represented: the purification and the actual opening of the mouth. These were probably the most crucial parts of the ceremony, and a depiction of just these episodes would have served as an abbreviation of the entire ritual.[53]

While in the Old Kingdom the ritual was performed on royal statues and took place in the sculptor's workshop, many of the New Kingdom scenes show the opening of the mouth itself taking place in front of the tomb, at the cult chapel. It is difficult to be certain how the ceremony was enacted in the Middle Kingdom for a person of the middle class, but we can expect that the coffin of Dedet, or perhaps a small statue or figurine, would be propped up before the tomb or in the cult chapel. Small wooden statues have been found in the cemetery of Haraga, including that of a standing woman with her hair styled in a "Hathor" style or wig – a tripartite, shoulder-length flip style typical of the Middle Kingdom – with her name carved on the base.[54] Dedet may have been provided with just such a simple yet effective statue.

The *sem* priest who was responsible for many of the procedures would have been her eldest son, Senbubu, dressed in the traditional leopard skin to play the role of Horus reanimating his mother, the Osiris Dedet. He would purify her a final time with oils and incense, and touch her mouth and eyes with various implements, including an adze (a sculptor's tool) made of meteoric iron; a *pesesh-kaf*, which looks like a forked blade made of obsidian, black stone, or metal and is thought to have originated from a tool used to cut the umbilical cord of a newborn; a serpent blade or wand made of red stone such as carnelian; and the haunch or leg of a calf. Our knowledge of these comes not only from textual and representational sources, but also from examples that have survived usually in the form of amulets, models, or even entire kits that were placed in Old and New Kingdom tombs. Some of the kits included small vessels meant for pouring out water and milk for the deceased.[55] The ritual is thus very much focused on an almost literal rebirth of the deceased, whereby the umbilical cord is cut, the senses are open for the first time to allow the individual to interact with a new environment, and the first sustenance is in the form of milk.

## Offerings

Having had her senses awakened, and having symbolically undergone a successful rebirth, Dedet was now ready to share a final meal with the living by the tomb. The eldest son was again responsible for organizing the provisions, which would be brought by relatives. We cannot be sure what was consumed, but it was likely the same foods that appear on the offering formula and that in the Predynastic Period and Old Kingdom had been actually left in the tomb. These included meat, cakes, fine bread, and beer – foods that were not necessarily the staples of everyday life for a woman such as Dedet (meat was certainly rare), but that were reserved for special occasions and were fit for sustaining one who herself had become divine. How these provisions were acquired is unclear. The family members, perhaps her sisters if any still lived, or her daughter Hedjerit, would have been responsible for baking the bread and cakes. In this case, the family may have had to obtain special molds required for the creation of ceremonial white bread, or perhaps this was acquired from the local temple, along with portions of meat.

Another possibility is that the bread that was shared at the funeral was the same bread that was used in daily life, and the special bread was offered symbolically through the offering formula. Unfortunately, all our surviving examples of actual bread come from elite tomb contexts (mostly from the New Kingdom), and without comparative evidence from settlements, we will never know if the same bread was used for the living as for the dead.[56] While elite funerals show male and female servants bringing the funeral goods, Dedet would have relied on her family. The items would have been gathered at the home, and distributed for carriage by the family members to the tomb.

Broken pottery found at the cult chapels of other non-elite cemeteries, such as that of Dra Abu el-Naga, suggests that the meal might have been physically repeated at later times, or perhaps the pottery remains were left there after the funeral. In addition, it appears that a single cult chapel could be used by the families of a number of individuals, as bodies far outnumber the chapels. The offering cult would be renewed by surviving relatives (or if one were wealthy enough one could pay priests to continue to provide this service) at festivals of Thoth and Sokar[57] as well as the *wag* festival. The latter seems to have been a festival of the dead that was held according to a lunar cycle,[58] and was located both in the official precinct of the temple as well as in lower-order cemeteries. One stela from the cemetery of Haraga includes in its offering formula a list of offerings to be given "every day forever, at the monthly feast and the half-monthly feast, at the *wag*-feast, at the feasts of Thoth, at every feast during eternity."[59] Textual evidence shows that bread and beer were the staples at these maintenance rites. In particular, the contracts that have survived from the Twelfth Dynasty made by the nomarch of Asyut, Djefai-Hapy, show us the complex redistributive system that could be arranged in order to insure the maintenance of perpetual offerings on the correct dates.[60] The majority of Egyptians, however, would rely on the beneficence and goodwill of their relatives to maintain their needs.

In any event, provisions would also be magically supplied to the *ka* of the deceased[61] for eternity, by means of immortalizing the words of the offering formula in stone. The initial recitation of the formula served to activate the offerings, and thereafter they would always be available to the deceased. Just to be sure, those with the means would also erect a stela with the formula in the accessible part of the tomb – in the cult chapel. In this way, every time a passerby recited the text, it would be magically reactivated. Although the remains of only nine stelae, which varied in quality, were found in the area of Haraga, it may be no coincidence that all of them were found in a single cemetery. This area, on higher ground, was probably reserved for those with more means.

In the Middle Kingdom, although the details ranged greatly, as did the skill of the sculptors and artists who created them, tomb stelae were generally relatively uniform. Some mimicked the shape of the false door that could be found in tombs,[62] but most were slabs of stone with a rounded top and straight sides and bottom. They could be either installed in the wall of the cult chapel, or erected as free-standing. The arrangement of their content reflected the cosmos in miniature – the top represented the arc of the sky and often contained divine symbols, while the lower section contained the text and at least one image of the deceased. While some stelae were crude, and contained little more than a sketch of the owner, the name, and perhaps the basic offering formula, others included the three main texts. The offering formula, which is also known to us by its opening lines, *hetep dj nesu* "an offering that the king gives," invokes the gods, lists the offerings, and names the deceased. A typical example was found on the stela of a woman buried at Haraga.[63]

An offering which the king has given, and Osiris, Lord of the Sacred Land, and an offering that Hathor, Lady of *Tep-jhu*[64] has given:

A voice offering of bread, beer, oxen, fowl, alabaster, linen, cool water, incense, oil, offerings and provisions, everything sweet, everything good, all growing things, everything pure, all oblations,

For the *ka* of the revered one before Anubis, the lady of the estate, this Jtnihab, the true-of-voice,[65] who was born of Hadj, true-of-voice, the possessor of reverence.

An appeal to the living could also be included, offering blessings in return for the recitation of the formula by the visitor.[66]

Oh you living ones who are upon earth, every pure priest, every high priest, every *ka*-servant who may pass by this tomb in the necropolis in faring north or south, your king shall honor you, your gods shall love you, you shall transmit your offices to your children;

As you say "A thousand of bread, a thousand of beer, a thousand of oxen, a thousand of fowl . . ."

And finally, a brief autobiography highlighting the individual's career and service to the king would be included on the stelae of the elite.

If Dedet was able to have a stela of her own, it would like have been a simple one, probably less complex than this Middle Kingdom example (Fig. 9.4) belonging to the "lady of the estate" Jtnihab, whose offering formula is given above. Her limestone stela was dedicated by her eldest daughter "Jmwias," who is depicted with "her beloved son Renefsoneb" on her lap. It is unclear whether this is dedicated by the eldest daughter because Jtnihab had no son or husband to perform this task, whether her daughter was older than any sons, or whether daughters dedicating stelae to their mother was a common practice in this area. We can expect that if Dedet had a stela, hers would have been dedicated by her eldest son, Senbubu, or her husband. The tomb stela would be erected outside the tomb itself, within or by the superstructure (depending on its size).

With the animating and offering rituals complete, the coffin would have been lowered into the tomb, probably by means of ropes. Eventually, more chambers would be added for her husband and some of her surviving children, but for the moment, we can imagine that her shaft contained a single chamber that awaited her coffin. It has recently been questioned whether family and any other members of the funeral procession stayed while the coffin was being lowered, or whether the burial occurred after the rituals were complete and the relatives had gone. It is now evident that many of the tombs were immediately plundered, and this certainly would have been easier before the tomb had been sealed, but after any witnesses had left.[67] If this is the case, then we must assume that the burial goods would have been left with the necropolis workers to place in the chamber with the coffin. And in the Middle Kingdom, even for the poorest individuals, at least some items were left with the deceased.

**Figure 9.4** Drawing of stela of Jtnihab from Haraga tomb 124 (Engelbach 1923) (courtesy of JJ Shirley).

## Burial Goods

There is no evidence of who made the decision of what was to be left in the tomb, but it is likely that an adult such as Dedet would have set aside or indicated some of the items that should be buried with her, and the rest of the choices would have been left to the family. Evidence from Middle Kingdom cemeteries show that there was a change in burial customs late in Dynasty 12, sometime during the reign of Senusret III, particularly in tombs of the elite.[68]

As an example of the contents of an elite Twelfth Dynasty tomb, the body of an overseer of troops by the name of Sep was wrapped in linen with a mummy mask placed over it, then laid in an anthropoid coffin, which was set within a rectangular one. The surviving grave goods surrounding the coffin included a canopic chest, three jars, two big clay plates, a painted wooden table with three cartonnage vessels, a brightly colored cartonnage offering table, three models of religious boats, and a model granary. Judging from the remains from Haraga and Riqqa, Dedet's family would have provided objects from 11 major categories.[69] These included furniture designed for burial use, such as coffins and canopic chests; furniture created for the cult chapel, such as offering tables,[70] stelae, and statuary; ceramic vessels of various shapes and sizes; non-ceramic vessels; jewelry, including amulets; animal and human figurines; domestic items, such as household furniture and tools; specialized tools, such as adzes, chisels, and mallets; materials that were inscribed, such as papyrus, ostraka, and seals; cosmetic items, such as kohl pots, kohl sticks, and a mirror; and miscellaneous items, such as games.

Clay models of homes and of offering tables were also prevalent in poorer tombs of this time.[71] Offering trays were found by Petrie still in Lahun, providing us with examples of the type that might have been buried in the tomb of an Egyptian like Dedet. The small clay model (Fig. 9.5) was shaped as a courtyard with miniature representations of the most important provisions for the deceased: the head of an ox, a haunch, loaves of bread, cakes, lettuce, and a *hes* or libation vase.

Another tray found by Petrie includes models of a bird, both flat and cone-shaped bread, and what he interpreted as radishes.[72] The trays were shaped with a spout or funnel at the bottom to drain the water that would become magically charged as it was poured down over the top to run over each of the items, thus activating them as well. Because these models contained all the offerings necessary for the afterlife, as well as a surface on which to perform the rituals, for those families who only had a tomb shaft and chamber, placing the model at the entrance could recreate the entire requisite environment.[73]

Some tombs in other Middle Kingdom cemeteries also yielded small numbers of mummiform human figurines which were either left uninscribed, or had on them the owner's name or a short spell. These probably represented the deceased, and were precursors to the later *shabti* figurines that would act as workers in place

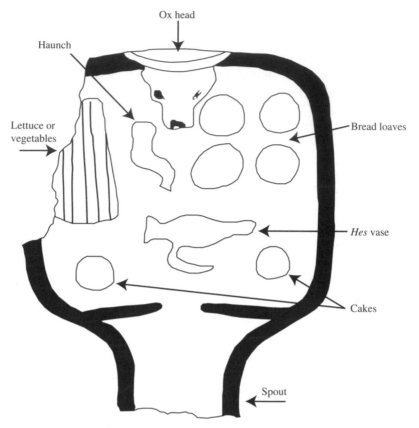

Ox head

Haunch

Lettuce or vegetables

Bread loaves

*Hes* vase

Cakes

Spout

**Figure 9.5** Drawing of offering tray after Petrie et al. 1890, 25, pl. XIII 102; now EGY274 (h. 2.6.0 cm × l. 30.8 cm × w. 24.8 cm) (courtesy of JJ Shirley).

of the deceased. The rarity of these figurines and the fact that only one or at best two might be found in a tomb suggest that just having one was an indicator of high status.[74]

After the reign of Senusret III, wooden models ceased to be included, and indeed few if any objects were included that had been specifically designed for funerary use. Instead there was a shift toward providing a wide variety of items of everyday use. Ironically, these were the types of items that were found in poorer graves from the First Intermediate Period and Middle Kingdom, though in lesser numbers: jewelry, cosmetic items, as well as vessels like this stone offering stand (Fig. 9.6). The new trend was for the inclusion of artifacts with a potent religious and magical function. These included the figures of naked humans (both women and men; Fig. 9.7) and of animals such as dogs, cats, hedgehogs, lions, cows, frogs, apes, and hippopotami. Because these are also found in settlement

**Figure 9.6** Stone offering stand UC6376 from Late Middle Kingdom Haraga tomb 112 (h. 2.3.0 cm × d. 9.1 cm) (courtesy of the Petrie Museum of Egyptian Archaeology).

**Figure 9.7** Figure of man UC6359 from Late Middle Kingdom Haraga tomb 112 (h. 3.7 cm) (courtesy of the Petrie Museum of Egyptian Archaeology).

and temple contexts, it is likely that their function was not specifically funerary, but that they were used for religious rituals in life.

Often made of faience, hippo figures in particular have become recognized as icons of Late Middle Kingdom burials.[75] Hippopotamus birth tusks were also included in the burials, perhaps again emphasizing that death was but a stage leading to rebirth in the afterlife, a process that was as fraught with danger for those in the beyond as it was for those on earth. At the cemetery of Haraga during the Thirteenth Dynasty, the appearance of semi-precious materials in graves decreased dramatically, while the use of faience increased.[76] This change was mirrored in other contemporary necropolises such as those of Riqqa and Abydos, leading scholars to suggest that this new trend represents a decrease either in access to mineral sources or in religious burial beliefs.[77] Whether originally politically motivated or due to changes in access to resources, the roughly concurrent changes in coffin types, body position,[78] and type and material of burial goods certainly point to alterations in burial customs that either reflected or necessitated a shift in religious beliefs regarding those customs.

In terms of Dedet's burial, we might expect that as she was not a member of the elite, her burial would not have included items made of precious substance anyway. Surprisingly, the evidence from Haraga shows that, as noted above, materials that usually represent material wealth, such as gold, copper, amethyst, and carnelian, were found in all different sizes of graves, and different types – even in the poorest shallow graves that were found in the wadis. Neither did the fact that she was a woman make any difference. As mentioned above, nine stelae were found in Haraga, but with one exception their original findspots are not known, therefore they cannot be assigned to individual tombs and studied within their archaeological context and that of other associated finds. The one exception, however, was found within the grave of a *nebet per*, a "lady of the estate," that is a woman of some means and power. Richards, who has been reanalyzing Middle Kingdom mortuary data, notes that "not unexpectedly, this grave also contained one of the more diverse and costly assemblages in Cemetery A, including silver jewelry, stone vessels, scarab amulets, cosmetic implements, and a large number of ceramic vessels."[79] Just as the cemeteries did not show a difference based on gender in terms of number of burials or location, neither do they show any difference in terms of goods. It seems that in death and in the afterlife, women and men had equal opportunities.[80] Their burials could be equally wealthy, or equally poor.

But for the living, burial practices afforded the opportunity not only for family members to grieve for their loved ones and to insure a safe transition to the afterlife, but also offered a way for the family to express their wealth and social status. For example, we might expect that a family with a high socio-economic status would have a large tomb, high on the hillside, with a diverse range of burial goods made of costly materials. Recent research at middle-class cemeteries surprisingly shows "there was no secure correlation among tomb size, wealth, and diversity . . . These data suggest, therefore, that grave size, wealth, and diversity were three different ways in which Middle Kingdom Egyptians could express wealth or social status in the mortuary arena."[81] Thus, a large tomb might have a limited range of burial goods, while some of the poor, shallow graves had articles of surprisingly costly material.

In addition, there seem to have been at least five levels of different burial practices, reflecting that although there was a strict demarcation between those buried in the wadis and those buried in the higher cemeteries, there were gradations within each of these ranges as well.[82] In this way, archaeological evidence from cemeteries can shed light on the life of the living that is hidden behind much of the textual rhetoric and ideology. Discussions of Egyptian society often present us with a model based on a pyramid with the pharaoh and royalty at the top, followed by the elite and officials, craftsmen, and then at the bottom a mass of poor as farmers and peasants. The mortuary data from the Middle Kingdom shows that the reality was much more complex – the levels were traversable to some extent, and wealth and social status were not necessarily synonymous or represented in the same way.

Dedet's family would have presented her socio-economic standing in as positive a light as possible. As a woman of perhaps the middle to upper tier of the middle class, her wrapped body would have been placed in a plain, uninscribed wooden coffin and buried in a small shaft tomb along with perhaps her favorite copper mirror with the head of Hathor; a small serpentine stone vessel; an alabaster kohl pot and bone applicator; two necklaces, one with beads of turquoise, carnelian, and faience, one with shells, amulets of Bes, and the eye of Horus; a small faience dog; a wooden headrest; and possibly even the same hippopotamus birth tusk that aided in the birth of her last son, but ultimately failed to insure her own survival.

Perhaps her son arranged for her to have a rough limestone stela inscribed with the offering formula, her name, and her image erected in front of the small mud-brick superstructure that served as a cult chapel in miniature. This chapel would have served as the site for memorial services and reactivation of the offering cult for all of the family members who would eventually be buried in this tomb. It may be that it would also have served for another nearby tomb that would house for eternity the bodies of another family, or other relatives. Finally, the chapel would act as a liminal zone between the land of the living and that of the dead. Family members would continue to make offerings for the dead not only as a filial duty, but also out of concern that if they did not, the deceased might return as an angry *akh*, one of the dead that was responsible for various ailments, headaches, and nightmares. Indeed, this is stated in one letter to the dead inscribed on the inside of a bowl: "It is for the protection of one who is on earth that funerary offerings are made."[83]

## Death as Friend and Foe

For an Egyptian such as Hedjerit, death and the dead were an integral part of everyday life. Once again, ideology and presentation reveal one aspect of death, but individual attitudes may vary. The living mourned the loss of a loved one, yet looked forward to rejoining them in the afterlife. For one who was sick, death could be both frightening and concurrently looked upon with relief as an opportunity to share in divinity. A unique text from the Middle Kingdom expresses both of these conceptions. Generally known by Egyptologists as *The Dialogue of a Man and his Soul*, this is one of the most eloquent pieces of Egyptian lyric literature, and manifests complex philosophical ponderings on the nature of death and the afterlife. The text is long and so only a few excerpts will be given here.[84] The beginning is unfortunately lost, and so it begins immediately with the speaker's response to his soul. Judging from this response, his soul has apparently been trying to convince the man that death is not something to be looked forward to at all, and the soul is threatening to abandon the speaker. The man responds by emphasizing the transitory nature of life on earth and calls upon the gods to support him and to ease his suffering: "He should stay close to me on the Day of Pain! . . . Life is a transitory time: the trees fall. . . . It would be a sweet relief, if the gods drove off the heaviness of my body!"

The *ba* responds to the man by reminding him that he is human and should appreciate life. The man responds by reminding his soul that it needs him just as much as he needs it, and that they will depend on each other after death. The soul responds by advising the living man that even the grandest funeral monuments of stone eventually perish and are forgotten:

> If you call burial to mind, it is heartbreak;
> it is bringing the gift of tears, causing a man misery;
> it is taking a man away from his house,
> and throwing him on the high ground.
> You will not come up again to see the sunlight!
> They who built in granite,
> who constructed pavilions in fair pyramids, as fair works,
> so that the builders should become Gods –
> their altar stones have vanished . . .
> Follow the happy day! Forget care!

The soul then provides two parables to illustrate his point, but the man responds with a series of laments. The first emphasizes how, quite literally, at this point life stinks:

> Look my name reeks,
> look, more than the smell of bird-droppings
> on summer days when the sky is hot. . . .

After eight of these stanzas, the speaker proceeds to lament his utter loneliness:

> Who can I talk to today?
> I am weighed down
> with misery for want of an intimate friend.
> Who can I talk to today?
> For wrong roams the earth;
> there is no end to it.

After 16 such stanzas, the increasingly expressive man makes clear his longing to reach the afterlife, contrasting the reek of life with the fragrant scent of the afterlife:

# Death

> Death is to me today
>  like a sick man's recovery,
>  like going out after confinement.
> Death is to me today
>  like the smell of myrrh,
>  like sitting under a sail on a windy day.
> Death is to me today
>  like the smell of flowers,
>  like sitting on the shore of Drunkenness . . .

He finishes his persuasive speech with an emphasis on the ultimate triumph of passing through death successfully – that of being divine himself and of being everlastingly in the presence of God:

> But There a man is a living god,
>  punishing the wrongdoer's action.
> But There a man stands in the barque,
>  distributing choice offerings from it to the temples.
> But There a man is a sage
>  who cannot, when he speaks, be stopped
>  from appealing to the Sungod.

In the end, the man convinces his *ba*, who agrees that there must be a compromise between loving life and looking forward to the afterlife:

> Yet love me here, having put aside the West,
> and also still desire to reach the West, your body making landfall!
> I shall alight when you are weary;
> so shall we make harbour together.

The soul promises to indeed remain with the man when he reaches the afterlife, which is euphemistically referred to as the west, making landfall, and a safe harbor. Finally, the text ends with a colophon used by scribes to authenticate that they have correctly and precisely copied a text: "So it ends, from start to finish, as found in writing."

Whether or not Hedjerit or her mother, or even her literate brother, were familiar with the text cannot be known. Only a single copy has survived, and this may be simply due to random chance, or it may reflect its unpopularity. But whether or not the text itself was widely known, the feeling behind it is reflected in numerous other textual sources, from mourners' laments that bewail the loss of the deceased from the earth, to songs sung by harpers, some of which extol the afterlife while others bemoan the brevity of life on earth. Clearly, this ambivalence toward death was as much a part of the ancient world as it is of today's.

Indeed, it is ironic that to so many people today, the beliefs associated with death and the funerary rites of the Ancient Egyptians should appear alien and strange. For all humans, death is inevitable, feared at times, looked forward to at others, yet always inescapable. To deal with this final stage of life, all cultures develop some sort of rituals.[85] In most, although the details differ, many of the same basic practices are performed. Funeral processions are common, as are displays of grief. The corpse usually undergoes some sort of purification, whether it be at the hands of a priest, or of an embalmer, or of members of the household washing it. The deceased is usually clothed in a specific manner, whether with favorite garments, or in specifically marked funeral attire. The body is placed in a specific container in a particular position, and taken to its final resting place, where it is to be eventually buried or burned. Funeral feasts are common, and often they are shared with the dead. This can happen once, or it can happen for a set number of days, or even as an annual event. Communication between the living and the dead may continue long after the actual funeral, either in private or as part of the larger community. The Mexican *Día de los Muertos* "Day of the Dead" is a happy cultural event that lasts for three days from October 31 to November 2, while in another culture an individual may prefer to sit quietly at the grave or memorial to the deceased on a special day.

Modern parallels can even be found for the practice of writing letters to the dead. To this day letters are left at the Vietnam War Memorial as well as at spontaneous shrines set up as memorials to commemorate victims of sudden or violent death. While the content may to a large extent differ from those of the Ancient Egyptians in that the modern ones do not usually ask for favors from the deceased, the letters all share the intense desire on the part of the survivor to maintain an intimate reciprocal connection with their loved one.

## Aftermath

For in the end, life does go on. For Hedjerit and her family there remained the problem of raising a now motherless child. Perhaps the seeming prevalence of wet nurses in Ancient Egypt was due in part to the high mortality rate for mothers. From what we know of the Egyptians, they would not abandon the infant. All the evidence, both archaeological and textual, indicates that he would have continued to be cared for as a precious member of the family and the community. One account from the New Kingdom includes the fees that a man pays for a wet nurse, and it ends with the statement by the father that "As Amun endures, as the Ruler, l.p.h. endures, my three daughters will not be taken from me, and I will not be taken from them." Whether this man lost his wife through divorce or death is uncertain, but the man clearly intends to care for his daughters himself, even though at least one has not yet been weaned.[86]

In the case of a man with older daughters, the primary care of a neonate may have been the responsibility of the eldest one, in this case Hedjerit, or it may have been shared among aunts, in-laws, and even servants. Hedjerit's father, Sasopedu, while mourning the loss of his "great wife" Dedet, would probably have eventually remarried. There is no evidence as to whether this could happen immediately, or whether decorum required a set period of celibacy between marriages. That remarriage was fairly common is clear from tomb inscriptions where an individual is named along with more than one spouse. In the case of men in particular, while this could be interpreted as reflecting polygamy, there is no substantiating evidence for this. Instead, it is highly likely that rather than being concurrent, the wives were consecutive. This is an expected repercussion of having a high maternal mortality rate. It also helps to explain the seemingly large number of children that are enumerated on some tombs. After Sasopedu remarried, his new wife may have borne more children to him, and if she were older, she may even have brought some of her own into the household.

As for Hedjerit herself, just a few years after the death of her mother, she too would reach a new stage in her life. She might now have acquired some of her own wealth, for women, as well as men, could write wills passing on their own personal property to their children, and could likewise choose to disinherit any that had displeased them.

While no comparable example has yet surfaced from the Middle Kingdom, a New Kingdom will left by a woman by the name of Naunakht presents us with one detailed specimen. At a very young age Naunakht married Qenherkhopshef, a well-known and rather older scribe in the village of Deir el-Medina who himself had been adopted by a childless couple there. When Qenherkhopshef died childless himself, Naunakht, having inherited his property, estate, land, and library, as well as retaining whatever she came into the marriage with, was now a widow of some means. She remarried and the couple had eight children.[87] In her will, she selectively decided how to distribute this inheritance. In this case she bequeathed her goods to some children, but some had obviously seriously displeased her, and these she completely disinherited. This would have had a significant impact on the children, for the inheritance would have included not only the goods and land she brought into the marriage, but also the one-third of the community property from her current marriage to which she had a claim. Naunakht made her will when she was old and knew that death was approaching. Knowing that bearing a child was always dangerous, Dedet may have made a similar will, or she may not have felt the need to bequeath her goods in any particular fashion – we will never know. In either case, with the death of her mother Hedjerit would have begun to secure some of her own possessions. These, along with the household and working skills she had acquired while still a child by our standards, would now help her as she approached adulthood.

## Notes

1 This phrase probably refers to tying the sidelock into a pony tail or braid, and indicates that the individual has not yet reached adulthood.
2 As explained below, the deceased was respectfully referred to as "revered" and as "true-of-voice," in much the way we refer to the dead as "the late X."

3 According to P. Ebers 838, if on the day of birth the child cries "*ny*," then it will survive (Westendorf 1999 vol. 2, 688).

4 According to one myth, when Ra, the sun god, grew weary of mankind plotting against him, he summoned his daughter Hathor, in her form of Sekhmet, the Powerful One, to destroy all humans. She ravaged mankind in a rage until she fell asleep. The sun god relented, but realized he would have trouble leashing the savage bloodthirst of the goddess. He therefore ordered that a depression in the desert be flooded with red beer that still had chunks of mash in it to resemble blood and gore. When Sekhmet awoke, she quenched her thirst in what she thought was a pool of blood, but the alcoholic beverage quickly pacified her, causing her to sleep peacefully and forget her rage. Thus mankind was spared.

5 Tait is the goddess of weaving, and the knotted fabric was therefore in her domain. For knotting in magic see Wendrich 2006, 243–69.

6 This is based on a spell from the New Kingdom in P. British Museum 100059 [41] 13, 14. See the translation in Borghouts 1978, 24.

7 This was one of the euphemisms for death in Ancient Egypt, which expresses the concept of reaching the shore of the west on a ferry.

8 Nerlich et al. 2002; Nerlich and Zink 2001.

9 For the latter see for example Assman 2005, 410–17. Yet even Assmann devotes only eight pages to the problem (and then his focus shifts to Christianity).

10 This name is also translated more accurately as "Sanehat," which means "son of the sycamore."

11 Translation from Parkinson 1998, 36.

12 Ikram and Dodson 1998, 196–7. In later times, the full outstretched body of the sky goddess was painted on the inside of the lid.

13 It has been suggested that these dancers performed as cemetery guards, or gave permission for entry, or that they were beings from the afterlife who would bring the deceased to the beyond, or that they were the actual spirits of kings coming into this world, or that they supervise some of the critical funerary rituals, or that they represented the ferryman helping the deceased to safely reach the final mooring (an Ancient Egyptian euphemism for crossing through death and entering the afterlife). Most of the discussions can be found summarized in Reeder 1995.

14 Royal cemeteries of the Twelfth and Thirteenth Dynasties usually focused on the pyramid complex of the pharaoh, with his family members buried closest in smaller pyramids, then the highest-ranking officials.

15 The moment when Osiris is killed is never depicted in myth, nor is the moment of death of any Egyptian depicted or described.

16 Fischer 2000, 8.

17 Robins 1993, 132–3.

18 R. Friedman 1998.

19 Taylor 2001, 57.

20 Hall 1985.

21 Grajetzki 2003, 51, notes that there is less evidence for the poorer levels of society in the Middle Kingdom than in the preceding time periods.

22 Richards 2005, 81–4.

23 Depictions of the funeral carts show them drawn by oxen, but these depictions reflect the practices of the elite. It is possible that the more readily available donkeys were used for the poorer classes.

24  Sweeney 2001.
25  Engelbach 1923.
26  Nearly all of the Ancient Egyptian tombs were plundered at some point in the millennia since their initial use.
27  A wadi is a valley or ancient river course that has long dried.
28  For this and the following see Richards 2005, 90–7.
29  The bibliography on Ancient Egyptian autobiographies is extensive. For an overview see Gnirs 1996.
30  Richards 2005, 96.
31  Richards 2005, 118.
32  Richards's research (2005) focused on Riqqa to the north of the Fayum, and Abydos in Middle Egypt.
33  Richards 2005, 90–7.
34  Richards 2005, 124.
35  Whether the right to dig a shaft tomb in a particular location was granted by the state, local officials, or the community is unclear. See Richards 1999, 93–5.
36  Grajetzki 2003, 49–61; Bourriau 2001.
37  Grajetzki 2004, 40–6.
38  The Coffin Texts disappear for about a hundred years after the reign of Senusret III, only to reappear on the outside of coffins.
39  CT (Coffin Text) 336 is a unique text found on the cedar-wood coffin of Gua. The translation is that of Forman and Quirke 1996, 88.
40  As mentioned in chapter 7, Atum is the original creator god, who was spontaneously self-created from the fertile, primeval, watery abyss of Nun. He was the first of the Ennead – the first group of nine gods. He embodied both the male and the female generative forces and by masturbating he was able to produce air (personified by the god Shu) and moisture (personified by the goddess Tefnut). This primeval couple in turn produced the earth (Geb) and the sky (Nut). This first couple to be associated with the earthly realm gave birth to Osiris (god of the dead), Isis (his wife and a great magician), Seth (the aggressive god associated with the desert and the wild), and Nephthys (who often worked in tandem with her sister Isis).
41  Faulkner 1973 vol. 3, 86.
42  Coffin Text 75 (author's translation).
43  The titles of many spells were written in red ink (rubric), indicated here by the underline. The *ba* is the part of the soul of the individual that is mobile in the afterlife, and it is thus often depicted as a bird with the face of the deceased. The *ba* is also associated with power, and is one of the elements that differentiates humans from gods. For where a human has but one *ba*, the gods have many *baw*, and their power can be turned against a recalcitrant human.
44  The emphasis here is on Shu (and by identification the speaker, who is the deceased) being the first creator god – there was none before him, therefore nobody brought him into existence. This is another example of the fluidity of Egyptian myth and beliefs. In some myths it is Atum who is self-created, and he produces Shu. Here, Shu plays the same role as Atum.
45  This is a most powerful image of the deceased being so integrated with the creator god that he is the very breath of life that lies within the god, and is then dispersed with every breath to provide life to others.
46  This last line summarizes and reasserts the point of the entire composition.

47 The seminal work on this ritual remains Otto 1960. Substantial commentary on this work can be found in Helck 1967. More recent interpretations can be found in Fischer-Elfert 1998; Roth 1992 and 1993; Schulman 1984.

48 Bjerke 1965.

49 Otto 1960 vol. II, 6–7; Bjerke 1965, 206–7.

50 Schulman 1984.

51 Otto 1960 vol. II, 2.

52 Bjerke 1965, 203–4.

53 Bjerke 1965.

54 Engelbach 1923, 12–3, pl. XVIII.

55 See the Old Kingdom example catalog #18 in J. Allen 2005, 28.

56 Samuel 2000, 542.

57 The festivals to Thoth (the god associated with judgment) and Sokar (the god associated with the most secret region of the farworld, or *duat*) are well attested in Middle Kingdom documents and were discussed in the chapteron religion.

58 The date of the festival has been the subject of Egyptological debate. See Krauss 1998; Luft 1992b and 1994.

59 Engelbach 1923, 27.

60 Spalinger 1985.

61 This was the part of the soul that was associated with physical needs such as nourishment. One of the words in Egyptian for provisions was *kau*.

62 Elite tomb chapels often incorporated a false door – it was carved, but did not open – with an offering table before it. This door was for the use of the *ka* of the deceased, to enable him or her to come back to the chapel and retrieve any offerings left there.

63 Stela from the Middle Kingdom tomb 128 in Engelbach 1923, pl. XVI; LXXIII.

64 Modern-day Atfih, located near the Nile east of Lahun. The name in Ancient Egyptian means "head of the cows," and is therefore associated with Hathor.

65 The element of judgment was already present in the Middle Kingdom, and the deceased's name is followed by the epithet *maa-kheru* "true-of-voice," which indicates that the deceased has successfully passed through death and is now justified and reborn.

66 Reconstructed from a stela fragment from Haraga in Engelbach 1923, pl. LXXII, 1.

67 Willems 2001, vii–viii.

68 For this and the following summary see Grajetzki 2003, 49–61.

69 Richards 2005, 85.

70 Offering tables were often made of stone, and were carved with representations of food for the deceased. Ones of clay have also been found.

71 Grajetzki 2003, 52–3.

72 Petrie et al. 1891, 9, pl. IV 20, 23.

73 Taylor 2001, 106–7.

74 Taylor 2001, 117.

75 See for example the famous "William" of the Metropolitan Museum of New York.

76 Richards 2005, 84.

77 Richards 2005, 106.

78 Bourriau 2001.

79 Richards 2005, 94.

80  This equality is also reflected in the Coffin Texts, which were applicable to women as well as men.
81  Richards 2005, 114.
82  Richards 2005, 123.
83  Gardiner and Sethe 1928, 5, pls. IV, IVa.
84  The translation is excerpted from Parkinson 1998, 151–65.
85  Parker Pearson 2001.
86  A. McDowell 1999, 36.
87  Her oldest son was named after her first husband Qenherkhopshef, perhaps indicating the fondness she had had for her late spouse.

# 10

# Love

*It happened one day as I lay down at home, pretending to be ill, that he stopped at my door. His voice was like pomegranate wine when he said to me "My sister,' your breasts are mandrakes, your hair is a lure, your lips the bud of a lotus." As he passed by on the road, my heart leapt to burst forth like a red fish in a pond, and I wished to become the mistress of his house. Love of him was my sole concern and I waited for the approach of the day when my heart would meet his heart.*

## Transitions

The passage from the state of childhood to that of being an adult is ceremonially marked in many cultures.[2] Some rituals focus on the coming out of a single individual while others involve a group of either boys or girls – more rarely both sexes are initiated together. Rather than being based on any set chronological age, the event is often based on the obvious physical manifestations of changes occurring within the body. For girls this includes the development of breasts, an increase in hair growth on the body, and most obviously, the onset of menstruation. The transformation in boys is usually marked by a change in voice, more body and facial hair, increased growth, and genital changes.

In Egyptian art, the changes were represented by the portrayal of specific clothing, hairstyles, and activities. Individuals who had reached adulthood were no longer shown naked, but wearing clothing befitting their rank, status, and employment. Most importantly, the sidelock, that distinctive emblem of childhood for both boys and girls, was replaced by unbound hair or a wig. In texts as well, the sidelock was used as a marker of youth. Officials proudly proclaimed the sensitive tasks and supervisory roles that the king had assigned to them while they still wore a sidelock, while they were still tying the fillet around their braid.

If there was any puberty ritual practiced in Lahun, it probably featured removing the sidelock of youth. Whether the hair was cut off by a barber, priest, official, relative, or by oneself, and whether it was part of a public performance or a private rite, in the end the result would be the same. Appearing in public without the sidelock was a conspicuous announcement of having attained a new stage of life.

Boys in many cultures have been initiated into adulthood by the rite of circumcision. There is some evidence that Ancient Egyptian boys were circumcised when they reached puberty, but it is ambiguous at best. The forensic evidence relies on enough flesh remaining on the corpse in order to make a definitive determination either way. Some royal mummies were circumcised, but re-examination of others shows that this was by no means a universal practice. Representational evidence depicts some men as circumcised, others as not, suggesting that it was by no means a universal or even common practice among any of the classes or ranks. Arguments have been made that some scenes that have been interpreted as depicting an operation on the penis were not meant to illustrate circumcision, but rather ritual cleaning.[3] The textual evidence is equally unclear, and at best indicates that some boys were circumcised upon reaching adolescence up until the New Kingdom, at which point even the textual references become rare.[4]

Although mutilation of girls' genitals when they reach puberty is commonly practiced in Middle Eastern and African countries today (including Egypt), there is no evidence for any of these practices in pharaonic Egypt. While classical authors have commented on female circumcision as an Egyptian custom, Dominic Montserrat, in his study on sex and society in Greco-Roman Egypt, notes that this may be a case of the authors wishing to emphasize the alien nature of Ancient Egypt.[5] Bearing in mind that the absence of evidence cannot absolutely provide evidence of absence, when evidence can reasonably be expected but is not existent, then the logical inference is that this meaningful zero should be taken as evidence for the absence of an effect. In the case of female genital mutilation, the mortuary remains fail to provide evidence, though as is the case with male circumcision, recognition of the practice partly relies on the survival of enough flesh on the corpse. Because the effects of female genital mutilation have numerous and severe medical consequences, especially in terms of fertility and chances for successful childbirth, it might be expected that these effects would have been mentioned in the lengthy Gynecological Papyrus that was found in Lahun or in other medical texts. But in this area, the papyri remain notably silent, even though, as Montserrat points out,

> these deal with such an extensive range of problems associated with women's reproductive organs that remedies for botched circumcisions, clitoridectomies or infibulations would surely have been included if such customs had been prevalent. The medical employment of vaginal contraceptive pessaries, and the insertion of fairly large objects such as onions and heads of garlic for cures and birth prognoses, would

be difficult if the women were badly scarred and vulvally contracted from genital operations. Contraceptive pessaries, whether in the form of some kind of solid tablet or a cervical plug made of fabric, were also probably fairly large devices filling the rear projection of the vagina and the area around the opening of the uterus.[6]

Thankfully, it is highly improbable that a girl such as Hedjerit would have had to undergo any such painful procedures at the onset of puberty.

For a girl, the onset of menstruation is one of the most obvious indicators that a new stage of life has been reached and that she can now conceive. In Ancient Egypt, if there were any rituals associated specifically with the onset of a girl's first cycle, marking her initiation into womanhood, they were unrecorded. This may be because they were considered secret, or because the subject in general was simply not considered important enough to be recorded by the male scribes. On the other hand neither was menstruation considered taboo. As previously mentioned, laundrymen cleaned women's garments, including the linen cloths that were used as feminine towels.

The Egyptian word *hesmen* is usually translated as menstruation, and appears in a number of administrative texts from the New Kingdom settlement of Deir el-Medina. The texts include records of the absences of workmen for reasons connected with the *hesmen* of a daughter or spouse, a property transfer deed, a record of festival provision, and one recording a gift being brought. Scholars differ in their opinions as to whether *hesmen* refers only to menstruation, or whether it also refers to any vaginal discharge or bleeding. Thus, depending on the interpretation, arguments have been set forth for the existence of a ceremony welcoming a girl's first cycle, monthly group rites based on the theory of menstrual synchrony,[7] postnatal purification, or even induced or involuntary miscarriage.[8] Some of the documents suggest that *hesmen* was a happy event, others indicate it was an inimical occurrence. Whatever it was, it is noteworthy that it was considered a legitimate reason for a man to be absent from work and to presumably provide support to the woman in his life affected by this experience.

Some religions have strict regulations and taboos regarding menstruating women, but these were not a feature of Ancient Egyptian religion. Nevertheless, artifacts that have survived in domestic or cult contexts and that seem to reflect the concerns of women are sometimes hastily connected with menstruation, and explained by unwarranted, curious theories. The most extreme example may be the interpretation of one assemblage consisting of two model clay beds, parts of two female figurines, and a stela depicting a woman wearing a cone on her head leading a young girl before the hippopotamus goddess Taweret. The artifacts were all found in a small room under the stairs in one house in Amarna.[9] On the basis of this single group and its findspot it has been postulated that women were segregated during their menstruation, further prompting one scholar to present a dark and dubious reconstruction of Egyptian women leading lives that consisted of "frequent childbirth and death, punctuated by squatting in the cupboard under the stairs during menstruation."[10] With no corroborating evidence, this is an unlikely scenario. Indeed, these kinds of areas are typically inviting to children – perhaps the assemblage represents a child's "secret stash." In an Egyptian town like Lahun, menstruation is unlikely to have been taboo or secret, neither was it likely celebrated. For a young woman like Hedjerit, it may have simply been an ordinary part of life.

## Sexuality

Whether or not the event was formally acknowledged, it is likely that soon after reaching sexual maturity a girl would be considered to be a young adult and of marriageable age. With no evidence that any sort of genital mutilation was practiced, we can imagine that women such as Hedjerit and the young men who had reached puberty began to be sexually attracted to each other. But in the areas of love, romance, and sexuality, we are again hampered by a dearth of evidence from Lahun, and indeed from the Middle Kingdom. With the exception of specific religious scenes such as the conception of Horus, or the act of creation featuring the earth god Geb and the sky goddess Nut, sexual acts themselves were not explicitly portrayed in formal art. And while erotic doodles on ostraka, papyrus, or stone illustrating couples engaged in sexual intercourse have survived, they date mostly to the New Kingdom and later. A possible exception is an inscription of a man and a woman obviously engaged in sexual intercourse on a bed that was found on the wall of a Middle Kingdom tomb at Beni Hassan.[11] Although it was copied in the nineteenth century of the common era, it has since been erased, and we cannot verify whether the sketch was contemporary with the tomb, or whether it dates to much later.

The New Kingdom (specifically the Ramesside period that followed the Amarna period) provides us with our earliest surviving examples of love poetry. The compositions are complex, and like all poems, are multivalent. Some of them make extensive use of wordplay that is unfortunately lost in translation. In one series, the beginning of each stanza includes the number of the stanza, or a homophone[12] of it, and at the end of the stanza that word or another homophone is repeated. Some poems are written as a dialogue between a man and a woman, but even these poems were likely composed by male scribes who were well versed in literary technique.[13] Nevertheless the poems capture the ideals of beauty, love, and romance that were prevalent three thousand years ago. One young woman's longing and desire to be in the physical presence of her beloved is evident in the following.

> O beauteous youth, may my desire be fulfilled
> To become the mistress of your house.
> With your hands resting upon my breasts,
> You have spread your love over me.

> I speak to my innermost heart
> With the prayer that my lord may be with me this night.
> I am like one who is in her tomb,
> For are not you alone my health and my life?
> Your touch brings the joy of my well-being,
> The joy of my heart seeking after you.[14]

The helpless yet rapturous feeling of being in love is a common theme, as seen in this passage from the point of view of the man:

> (How) intoxicating are the plants of my garden!
> [The lips] of my beloved are the bud of a lotus,
> Her breasts are mandrakes,
> And her arms are ornate [. . .]
> Behold, her forehead is a snare of willow,
> And I am a goose.
> My [hands are in] her hair as a lure,
> Held fast in the snare of willow.[15]

A mixture of romantic love and earthy sensuality is present in many of the poems, and while these were likely written by the elite literati and enjoyed in the royal courts, their themes would have been familiar to those in love at all levels of society, and during all time periods.

No love poetry remains from the Middle Kingdom, but a fragment of a tale survives which relates an encounter between a herdsman and a goddess. Only the middle of the story remains, and when we join the protagonist, he relates to his fellow herdsmen what transpired as he was in a field by a lake:

> See, all of you, I went down to a pool which is close [to] this lowland, I saw a woman there, whose physique is not that of (ordinary) humans; my hair went on end as I stared at her locks (?), for the smoothness of her skin I would never do what she had said (otherwise but) awe of her pervaded my body.[16]

We do not know what the goddess wanted him to do, but he leaves and encourages his fellow herdsman to cross the water to rest for the night. For some unknown reason, however, in the morning he goes back to the lake again

> The day broke then the next morning (?) and it was done as he said: this goddess did meet him when he went forward to the lake, and she did strip off her clothing and shake her hair loose.

Inconveniently the text breaks off again at this point, and we are left in the dark as to what happens next. The shedding of the goddess's clothes and loosening of her hair[17] suggest it was something of a sexual nature, but we cannot be sure.

However, we can be sure that sex was a part of the daily life of both Egyptian men and women. And while sexual intercourse was important for the purposes of procreation, sex was also enjoyed purely for pleasure. The act itself was referred to by the verb *nek*, while one of the more common euphemisms was "spending a happy day." There does not seem to have been any prohibition on sex outside of marriage, or against intercourse with people of the same sex.[18] One controversial love poem may have involved a man who was irresistibly attracted to a young charioteer.[19] Another text, a tale from the Middle Kingdom, features a king spending amorous nights with his general, even throwing a stone up at his lover's window for him to let down a ladder and allow him clandestine entry.[20] A Middle Kingdom fragment from Lahun relates how the god Horus himself, encouraged by his mother Isis, uses the fact that Seth is sexually attracted to him to trick his rival.[21] After Seth tells Horus "how beautiful your buttocks are, broad of legs," Horus tells his mother that Seth is trying to have sex with him. She advises him to:

> resist when he has entered it; after he tells you it again, then you should tell him, it is much too difficult for me because you are heavier than I am, my strength cannot shoulder your strength – that is what you should say to him; after he has placed his strength on you, then you should push your fingers between your buttocks . . .

and she tells him to take "that seed that comes from his phallus without letting Ra see it." The seed that Horus captures is later used to humiliate his uncle Seth, and strengthen Horus's claim to the throne of Egypt. The sexual escapades are treated humorously in these literary texts, but there is no indication that they were prohibited.

The desire for sex for reasons other than procreation is also indicated by the recipes for contraceptives that are listed among the treatments for various discharges and ailments of the vagina in the Lahun Gynecological Papyrus as well as later medical texts. One Lahun prescription for preventing pregnancy[22] involves sprinkling "crocodile dung, chopped over *hesa* and *awyt*-liquid," while another specifies "a *hin* of honey, sprinkle over her vagina, this to be done on a natron bed."[23] It would not be surprising to find that this was effective, for one can imagine that putting any type of dung near the vagina would quickly quench any amorous advances. The Ebers papyrus includes a section that is even more clear: "Beginning of the prescriptions prepared for women/wives to allow a woman to cease conceiving for one year, two years or three years: *qaa* part of acacia, carob, dates; grind with one *henu* of honey, lint is moistened with it and placed in her flesh."[24]

Although these prescriptions are found in texts, it is unlikely that the knowledge of contraceptives was limited to an elite group of literate men. Contraception and timed pregnancy are often parts of the realm of unwritten lore and common knowledge that is transmitted orally. Whether breast-feeding was used as a way to avoid pregnancy is debatable. Lactation itself is not an effective method – the World Health Organization has demonstrated that it does suppress fertility, but only for a maximum of six months, and even then only if the child is exclusively breast-fed and if other strict conditions are met. There could, however, have been cultural conventions for avoiding sex while a woman was still breast-feeding that are not apparent in the surviving documentation. The fact that in Ancient Egypt other methods for preventing pregnancy were recorded indicates that contraception was a formally sanctioned practice, and was not a transgression of any kind. As there is no indication that virginity was required for marriage, young men and women of Lahun would likely have experimented with sex and fallen in love as people do around the world.

## Marriage

For the most part our understanding of marriage in Late Middle Kingdom Egypt is based on negative evidence. There is no indication that marriages were arranged by a third party, or negotiated with other family members such as the father. No ceremonies, festivities, or celebrations are described or depicted, but from this we should not infer that they did not take place – cohabitation and partnerships are acknowledged in many ways in various cultures without leaving behind any material manifestation. The lack of records does, however, indicate that marriages or unions between adults did not need to be legitimated or acknowledged either by the state or within a religious context. The terminology is equally unclear, and the word that we translate as "wife," *hemet*, is also the word for "woman." This is the term that commonly appears in the legal contracts, accounts, and letters from Lahun.

But from the Middle Kingdom onward a second, less popular designation could be used, *hebsut*, sometimes in contexts where we would expect to find *hemet*.[25] In some cases both are used, but in a different context, so for example, *hebsut* seems to occur less frequently on monumental sources such as stelae than in letters and administrative texts. One suggestion has been that *hemet* referred to a man's first wife, while any other wives he may have had, after divorce or death of the first one, were referred to as *hebsut*.[26] Others have suggested that a *hebsut* was a woman who was cohabiting with a man but was not formally married.[27] With the little data available, perhaps the most that can be said is that during the Middle and New Kingdoms, there was a difference in the relationship, but that it had little impact on the daily lives of the women designated by those terms.[28] The texts from Lahun do not seem to use *hebsut* at all, whereas *hemet* does occur, implying that whatever differentiation may have developed between the terms later, in Middle Kingdom Lahun it had no significance.

Another problematic term is *nebet per*, "mistress of the house." As opposed to *hemet*, *nebet per* occurs mostly in formal monumental sources such as stelae (particularly from the Middle Kingdom) or on tombs. The expression has been interpreted as being a title for any female family member, a female head of household, or a formally married wife who gives birth to the main heirs of the husband's property. It is often associated with elite women, and has also been thought to refer to the wife's role as manager of the estate. Others have suggested that it was purely an honorific title. A minority suggest that the *nebet per* need not necessarily be married.[29] In the few instances where it appears in the Lahun texts, it is used as a filiation in a census lists of employees, or in letters.[30] The single known word for husband, *hi*, on the other hand, occurs rarely in any texts, mostly because so much of our data derives from tombs that were owned by men, who did not therefore refer to themselves as "husband."[31]

The lack of data and the inconsistency of terminology also leave open the possibility that a wide range of levels of relationship could exist between a couple in the Late Middle Kingdom. In a recent study based on the more plentiful data from the New Kingdom workmen's village of Deir el-Medina, Jaana Toivari-Viitala pointed out that the perception that there are only two choices for relationships – married and unmarried – is not valid even in modern western culture.[32] Couples in the modern world, whether hetero- or homosexual, describe themselves as casually dating, being in exclusive relationships, living together, partnered but not cohabiting, or married by common law, or by a purely religious or a purely civil ceremony, or by both. There are also many serious relationships that involve more than two individuals at the same time. In Ancient Egypt

> it is not unthinkable that the relationships between men and women existed in terms of a continuum, which was delineated by the duration of the cohabitation as well as the number of procedural formalities and property arrangements. In such a situation, the relation between a man and a woman could at one end of the continuum be brought about by a passing through of all necessary formal states, such as (formal) negotiation between the two concerned families, provision of marriage payments, and perhaps even oaths taken to guarantee the rights of the wife. At the other extreme, a man and woman would "just" move to live together. In this latter case the nature of the relationship could be defined and redefined, if it, for example, continued over a longer period of time, resulted in children being born, and/or if it at some stage also led to formal negotiations, provision of bride wealth and dowry and/or other property settlements.[33]

In Late Middle Kingdom Lahun as well, individuals could engage in a variety of dynamic relationships with others. Houses were physically modified in size to cope with growing families or the integration of additional family members and even servants. In general, it seems that when a woman married, she moved into her husband's home, and some of the smaller and medium-sized homes in Lahun clearly show that walls were removed in order to enlarge them, sometimes by merging two homes into one. Likewise, households could shrink in size due to death, or in the case of married couples, due to divorce. Ironically, we know more about methods of divorce in pharaonic Egypt than we do about the process of marriage, in large part because the dissolution of a marriage usually entailed a division of property and had an impact on children or led to legal squabbling. The evidence is again mostly from the New Kingdom and later, and we cannot be sure that the process was the same in the Late Middle Kingdom. Nevertheless, it is likely that within a few years of reaching childbearing age, Hedjerit would have left her father's home, and moved into the house established by her husband, ready to start a new family.

## Inheritance and Property Transfer

While there are no documents formalizing a marriage at the non-royal level (marriages of the pharaoh had significant political ramifications and were treated differently), there are extant copies of legal documents that were used to clarify and formalize more difficult or unusual arrangements for disbursing property. These *imyt-per*[34] or (land-)transfer documents were used from the Old Kingdom through the Late Period in various situations, not necessarily only for married couples. In terms of property inheritance, the usual and default rule in pharaonic Egypt was that upon the death of a married man, the male and female children would inherit equally and automatically two-thirds of the property of their deceased parent, with the wife receiving one-third. In the case of divorce, the wife would receive one-third of the community assets, and would retain possession of any private property she might have inherited from her own parents or from previous marriages. Either parent could also disinherit one or some of their children if they wished. As mentioned earlier, if any children failed to help take care of their parent's burial (or indeed neglected to care for their aging parents), they ran the risk of losing their right to the inheritance, and legal cases could ensue.[35] Because the transfer contracts (and indeed any legal documents) were written only in the case of exceptional circumstances, we can only infer the usual processes from a limited number of cases. Nevertheless, their meticulous detail can provide us with insight into spousal and family relationships.

One such document found in the town of Lahun provides us with a clear picture of some of the inheritance arrangements of a man named Wah, who worked as a priest at the local temple.[36] While he must have had another occupation as well, his most important title was *"wab* priest and overseer of the phyle of Sopedu." Thus he was not only a priest on his own, but also in charge of one of the shifts of priests (the phyle). The first document consists of a summary of an earlier contract wherein his brother, a minor official whose nickname was Ankhren, bequeathed all of his own possessions, including any fields, dwellings, personal possessions, staff, and servants, to Wah. At the time, it is likely that Ankhren had no children of his own, but did have at least one other sibling, and wanted to insure that all his assets would go to this particular brother instead of the other(s).[37]

> Copy of the *imyt-per* which the trustworthy seal-bearer of the controller of works, Ankhren, made:

# Love

"Year 44, second month of summer, day 13.[38]

The *imyt-per* made by the trustworthy seal-bearer of the controller of works of the north district, Shepsut's son Ihiseneb, who is called Ankhren:

'All my possessions in the field or in town will go to my brother, the *wab* priest and overseer of the phyle of Sopedu, Lord of the East, Shepsut's son Ihiseneb, who is called Wah. All my dependents will also go to this brother of mine.'"

The original of the document was deposited in the records office, and a copy was filed in the "office of the Second Reporter of the South" on the same day it was completed. Wah here began his own document with a summary of his brother's *imyt-per*, to clarify what was at stake and to legitimize his right to further transfer all the property as he chose. In order that there not be any potential for disputes, the identities of all the individuals are clearly indicated by their parentage (in this document the filiation is via the mother), their full name, and their nickname. This is particularly important in this document as the two brothers Ankhren and Wah shared the same full name: IhiSeneb.

When Wah himself felt his own death approaching, but had as yet no children, he in turn insured that when he died all of the assets that he inherited from his brother would be passed on to his wife. Without such a document, she would have inherited only one-third of the assets that they jointly acquired, but not his private property. The compact was likely written shortly after or just prior to the actual marriage. Note that this contract is specifically between Wah and his wife Teti, and does not involve any third parties, except as witnesses.

Year 2, second month of the inundation, day 18.

The *imyt-per* which the *wab* priest and overseer of the phyle of Sopedu, Lord of the East, Wah made:

"I am making an *imyt-per* for my wife, a woman of the town of Ges-jaby, SatSopedu's daughter Sheftu, who is called Teti, consisting of all the property which my brother, the trustworthy seal-bearer of the controller of works, Ankhren, gave to me together with all of the goods of his estate that he gave to me. She may give them, as she wishes, to any of the children whom she will bear to me. I am giving her the four Asiatics given to me by my brother, the trustworthy seal-bearer of the controller of works, Ankhren. She may give them to any of her children as she wishes. As for my tomb, let me be buried in it together with my wife, without letting any man at all interfere. As for the rooms which my brother, trustworthy seal-bearer of the controller of works, Ankhren, built for me, my wife shall live therein without being evicted from there by anyone."

The document was then formally witnessed by three individuals whose titles and names are given. Legally then, Wah insured that his wife, Teti, would inherit not only the property and movables that he had inherited from his brother but also the four Asiatic dependents who were tied to the household. In turn, Wah specified that Teti should be able to bequeath these items as she wishes, as long as they go to any children that they might bear together (as opposed to any she might bring into the marriage, or that she might bear in the future with another husband). In addition, the children are specified as ones that he will bear with her, not any that he may have had or might have in the future from any other women.[39] In effect, the document protects the bloodline of both parties, by insuring that only the children they had together would inherit. In addition, it guaranteed the continued well-being of Teti. Normally, a widow would not have any decisions to make in this regard – as we have seen, the children would automatically have a right to two-thirds of their father's possessions, and she would be entitled only to one-third of their communal property.

Wah also made sure that Teti would have a place to be buried regardless of any future changes in her circumstances. The actual burial would still need to be performed by any children they might have, but those children would have an even greater vested interest in insuring a proper burial for their mother, for if they did not, she could disinherit some of them if she chose. And as a final safeguard for his wife, Wah provided Teti with a place to live for the duration of her life. A final addendum to the document (in different handwriting) suggests that they did at least have one child together: "It is the deputy, Gebu, who will act as the guardian of my son." Wah insured that his son, while still a youth, would have a male to look after his future career and social interests. Women had equal legal rights, but did not have equal power in terms of status and wealth.

With the high infant and maternal mortality rate, there must have been a good number of complex family situations in Ancient Egypt. Somebody like Hedjerit's father might well have drafted one of these *imyt-per* documents to insure the disbursement of his own property either to his children by his first wife or to the ones of his second wife, or to insure that his second wife was provided for in any event. Hedjerit and her husband, however, might not have had a need for any special contract and might have focused on conceiving the children that they would expect to care for them in their old age and to provide them with a proper burial.

## Conception

The Egyptians were well aware that copulation between a man and a woman was required for procreation, but in many ways it was the male who was believed to be responsible for fertility through his sperm.[40] This is reflected in the various cosmogonies which feature a male creator god being able to initiate creation by himself. In one of the major myths, after coming into existence on his own from the watery chaos called Nun, the creator god Atum masturbated with his hand to bring forth the first divine couple. The hand of the creator god is later associated with the feminine principle, and the title "hand of god" becomes an important one for elite women in the New Kingdom. In similar fashion the deity associated with the earth (Geb) was not female as it was in many cultures, but obviously and resolutely male. All the gods who embodied the concept of fertility, such as Osiris, Min, and Geb,[41] were depicted with erect phalluses. It is thus the god and his seed that supply the dynamic energy required for life, while he is stimulated by the woman.

How far this religious belief was translated into daily life and acted upon is another matter. Teaching texts such as the *Instructions of Ptahotep*, composed to guide any nobleman in appropriate behavior for elite society, instruct the young man to take care of his wife for she is "a field for her lord." A New Kingdom document from Deir el-Medina discussing the case of an adulterous man even uses the phrase "he made her pregnant," emphasizing the active role of men in begetting children.[42] This could also explain the purpose of phallic objects that have been found in shrines devoted to Hathor, the Egyptian goddess of love and sexuality, and that have been published by Geraldine Pinch.[43] These artifacts are made primarily of wood, though stone and faience examples are also attested. Little research has been carried out on them. As Pinch notes, early excavators seemed to be embarrassed by them and failed to record them, shunting them aside or at best attributing to them a late date in order to explain their presence as a foreign import. Museums have also been loath to display them, and they are notably absent from art and auction houses. Nevertheless, they were important enough to the Ancient Egyptians to have been left at sacred spots. Without further research, their precise function is not known, but they were probably deposited, by either men or women, as votive offerings to the goddess to stimulate male potency and fertility. Pinch suggests that they were left during a specific festival, perhaps the one "celebrating the union of Hathor, the Hand of Atum, with the masculine creator deity."[44] Although these date to the New Kingdom, trips to the dusty storerooms of museums and more careful reading of old excavation reports may reveal more examples, possibly from the Middle Kingdom.

Notwithstanding the role of men in conception, it was certainly known that without a fertile woman, conception could not take place. From all time periods of Ancient Egypt, including the Middle Kingdom, a variety of female figurines has been found. Most are nude, some wear wigs, sometimes their breasts and pubic regions are emphasized, and some suckle children. Pinch has classified these into six main categories, and notes that they have been found in domestic, funerary, and religious contexts, and that all of the types have been found in shrines devoted to Hathor.[45] It is unlikely that they all had the same function, but some of the types were likely connected to insuring fertility and a successful birth. Two of these types were found in Lahun, varying from the mud doll-like figurines with hair extensions that were previously discussed, to figures made of faience (classified by Pinch as type 1). The latter often had the pubic area emphasized with black dots, and they may have jewelry such as necklaces and bracelets, or strings of cowrie shells on their hips. Other parts of

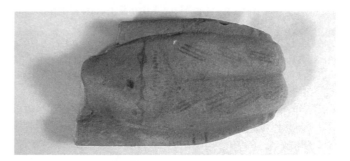

**Figure 10.1** Fragment of faience female figurine UC16723 (h. 6.5 cm) (courtesy of the Petrie Museum of Archaeology).

the body could also be decorated, in particular the thighs, with tattoo-like markings (Fig. 10.1).

If these were associated with fertility as has been suggested, we can imagine a woman like Hedjerit or her husband or perhaps both of them together acquiring one from a craftsman who specialized in working faience, for help after failing to conceive. The figurine may have been used in a household ritual or perhaps simply placed in a bedroom where its power could help stimulate the couple's fertility. In the New Kingdom, figures such as these could also have been presented as a votive offering at the local temple to help in petitions for a successful conception or childbirth. But as none of the figures was found in Nile valley temples in the Middle Kingdom to Second Intermediate Period, it seems that they were used primarily in domestic cults at Lahun.[46]

It is not only fertility figurines that testify to the difficulties women had in conceiving children. In the Gynecological Papyrus from Lahun, seven of the surviving 34 cases (that is, one-fifth) are devoted to determining whether or not a women was even capable of giving birth. These begin with the unambiguous heading: "Determining a woman who will conceive from one who will not."[47] Many of these were based on visible signs at the mouth, which was thought to be linked to the womb. To reveal how many births a woman will have, one section instructs the woman to sit "on earth smeared with dregs of sweet beer, put fruit" somewhere, but if she "ejects, she will give birth and for every ejection which comes from her mouth, each is one birth [. . .]. If she does not eject though, she will never give birth." Another fragmentary case involves reciting a formula over a substance which is to be presumably placed in the body, and "if it comes down from her nostril, she will give birth. If it comes down from her vagina, she will give birth. If then [. . .] she will not give birth for ever."

The lack of menstruation over an extended time period (amenorrhea) when not accompanied by the visible signs of pregnancy was recognized as a medical

problem and was discussed in the Ebers Papyrus.[48] Various menstrual distur-
bances, vaginal discharge, and uterine ailments were sources of concern in many
of the medical papyri, and these relate diverse methods for keeping female organs
healthy.[49] Because the Egyptians envisaged a direct route from the woman's
uterus to other parts of the body, many of the symptoms were in organs that we
consider to be unrelated. For example, if a woman suffered from an aching neck
and her eyes were in such pain that she could not see, the diagnosis was that it
was a "discharge of the uterus in her eyes."[50] This was treated by "fumigating
her with incense and fresh oil, fumigating her vagina with it, and fumigating her
eyes with goose leg fat," and by having her eat the fresh liver of a donkey.

If all the positive predictions came true and the fertility figurine worked, then
once she was pregnant Hedjerit could also try to determine the sex of the unborn
child. This procedure (unfortunately now very damaged) in the Lahun Gynecological Papyrus was described as for "determining the child to be born in the
uterus of the woman."[51] Whichever sex was predicted, it is clear both male and
female children were equally desired and welcomed.

During her pregnancy, there is no evidence to indicate whether or not Hedjerit
would continue with her usual work as is the case in modern Egyptian villages,[52]
or whether any special precautions were taken, such as avoidance of heavy labor
or a change in diet. Barring any evidence, we can only speculate on the life of a
woman who was pregnant. In terms of the pervasive religious practice, now that
conception was insured there may have been a change in the focus of petitions
to the gods within the home. Having proven to be effective, a nude female figurine whose function was to stimulate sexuality and fertility perhaps would have
been brought to a shrine in gratitude to the divine, or passed to another couple
hoping to conceive, or kept in hopes of promoting future fecundity for the couple
or eventually their children. As the nature of the problem shifted from fertility
to a safe and sound delivery for both mother and child, prayers would be chan-
neled through different sources, perhaps protective apotropaic figures such as
that of the hippopotamus goddess Taweret or the dwarf deity Bes.

When the time came for Hedjerit to give birth, it is possible that her husband
would have been with her – if not at the delivery itself, then close by. While
attendance lists from Lahun do not provide details for the workers' absences,
registers from Deir el-Medina are more detailed. Fragments of journals have
survived that explicitly record the names of men who were absent because their
wives were in childbirth.[53] In one case, the man was listed as being away for three
days.[54] Whether this was a typical scenario, or whether the allowance was granted
for particularly difficult deliveries, is unclear. The question also remains whether
this granting of "paternity leave" was a feature of life peculiar to the New
Kingdom workman's village of Deir el-Medina, or whether it was typical of
life in a Late Middle Kingdom village such as Lahun as well. The birth of any
Egyptian child was a momentous event, and it is possible that the birth of
Hejerit's child would have been attended by her husband, as well as relatives and
midwives.

## Conclusion

Although they were not of royal or noble birth, individuals such as Hedjerit and her family represented a large segment of the population of Late Middle Kingdom Egypt. All members of her family participated in conserving *maat*, the fundamental order of Egypt, by their social interactions, contributions to the economy, and loyalty to the king. While the pharaoh provided them with protection and resources, it was understood that although he was divine, he was no less dependent on the citizens of Egypt: "It is people who bring what there is into being. We live as men who have by their labor. If there is a lack of it, poverty takes power."[55] While we cannot hope to know all the details, the artifacts that have been left behind can provide glimpses of the everyday lives of these people of Ancient Egypt.

This book presents one reconstruction of daily life based on the Middle Kingdom town of Lahun. Rather than addressing big historical or anthropological questions, it attempts to follow the life of one individual and her family to help us understand Ancient Egypt. As the Egyptians themselves understood, it was not the singular great events that maintained *maat*, but the everyday actions of the gods, the king, and all people. Cultural values, traditions, norms, beliefs, and practices begin to be instilled in children from the moment of their birth, and are refined and further transmitted year after year. The continuation of life, the passing of beliefs, practices, customs, and knowledge from one generation to the next, is the single most critical factor for the preservation of a civilization. The concept of the cycle of continuity is expressed in the song of an Ancient Egyptian harper:

> For a generation passes,
> and another remains, since the time of the ancestors,
> those gods who existed aforetime,
> who rest in their pyramids,
> and the blessed noble dead likewise,
> buried in their pyramids.[56]

Thus, as Hedjerit waited for the cry of her own child announcing its successful entry into the world, she was in effect insuring the perpetuation of the essential nature of Ancient Egyptian culture.

## Notes

1  The Egyptian word for "sister" *senet* was also used for lover and close companions.
2  Kamp 2001.
3  Grunert 2002.

4   R. Janssen and Janssen 1990, 90–7.
5   Montserrat 1996, 42–4.
6   Montserrat 1996, 43.
7   Wilfong 1999. While this theory remains popular, it has now been largely discredited. See Strassmann 1999a.
8   For a full discussion of all these see Toivari-Viitala 2001, 162–8.
9   Kemp 1989, 305.
10  Montserrat 1996, 48.
11  Manniche 1987, 34, though she does not cite the publication.
12  Words that sound the same but have a different meaning.
13  Mathieu 1996.
14  From Papyrus Harris 500, part of the "Songs of Pleasant Entertainment for Your Beloved, the Chosen of your Heart, When She Comes from the Field" in Simpson 2003, 314.
15  From the Papyrus Harris 500 in Simpson 2003, 309.
16  Quirke 2004a, 180.
17  Women's hair, in particular bound hair being released, seems to have had erotic overtones for Ancient Egyptian men.
18  For the most thorough discussion see Parkinson 1995.
19  Simpson 2003, 324; Lichtheim 1976, 183; Foster 1974, 50–1; Gillam 2000.
20  *The Tale of King Neferkara and General Sasnet* in Quirke 2004a, 168.
21  The following passage is adapted from Quirke 2004a, 181.
22  UC 32057 in Collier and Quirke 2004, 62.
23  A *hin* or *henu* is an Egyptian unit of measurement equal to 450 ml. Natron, as mentioned in chapter 9, is the salt that was used for drying the body in preparation for mummification.
24  Nunn 1996, 196.
25  Robins 1993, 60–2.
26  Robins 1993, 62.
27  Toivari-Viitala 2001, 34–5.
28  Toivari-Viitala 2001, 32–8.
29  For the above see Toivari-Viitala 2001, 15–16 and notes.
30  UC32170 in Collier and Quirke 2006, 44–5.
31  Robins 1993, 60.
32  Toivari-Viitala 2001, 15–95.
33  Toivari-Viitala 2001, 84–5.
34  Literally this means "that which is in the house."
35  Robins 1993, 132–3.
36  The following analysis relies largely on the interpretation of Johnson 1999.
37  Johnson 1999, 170. The following translation is based on Johnson and UC 32058 in Collier and Quirke 2004, 104–5.
38  The date is given according to the Egyptian tradition of counting from the 1st year of the current pharaoh's reign, providing the month and season, and the day.
39  Johnson 1999, 171.
40  Roth 2000.
41  Osiris was the god of the dead, Min was one of the earliest attested deities and a god of fertility, while Geb was the god of the earth.

42   Toivari-Viitala 2001, 171.
43   Pinch 1993, 235–45.
44   Pinch 1993, 245.
45   Pinch 1993, 225.
46   Pinch 1993, 221.
47   UC 32057 (column 3, 12–25) cases 26–32 in Collier and Quirke 2004, 63–4.
48   Ebers 833 (Nunn 1996, 196–7).
49   Westendorf 1999 vol. 1, 411–38.
50   UC 32057 (column 1, 1–5) case 1 in Collier and Quirke 2004, 58.
51   UC 32057 (column 3, 2–3) case 19 in Collier and Quirke 2004, 62.
52   Morsy 1982.
53   Toivari-Viitala 2001, 172–3.
54   A. McDowell 1999, 53.
55   From the *Loyalist Teaching* in Quirke 2004a, 110.
56   From the *Harpist's Song* in Parkinson 1991, 145.

# Bibliography

Adams, M. D. (1998) "The Abydos settlement site project: investigation of a major provincial town in the Old Kingdom and First Intermediate Period," in *Proceedings of the Seventh International Congress of Egyptologists, Cambridge, 3–9 September 1995* (ed., Eyre, C. J.), Leuven: Peeters: 19–30.

Adetunji, J. A. (1996) "Infant mortality levels in Africa: does method of estimation matter?" *Genus* 52: 89–106.

Allen, J. P. (2002) *The Heqanakht Papyri.* New York: Metropolitan Museum of Art.

— (2005) *The Art of Medicine in Ancient Egypt.* New York: Metropolitan Museum of Art; New Haven, CT: Yale University Press.

Allen, S. (1997) "Spinning bowls: representation and reality," in *Ancient Egypt, the Aegean, and the Near East: Studies in Honour of Martha Rhoads Bell.* Vol. 1 (ed., Phillips, J.), San Antonio, TX: Van Siclen Books: 17–38.

Altenmüller, H. (1965) *Die Apotropaia und die Götter mittelägyptens: Eine typologische und religionsgeschichtliche Untersuchung der sogenannten "Zaubermesser" des Mittleren Reichs.* Munich: Ludwig-Maximilians-Universität.

Anderson, R. D. (1995) "Music and dance in Pharaonic Egypt," in *Civilizations of the Ancient Near East.* Vol. 4 (ed., Sasson, J. M.), Peabody, MA: Hendrickson: 2555–68.

Angel, J. L. (1972) "Ecology and population in the Eastern Mediterranean," *World Archaeology* 4: 88–105.

Arnold, D. (2003) *The Encyclopedia of Ancient Egyptian Architecture.* London: I. B. Tauris.

Arnold, F. (1989) "A study of Egyptian domestic buildings," *Varia Ägyptiaca* 5: 75–93.

— (1996) "Settlement remains at Lisht-North," in *Haus und Palast im Alten Ägypten* (ed., Bietak, M.), Vienna: Verlag der Österreichischen Akademie der Wissenschaften: 13–44.

Assmann, J. (1975) *Ägyptische Hymnen und Gebete.* Zurich and Munich: Artemis.

225

# Bibliography

— (2005) *Death and Salvation in Ancient Egypt.* Ithaca, NY, and London: Cornell University Press.

Aufrère, S. (1991) *L'Univers minéral dans la pensée Égyptienne.* Cairo: Institut français d'archéologie orientale.

Bagnall, R. S. and B. Frier (1994) *The Demography of Roman Egypt.* Cambridge: Cambridge University Press.

Baines, J. (1983) "Literacy and Ancient Egyptian society," *Man* 18: 572–99.

Baines, J. and C. J. Eyre (1983) "Four notes on literacy," *Göttinger Miszellen* 61: 65–96.

Baker, B. J. (1997) "Contributions of biological anthropology to the understanding of Ancient Egyptian and Nubian docieties," in *Anthropology and Egyptology: A Developing Dialogue* (ed., Lustig, J.), Sheffield: Sheffield Academic Press: 106–16.

— (2001) "Secrets in the skeletons: disease and deformity attest the hazards of daily life," *Archaeology* 54: 47.

Baker, B. J., T. L. Dupras, and M. W. Tocheri (2005) *The Osteology of Infants and Children.* College Station: Texas A & M University Press.

Barber, E. W. (1994) *Women's Work: The First 20,000 Years. Women, Cloth, and Society in Early Times.* New York and London: W. W. Norton.

Behrmann, A. (1989, 1996) *Das Nilpfred in der Vorstellungswelt der Alten Ägypter.* Bern: Peter Lang.

Bietak, M. (1996) "Zum Raumprogramm ägyptischer Wohnhäuser des Mittleren und des Neuen Reiches," in *Haus und Palast im Alten Ägypten* (ed., Bietak, M.), Vienna: Verlag der Österreichischen Akademie der Wissenschaften: 23–44.

Bietak, M. and J. Dorner (1998) "Der Tempel und die Siedlung des Mittleren Reiches bei 'Ezbet Ruschdi. Grabungsvorbericht 1996," *Ägypten und Levante* 8: 9–40.

Bjerke, S. (1965) "Remarks on the Egyptian ritual of 'opening the mouth' and its interpretation," *Numen* 12: 201–16.

Blackman, A. M. and M. R. Apted (1953) *The Rock Tombs of Meir. Part 6, The Tomb-Chapels of Ukhhotpe Son of Iam (A, no. 3), Senbi Son of Ukhhotpe Son of Senbi (B, no. 3), and Ukhhotpe Son of Ukhhotpe and Heny-Hery-Ib (C, no. 1).* London: Egypt Exploration Society.

Blackman, W. (1925) "An Ancient Egyptian custom illustrated by a modern survival," *Man* 25: 65–57.

Boerma, J. T. (1987) "Levels of maternal mortality in developing countries," *Studies in Family Planning* 18: 213–21.

Borghouts, J. F. (1978) *Ancient Egyptian Magical Texts.* Leiden: E. J. Brill.

Bourriau, J. (1988) *Pharaohs and Mortals: Egyptian Art in the Middle Kingdom.* Cambridge and New York: Cambridge University Press.

— (2001) "Change of body position in Egyptian burials from the mid XIIth Dynasty until the early XVIIth Dynasty," in *Social Aspects of Funerary Culture in the Egyptian Old and Middle Kingdoms: Proceedings of the International Symposium held at Leiden University, 6–7 June, 1996* (ed., Willems, H.), Leuven and Sterling, VA: Uitgeverij Peeters and Dep. Oosterse Studies: 1–20.

Bourriau, J. and S. Quirke (1998) "The Late Middle Kingdom ceramic repertoire in words and objects," in *Lahun Studies* (ed., Quirke, S.), New Malden: Sia: 60–83.

Brunner-Traut, E. (1958) *Der Tanz im alten Ägypten nach bildlichen und inschriftlichen Zeugnissen.* 3rd edition 1992. Glückstadt: J. J. Augustin.

# Bibliography

Bryan, B. M. (1985) "Evidence for female literacy from Theban tombs of the New Kingdom," *Bulletin of the Egyptological Seminar* 6: 17–32.

Buikstra, J., B. J. Baker, and D. Cook (1995) "What diseases plagued the ancient Egyptians? A century of controversy considered," in *Biological Anthropology and the Study of Ancient Egypt* (eds., Davies, V. and Walker, R.), London: British Museum Press: 24–53.

Buzon, M. R. (2006) "Health of the non-elites at Tombos: nutritional and disease stress in New Kingdom Nubia," *American Journal of Physical Anthropology* 130: 26–37.

Caminos, R. A. and A. H. Gardiner (1954) *Late-Egyptian Miscellanies.* London: Oxford University Press.

Capel, A. K. and G. E. Markoe (eds.) (1996) *Mistress of the House, Mistress of Heaven: Women in Ancient Egypt.* New York: Hudson Hills Press and Cincinnati Art Museum.

Cartwright, C., H. Granger-Taylor, and S. Quirke (1998) "Lahun textile evidence in London," in *Lahun Studies* (ed., Quirke, S.), New Malden: Sia: 92–111.

Centers for Disease Control and Prevention (2002) "National Vital Statistics Report, Vol. 50, No. 15, September 16, 2002," www.cdc.gov/nchs/fastats/pdf/nvsr50_15tb34.pdf, accessed February 19, 2006.

Central Intelligence Agency (2006) "Online Factbook," www.cia.gov/cia/publications/factbook/rankorder/2091rank.html, accessed February 19, 2006.

Clark, G. (2005) *The Conquest of Nature: A Brief Economic History of the World.* Princeton, NJ: Princeton University Press.

Collier, M. and S. Quirke (eds.) (2002) *The UCL Lahun Papyri: Letters.* Oxford: Archaeopress.

— (eds.) (2004) *The UCL Lahun Papyri: Religious, Literary, Legal, Mathematical and Medical.* Oxford: Archaeopress.

— (eds.) (2006) *The UCL Lahun Papyri: Accounts.* Oxford: Archaeopress.

Dasen, V. (ed.) (2004) *Naissance et petite enfance dans l'Antiquité: Actes du colloque de Fribourg, 28 novembre–1er décembre 2001.* Fribourg: Academic Press; Göttingen: Vandenhoeck & Ruprecht.

David, R. (1986) *The Pyramid Builders of Ancient Egypt: A Modern Investigation of Pharaoh's Workforce.* London: Routledge.

Davies, N. d. G. (1943) *The Tomb of Rekh-mi-re at Thebes.* Reprint 1973. New York: Arno Press.

Decker, W. (1992) *Sports and Games of Ancient Egypt.* New Haven, CT, and London: Yale University Press.

Demarée, R. J. (1983) *The Ꜣḫ iḳr n Rꜥ-Stelae: On Ancestor-Worship in Ancient Egypt.* Leiden: Nederlands Instituut voor het Nabije Oosten.

Derriks, C. (2001) "Mirrors," in *The Oxford Encyclopedia of Ancient Egypt.* Vol. 2 (ed., Redford, D. B.), Cairo: American University in Cairo Press: 419–22.

deVries, M. W. and M. R. deVries (1977) "Cultural relativity of toilet training readiness: a perspective from East Africa," *Pediatrics* 60: 170–7.

Dewey, W. J. (1993) *Sleeping Beauties: The Jerome L. Joss Collection of African Headrests at UCLA.* Los Angeles: University of California, Los Angeles, Fowler Museum of Cultural History.

Dorman, P. F. (2002) *Faces in Clay: Technique, Imagery, and Allusion in a Corpus of Ceramic Sculpture from Ancient Egypt.* Mainz: Philipp von Zabern.

Dunand, F. (2004) "Les enfants et la mort en Egypte," in *Naissance et petite enfance dans l'Antiquité: Actes du colloque de Fribourg, 28 novembre–1er décembre 2001.* (ed., Dasen, V.), Fribourg, Göttingen: Academic Press; Vandenhoeck & Ruprecht: 13–32.

Dupras, T. L., H. P. Schwarcz, and S. I. Fairgrieve (2001) "Infant feeding and weaning practices in Roman Egypt," *American Journal of Physical Anthropology* 115: 204–12.

Elliot, Geraldine (1938) *The Long Grass Whispers.* New York: Schocken Books.

Engelbach, R. (1923) *Harageh.* London: British School of Archaeology in Egypt.

Erman, A. (1901) *Zaubersprüche für Mutter und Kind.* Berlin: Abhandlungen der Königliche Preussischen Akademie der Wissenschaften.

Eyre, C. J. (1999) "The village economy in Pharaonic Egypt," in *Agriculture in Egypt from Pharaonic to Modern Times* (eds., Bowman, A. K. and Rogan, E.), Oxford: Oxford University Press: 33–59.

Eyre, C. J. and J. Baines (1989) "Interactions between orality and literacy in Ancient Egypt," in *Literacy and Society* (eds., Schousboe, K. and Larsen, M. T.), Copenhagen: Akademisk Forlag: 91–119.

Ezzamel, M. (2002) "Accounting for private estates and the household in the twentieth-century BC Middle Kingdom, Ancient Egypt," *Abacus* 38: 235–62.

— (2004) "Work organization in the Middle Kingdom, Ancient Egypt," *Organization* 11: 497–537.

Faulkner, R. O. (1973) *The Ancient Egyptian Coffin Texts.* Warminster: Aris & Phillips.

Feucht, E. (1995) *Das Kind im alten Ägypten.* Frankfurt and New York: Campus Verlag.

— (2004) "Der Weg ins Leben," in *Naissance et petite enfance dans l'Antiquité: Actes du colloque de Fribourg, 28 novembre–1er décembre 2001* (ed., Dasen, V.), Fribourg: Academic Press; Göttingen: Vandenhoeck & Ruprecht: 33–53.

Filer, J. M. (1998) "Mother and baby burials," in *Proceedings of the Seventh International Congress of Egyptologists, Cambridge, 3–9 September 1995* (ed., Eyre, C. J.), Leuven: Peeters: 392–400.

Fischer, H. G. (1985) *Egyptian Titles of the Middle Kingdom: A Supplement to Wm. Ward's Index.* New York: Metropolitan Museum of Art.

— (2000) *Egyptian Women of the Old Kingdom and of the Heracleopolitan Period.* 2nd edition. New York: Metropolitan Museum of Art.

Fischer-Elfert, H.-W. (1998) *Die Vision von der Statue im Stein.* Heidelberg: Universitätsverlag C. Winter.

Fitton, L., M. Hughes, and S. Quirke (1998) "Northerners at Lahun: neutron activation analysis of Minoan and related pottery in the British Museum," in *Lahun Studies* (ed., Quirke, S.), New Malden: Sia: 112–40.

Forman, W. and S. Quirke (1996) *Hieroglyphs and the Afterlife in Ancient Egypt.* London: British Museum Press.

Foster, J. L. (1974) *Love Songs of the New Kingdom: Translated from the Ancient Egyptian by John L. Foster.* Austin, TX: University of Texas Press.

Franke, D. (2003a) "Middle Kingdom hymns, and other sundry religious texts," in *Egypt – Temple of the Whole World: Studies in Honor of Jan Assmann* (eds., Meyer, S. and Meyer, R.), Leiden: Brill: 95–135.

— (2003b) "The Middle Kingdom offering formulas: a challenge," *Journal of Egyptian Archaeology* 89: 39–57.

Friedman, F. D. (1994) "Aspects of domestic life and religion," in *Pharaoh's Workers: The Villagers of Deir el-Medina* (ed., Lesko, L. H.), Ithaca, NY, and London: Cornell University Press: 95–117.

Friedman, R. F. (1998) "More mummies: the 1998 season at HK43," *Nekhen News* 10: 4–6.

Gallorini, C. (1998) "A reconstruction of Petrie's excavation at the Middle Kingdom settlement of Kahun," in *Lahun Studies* (ed., Quirke, S.), New Malden: Sia: 42–9.

Gardiner, A. H. (1905) "Hymns to Amon from a Leiden papyrus," *Zeitschrift für Ägyptische Sprache und Altertumskunde* 42: 12–42.

— (1930) "A new letter to the dead," *Journal of Egyptian Archaeology* 16: 19–22.

— (1947) *Ancient Egyptian Onomastica*. London: Oxford University Press.

Gardiner, A. H. and K. Sethe (1928) *Egyptian Letters to the Dead: Mainly from the Old and Middle Kingdoms*. London: Egypt Exploration Society.

Germer, R. (1998) "The plant remains found by Petrie at Lahun and some remarks on the problems of identifying Egyptian plant names," in *Lahun Studies* (ed., Quirke, S.), New Malden: Sia: 84–91.

Gillam, R. (2000) "The Mehy Papers: text and lifestyle in translation," *Chronique d'Égypte* 75: 207–16.

Gilmore, G. (1986) "The chemical analysis of the Kahun metals," in *The Pyramid Builders of Ancient Egypt: A Modern Investigation of Pharaoh's Workforce* (ed., David, R.), London: Routledge: 215–25.

Gilula, M. (1978) "Hirtengeschichte 17–22 = CT VII 36m–r," *Göttinger Miszellen* 29: 21–2.

Gnirs, A. (1996) "Die ägyptische Autobiographie," in *Ancient Egyptian Literature: History and Forms*. Vol. 10 (ed., Loprieno, A.), Leiden, New York, and Cologne: E. J. Brill: 191–242.

Golden, M. (2004) "Mortality, mourning and mothers," in *Naissance et petite enfance dans l'Antiquité: Actes du colloque de Fribourg, 28 novembre–1er décembre 2001*. (ed., Dasen, V.), Fribourg: Academic Press; Göttingen: Vandenhoeck & Ruprecht: 145–57.

Goodman, A. H. and G. J. Armelagos (1989) "Infant and childhood morbidity and mortality risks in archaeological populations," *World Archaeology* 21: 225–43.

Gosline, S. L. (1999) *Archaeogender: Studies in Gender's Material Culture*. Warren Center, PA: Shangri-La Publications.

Grajetzki, W. (2003) *Burial Customs in Ancient Egypt: Life in Death for Rich and Poor*. London: Duckworth.

— (2004) *Harageh: An Egyptian Burial Ground for the Rich, around 1800 BC*. London: Golden House Publications.

— (2005) *Middle Kingdom of Ancient Egypt: History, Archaeology and Society*. London: Duckworth.

Green, L. (2001) "Hairstyles," in *The Oxford Encyclopedia of Ancient Egypt*. Vol. 2 (ed., Redford, D. B.), Cairo: American University in Cairo Press: 73–6.

Griffith, F. L. (1898) *Hieratic Papyri from Kahun and Gurob (Principally of the Middle Kingdom)*. London: Bernard Quaritch.

— (1910) *Catalogue of Egyptian Antiquities of the XII and XVIII Dynasties from Kahun, Illahun and Gurob*. Manchester: Sherratt & Hughes.

Grunert, S. (2002) "Nicht nur sauber, sondern rein: Rituelle Reinigungsanweisungen aus dem Grab des Anchmahor in Saqqara," *Studien zur altägyptische Kultur* 30: 137–51.

# Bibliography

Hall, R. (1985) "'The cast-off garment of yesterday': dresses reversed in life and death," *Bulletin de l'institut français d'archéologie orientale* 85: 235–44.

Harer, W. B. (1993) "Health in Pharaonic Egypt," in *Biological Anthropology and the Study of Ancient Egypt* (eds., Davies, W. V. and Walker, R.), London: British Museum Press: 19–23.

Harrell, J. A. and M. D. Lewan (2002) "Sources of mummy bitumen in ancient Egypt and Palestine," *Archaeometry* 44: 285–93.

Hayes, W. C. (1959) *The Scepter of Egypt: A Background for the Study of the Egyptian Antiquities in the Metropolitan Museum of Art*. New York: Metropolitan Museum of Art.

Helck, W. (1967) "Einige Bemerkungen zum Mundöffnungsritual," *Mitteilungen des Deutschen Ärchäologischen Instituts* 22: 27–41.

Hickmann, H. (1956) "La danse aux miroirs: essai de reconstitution d'une danse pharaonique de l'ancien empire," *Bulletin de l'Institut d'Égypte* XXXVII: 151–90.

Hofmann, T. (2005) *Zur sozialen Bedeutung zweier Begriffe für "Diener": bꜣk und ḥm*. Basel: Verlag Schwabe AG Basel.

Ikram, S. and A. Dodson (1998) *The Mummy in Ancient Egypt: Equipping the Dead for Eternity*. London: Thames and Hudson.

Insoll, T. (2004) *Archaeology, Ritual, Religion*. London and New York: Routledge.

Janssen, J. J. (2005) *Donkeys at Deir el-Medina*. Leiden: Nederlands Instituut voor het Nabije Oosten.

Janssen, R. and J. J. Janssen (1989) *Egyptian Household Animals*. Princes Risborough: Shire Publications.

— (1990) *Growing Up in Ancient Egypt*. London: Rubicon Press.

— (1996) *Getting Old in Ancient Egypt*. London: Rubicon Press.

Jaquet-Gordon, H. (1981) "A tentative typology of Egyptian bread moulds," in *Studien zur altägyptischen Keramik*. Vols. 11–24 (ed., Arnold, D.), Mainz am Rhein: von Zabern.

Jeffreys, D. G. (2003) "All in the family? Heirlooms in Ancient Egypt," in *"Never had the Like Occurred": Egypt's View of its Past* (ed., Tait, W. J.), London: UCL: 197–211.

Johnson, J. H. (1999) "Speculations on Middle Kingdom marriage," in *Studies on Ancient Egypt in Honour of H. S. Smith*. Occasional Publications vol. 13 (ed., Leahy, A.), London: Egypt Exploration Society: 169–72.

Kadish, G. E. (1979) "The scatophagous Egyptian," *Journal of the Society for the Study of Egyptian Antiquities* 4: 203–17.

Kamp, K. A. (2001) "Where have all the children gone? The archaeology of childhood," *Journal of Archaeological Method and Theory* 8: 1–34.

Kemp, B. J. (1989) *Ancient Egypt: Anatomy of a Civilization*. London and New York: Routledge.

— (2005) *Ancient Egypt: Anatomy of a Civilization*. 2nd edition. London: Routledge.

Killen, G. (1994) *Ancient Egyptian Furniture*. Warminster: Aris & Phillips.

Kloos, H. and R. David (2002) "The paleoepidemiology of schistosomiasis in Ancient Egypt," *Research in Human Ecology* 9: 14–25.

Koller, J., U. Baumer, Y. Kaup, and U. Weser (2005) "Herodotus' and Pliny's embalming materials identified on Ancient Egyptian mummies," *Archaeometry* 47: 609–28.

# Bibliography

Kóthay, K. A. (2001) "Houses and households at Kahun: bureaucratic and domestic aspects of social organization during the Middle Kingdom," in *Mélanges offerts à Edith Varga: "le lotus qui sort de terre"* (ed., Győry, H.), Budapest: Bulletin du Musée hongrois des Beaux-Art Supplément: 349–68.

Kraus, J. (2004) *Die Demographie des Alten Ägypten: Eine Phänomenologie anhand altägyptischer Quellen.* Göttingen: Georg-August-Universität.

Krauss, R. (1998) "Das Wag-Fest und die Chronologie des Alten Reiches," *Göttinger Miszellen* 162: 53–63.

Lacovara, P. (1992) "A new date for an old hippopotamus," *Journal of the Museum of Fine Arts, Boston* 4: 17–26.

Laubenheimer, F. (2004) "La mort des tout petits dans l'Occident romain," in *Naissance et petite enfance dans l'Antiquité: Actes du colloque de Fribourg, 28 novembre–1er décembre 2001* (ed., Dasen, V.), Fribourg: Academic Press; Göttingen: Vandenhoeck & Ruprecht: 293–315.

Lawergren, B. (2001) "Music," in *The Oxford Encyclopedia of Ancient Egypt.* Vol. 2 (ed., Redford, D. B.), Oxford and New York: Oxford University Press: 450–4.

Leitz, C. (1999) *Magical and Medical Papyri of the New Kingdom.* London: British Museum Press.

Leprohon, R. J. (1978) "The personnel of the Middle Kingdom funerary stelae," *Journal of the American Research Center in Egypt* 15: 33–8.

Lesko, L. H. (1990) "Some comments on Ancient Egyptian literacy and literati," in *Studies in Egyptology: Presented to Miriam Lichtheim.* Vol. 2 (ed., Israelit-Groll, S.), Jerusalem: Magnes Press: 656–67.

Lexová, I. (2000 [1935]) *Ancient Egyptian Dances.* Mineola, NY: Dover Publications.

Lichtheim, M. (1973) *Ancient Egyptian Literature. Vol I: The Old and Middle Kingdoms.* Berkeley, CA: University of California Press.

— (1976) *Ancient Egyptian Literature. Vol II: The New Kingdom.* Berkeley, CA: University of California Press.

Lilyquist, C. (1979) *Ancient Egyptian Mirrors: From the Earliest Times through the Middle Kingdom.* Munich and Berlin: Deutscher Kunstverlag.

Lloyd, A. B. (2006) "Heka, dreams, and prophecy in Ancient Egyptian stories," in *Through a Glass Darkly: Magic, Dreams and Prophecy in Ancient Egypt* (ed., Szpakowska, K.), Swansea: Classical Press of Wales: 71–94.

Loprieno, A. (ed.) (1996) *Ancient Egyptian Literature: History and Forms.* Leiden, New York, and Cologne: E. J. Brill.

— (1997) "Slaves," in *The Egyptians* (ed., Donadoni, S.), Chicago and London: University of Chicago Press: 185–220.

Luft, U. (1992a) *Das Archiv von Illahun. Briefe 1: Hieratische Papyri aus den Staatlichen Museen zu Berlin – Preussischer Kulturbesitz 1.* Berlin: Akademie Verlag.

— (1992b) *Die chronologische Fixierung des ägyptischen Mittleren Reiches nach dem Tempelarchiv von Illahun.* Vienna: Verlag der Österreichischen Akademie der Wissenschaften.

— (1994) "The date of the *Wagy* feast: considerations on the chronology of the Old Kingdom," in *Revolutions in Time: Studies in Ancient Egyptian Calendrics* (ed., Spalinger, A. J.), San Antonio, TX: Van Siclen Books: 39–43.

Lustig, J. (1997) "Kinship, gender and age in Middle Kingdom tomb scenes and texts," in *Anthropology and Egyptology: A Developing Dialogue* (ed., Lustig, J.), Sheffield: Sheffield Academic Press: 43–65.

Luy, M. (2003) "Causes of male excess mortality: insights from cloistered populations," *Population and Development Review* 29: 647–76.

Manniche, L. (1987) *Sexual Life in Ancient Egypt*. London and New York: Kegan Paul International.

Mathieu, B. (1996) *La Poésie amoureuse de l'Égypte Ancienne*. Cairo: Institut français d'archéologie orientale.

Meskell, L. (1994) "Dying young: the experience of death at Deir el-Medina," *Archaeological Review from Cambridge* 13: 35–45.

— (1999) *Archaeologies of Social Life: Age, Sex, Class et cetera in Ancient Egypt*. Oxford: Blackwell Publishers.

McDowell, A. G. (1996) "Student exercises from Deir el-Medina: the dates," in *Studies in Honor of William Kelly Simpson*. Vol. 2 (ed., Der Manuelian, P.), Boston: Dept of Ancient Egyptian Nubian and Near Eastern Art, Museum of Fine Arts: 601–8.

— (1999) *Village Life in Ancient Egypt: Laundry Lists and Love Songs*. Oxford and New York: Oxford University Press.

— (2000) "Teachers and students at Deir el-Medina," in *Deir el-Medina in the Third Millenium AD: A Tribute to Jac. J. Janssen*. (eds., Demarée, R. J. and Egberts, A.), Leiden: Nederlands Instituut voor het Nabije Oosten: 217–33.

McDowell, J. A. (1986) "Kahun: the textile evidence," in *The Pyramid Builders of Ancient Egypt: A Modern Investigation of Pharaoh's Workforce* (ed., David, R.), London: Routledge: 226–47.

Montserrat, D. (1996) *Sex and Society in Graeco-Roman Egypt*. London and New York: Kegan Paul International.

Morkot, R. (2005) *The Egyptians: An Introduction*. London: Routledge.

Morsy, S. A. (1982) "Childbirth in an Egyptian village," in *Anthropology of Human Birth* (ed., Kay, M. A.), Philadelphia: F. A. Davis.

Moses, S. (2004) "The children of neolithic Çatalhöyük: burial symbolism and social metaphor," *Çatalhöyük: Excavations of a Neolithic Anatolian Höyük*, www.catalhoyuk.com/archive_reports/2004/ar04_34.html, accessed May 29, 2007.

Müller, V. (1998) "Offering deposits at Tell el-Dab'a," in *Proceedings of the Seventh International Congress of Egyptologists, Cambridge, 3–9 September 1995* (ed., Eyre, C. J.), Leuven: Peeters: 793–803.

Murray, M. A. (2000) "Fruits, vegetables, pulses and condiments," in *Ancient Egyptian Materials and Technology* (eds., Nicholson, P. T. and Shaw, I.), Cambridge: Cambridge University Press: 609–55.

Nerlich, A. and A. Zink (2001) "Leben und Krankheit im alten Ägypten," *Bayerisches Ärzteblatt* 8: 373–6.

Nerlich, A., H. Rohrbach, and A. Zink (2002) "Paläopathologie altägyptischer Mumien und Skelette: Untersuchungen zu Auftreten und Häufigkeit spezifischer Krankheiten in verschiedenen Zeitperioden der altägyptischen Nekropole von Theben-West," *Der Pathologe* 23: 379–85.

Nicholson, P. T. and H. L. Patterson (1985) "Pottery making in Upper Egypt: an ethnoarchaeological study," *World Archaeology* 17: 222–39.

# Bibliography

Nicholson, P. T. and E. Peltenburg (2000) "Egyptian faience," in *Ancient Egyptian Materials and Technology* (eds., Nicholson, P. T. and Shaw, I.), Cambridge: Cambridge University Press: 177–94.

Nunn, J. F. (1996) *Ancient Egyptian Medicine*. Norman, OK: University of Oklahoma Press.

O'Connor, D. (1997) "The elite houses of Kahun," in *Ancient Egypt, the Aegean, and the Near East: Studies in Honour of Martha Rhoads Bell* (ed., Phillips, J.), San Antonio, TX: Van Siclen Books: 389–400.

Osborn, D. J. and J. Osbornová (1998) *The Mammals of Ancient Egypt*. Warminster: Aris & Phillips.

Otto, E. (1960) *Das ägyptische Mundöffnungsritual*. Wiesbaden: Otto Harrassowitz.

Panagiotakopulu, E. (2003) "Insect remains from the collections in the Egyptian Museum of Turin," *Archaeometry* 45: 355–62.

Parker Pearson, M. (2001) *The Archaeology of Death and Burial*. College Station, TX: Texas A & M University Anthropology Press.

Parkinson, R. B. (1991) *Voices from Ancient Egypt: An Anthology of Middle Kingdom Writings*. Norman, OK: University of Oklahoma Press.

— (1995) "'Homosexual' desire and Middle Kingdom literature," *Journal of Egyptian Archaeology* 81: 57–76.

— (1998) *The Tale of Sinuhe and other Ancient Egyptian Poems 1940–1640 BC*. Oxford: Clarendon Press.

— (2002) *Poetry and Culture in Middle Kingdom Egypt: A Dark Side to Perfection*. London and New York: Continuum.

Perraud, M. (1998) "Un raccord au Louvre: l'appui-tête E 4231 + E 4293 à figurations de Bès," *Revue d'Égyptologie* 49: 161–6.

— (2002) "Appuis-tête à inscription magique et *apotropaïa*," *Bulletin de l'institut français d'archéologie orientale* 102: 309–26.

Petrie, W. M. F. (1927) *Objects of Daily Use*. London: British School of Archaeology in Egypt.

Petrie, W. M. F., F. L. Griffith, and P. E. Newberry (1890) *Kahun, Gurob, and Hawara*. London: K. Paul Trench Trübner.

Petrie, W. M. F., A. H. Sayce, and F. L. Griffith (1891) *Illahun, Kahun and Gurob: 1889–1890*. London: D. Nutt.

Petrie, W. M. F., G. Brunton, and M. A. Murray (1923) *Lahun II*. London: British School of Archaeology in Egypt and Egyptian Research Account.

Picardo, N. S. (2006) "Egypt's well-to-do: elite mansions in the town of Wah-Sut," *Expedition* 48: 37–40.

Piccione, P. A. (1980) "In search of the meaning of Senet," *Archaeology* 33: 55–8.

Pinch, G. (1983) "Childbirth and female figurines at Deir el-Medina and el-Amarna," *Orientalia* 52: 405–14.

— (1993) *Votive Offerings to Hathor*. Oxford: Griffith Institute, Ashmolean Museum.

— (1994) *Magic in Ancient Egypt*. London: British Museum Press.

Polz, D. and S. Voß (1999) "Bericht über die 6., 7. und 8. Grabungskampagne in der Nekropole von Dra' Abu el-Naga/Theben West." *Mitteilungen des Deutschen Ärchäologischen Instituts* 55: 343–410.

Posener, G. (1960) "Une nouvelle histoire de revenant," *Revue d'Égyptologie* 12: 75–82.

Pusch, E. B. (1979) *Das Senet-Brettspiel im alten Ägypten*. Munich and Berlin: Deutscher Kunstverlag.

Quirke, S. (1988) "State and labour in the Middle Kingdom: a reconsideration of the term *ḥnrt*," *Revue d'Égyptologie* 39: 83–106.

— (1990) *The Administration of Egypt in the Late Middle Kingdom*. New Malden: Sia.

— (1997) "Gods in the temple of the king: Anubis at Lahun," in *The Temple in Ancient Egypt: New Discoveries and Recent Research* (ed., Quirke, S.), London: British Museum Press: 24–48.

— (1998a) "Figures of clay: toys or ritual objects?" in *Lahun Studies* (ed., Quirke, S.), New Malden: Sia: 141–51.

— (ed.) (1998b) *Lahun Studies*. New Malden: Sia.

— (2004a) *Egyptian Literature 1800 BC: Questions and Readings*. London: Golden House Publications.

— (2004b) *Titles and Bureaux of Egypt 1850–1700 BC*. London: Golden House Publications.

— (2006) *Lahun: A Town in Egypt 1800 BC, and the History of its Landscape*. London: Golden House Publications.

Randall, S. and T. LeGrand (2003) "Reproductive strategies and decisions in Senegal: the role of child mortality," *Population (English Edition, 2002–)* 58: 687–715.

Ranke, H. and W. Baumgartner (1935) *Die ägyptischen Personennamen*. Gluckstadt: J. J. Augustin.

Raven, M. J. (1987) "Puzzling Pataikos," *Oudheidkundige mededelingen uit het Rijksmuseum van Oudheiden te Leiden* 67: 7–19.

— (1997) "Charms for protection during the epagomenal days," in *Essays on Ancient Egypt in Honour of Herman Te Velde*. Egyptological Memoirs vol. 1 (ed., van Dijk, J.), Groningen: Styx Publications: 275–85.

Redding, R. and B. V. Hunt (2007) "Archaeozoology at Giza: pyramids and protein, of cattle, sheep, goats, and pigs," *Ancient Egypt Research Associates*, www.aeraweb.org/spec_ZOO.asp, accessed March 20, 2007.

Reeder, G. (1995) "The mysterious *muu* and the dance they do," *KMT* 6: 3.

Rice, M. (2006) *Swifter than the Arrow: The Golden Hunting Hounds of Ancient Egypt*. London and New York: I. B. Tauris.

Richards, J. E. (1999) "Conceptual landscapes in the Nile valley," in *Archaeologies of Landscape* (eds., Ashmore, W. and Knapp, A. B.), Oxford: Blackwell: 83–100.

— (2005) *Society and Death in Ancient Egypt: Mortuary Landscapes of the Middle Kingdom*. Cambridge: Cambridge University Press.

Ritner, R. K. (1990) "O. Gardiner 363: a spell against night terrors," *Journal of the American Research Center in Egypt* 27: 25–41.

— (1993) *The Mechanics of Ancient Egyptian Magical Practice*. Chicago: Oriental Institute of the University of Chicago.

— (1995) "The religious, social, and legal parameters of traditional Egyptian magic," in *Ancient Magic and Ritual Power* (eds., Meyer, M. and Mirecki, P.), Leiden, New York, and Cologne: E. J. Brill: 43–60.

— (1997) "Execration texts," in *The Context of Scripture. Vol. 1: Canonical Compositions from the Biblical World* (eds., Hallo, W. W. and K. Lawson Younger, J.), Leiden, New York, and Cologne: E. J. Brill: 50–2.

— (2000) "Innovations and adaptations in Ancient Egyptian medicine," *Journal of Near Eastern Studies* 59: 107–17.

— (2006) "'And each staff transformed into a snake': the serpent wand in Ancient Egypt," in *Through a Glass Darkly: Magic, Dreams, and Prophecy in Ancient Egypt* (ed., Szpakowska, K.), Swansea: Classical Press of Wales: 205–25.

Robins, G. (1993) *Women in Ancient Egypt*. Cambridge, MA: Harvard University Press.

Roccati, A. (1970) *Papiro Ieratico n. 54003: Estratti magici e rituali del Primo Medio Regno*. Turin: Edizioni d'Arte Fratelli Pozzo.

— (1997) "Scribes," in *The Egyptians* (ed., Donadoni, S.), Chicago and London: University of Chicago Press: 61–85.

Romano, J. F. (1989) *The Bes Image in Pharaonic Egypt*. New York: Graduate School of Arts and Sciences at NYU.

Ronsmans, C. (1996) "Birth spacing and child survival in rural Senegal," *International Journal of Epidemiology* 25: 989–97.

Rose, J. C. (2006) "Paleopathology of the commoners at Tell Amarna, Egypt, Akhenaten's capital city," *Memorias do Instituto Oswaldo Cruz* 101 (Suppl. II): 73–6.

Rose, J. C., G. J. Armelagos, and L. S. Perry (1993) "Dental anthropology of the Nile valley," in *Biological Anthropology and the Study of Ancient Egypt* (eds., Davies, V. and Walker, R.), London: British Museum Press: 61–74.

Rossel, S. (2006) "A tale of the bones: animal use in the temple and town of Wah-Sut," *Expedition* 48: 41–3.

Roth, A. M. (1992) "The *psš-kf* and the 'opening of the mouth' ceremony: a ritual of birth and rebirth," *Journal of Egyptian Archaeology* 78: 113–47.

— (1993) "Fingers, stars, and the 'opening of the mouth': the nature and function of the *nṯrwj*-blades," *Journal of Egyptian Archaeology* 79: 57–79.

— (2000) "Father Earth, Mother Sky: Ancient Egyptian beliefs about conception and fertility," in *Reading the Body: Representations and Remains in the Archaeological Record* (ed., Rautman, A. E.), Philadelphia: University of Pennsylvania Press: 187–201.

Roth, A. M. and C. H. Roehrig (1989) "The Bersha procession: a new reconstruction," *Journal of the Museum of Fine Arts, Boston* 1: 32–40.

— (2002) "Magical bricks and the bricks of birth," *Journal of Egyptian Archaeology* 88: 121–39.

Samuel, D. (1989) "Their staff of life: initial investigations on Ancient Egyptian bread baking," in *Amarna Reports V* (ed., Kemp, B. J.), London: Egypt Exploration Society: 253–9.

— (2000) "Brewing and baking," in *Ancient Egyptian Materials and Technology* (eds., Nicholson, P. T. and Shaw, I.), Cambridge: Cambridge University Press: 537–76.

Scharff, A. (1924) "Briefe aus Illahun," *Zeitschrift für Ägyptische Sprache und Altertumskunde* 59: 20–51.

Scheub, H. (1990) *The African Storyteller: Stories from African Oral Traditions*. Dubuque, IA: Kendall/Hunt.

Schott, S. (1958) "Eine Kopfstütze des Neuen Reiches," *Zeitschrift für Ägyptische Sprache und Altertumskunde* 83: 141–4.

Schulman, A. R. (1984) "The iconographic theme: 'opening of the mouth' on stelae," *Journal of the American Research Center in Egypt* 21: 169–96.

Schwarzman, H. B. (2006) "Materializing children: challenges for the archaeology of childhood," *Archaeological Papers of the American Anthropological Association* 15: 123–31.

# Bibliography

Scott, E. (1999) *The Archaeology of Infancy and Infant Death*. Oxford: Archaeopress.

Seipel, W. and Schlossmuseum Linz (1989) *Ägypten: Götter, Gräber und die Kunst: 4000 Jahre Jenseitsglaube, Schlossmuseum Linz 9. April bis 28. September, 1989*. Linz: Oberösterreichisches Landesmuseum.

Shaw, I. (ed.) (2000) *The Oxford History of Ancient Egypt*. Oxford: Oxford University Press.

Simpson, W. K. (1966) "The letter to the dead from the tomb of Meru (N 3737) at Nag' ed-Deir," *Journal of Egyptian Archaeology* 52: 39–50.

— (1970) "A late Old Kingdom letter to the dead from Nag' Ed-Deir n 3500," *Journal of Egyptian Archaeology* 56: 58–62.

— (ed.) (2003) *The Literature of Ancient Egypt: An Anthology of Stories, Instructions, Stelae, Autobiographies, and Poetry*. New Haven, CT, and London: Yale University Press.

Smith, S. T. (2003) *Wretched Kush: Ethnic Identities and Boundaries in Egypt's Nubian Empire*. London and New York: Routledge.

Spalinger, A. J. (1985) "A redistributive pattern at Assiut," *Journal of the American Oriental Society* 105: 7–20.

Sterling, S. (1999) "Mortality profiles as indicators of slowed reproductive rates: evidence from Ancient Egypt," *Journal of Anthropological Archaeology* 18: 319–43.

Stern, B., C. Heron, L. Corr, M. Serpico, and J. Bourriau (2003) "Compositional variations in aged and heated pistacia resin found in Late Bronze Age Canaanite amphorae and bowls from Amarna, Egypt," *Archaeometry* 45: 457–69.

Strassmann, B. I. (1996) "Menstrual hut visits by Dogon women: a hormonal test distinguishes deceit from honest signaling," *Behavioral Ecology* 7: 304–15.

— (1999a) "Menstrual synchrony pheromones: cause for doubt," *Human Reproduction* 14: 579–80.

— (1999b) "Polygyny, family structure, and child mortality: a prospective study among the Dogon of Mali," in *Adaptation and Human Behavior: An Anthropological Perspective* (eds., Cronk, L., Chagnon, N. A., and Irons, W.), New York: Aldine de Gruyter: 49–67.

Stuart-Macadam, P. (1992) "Porotic hyperostosis: a new perspective," *American Journal of Physical Anthropology* 87: 39–47.

Sweeney, D. (2001) "Walking alone forever, following you: gender and mourner's laments from Ancient Egypt," *NIN: Journal of Gender Studies in Antiquity* 2: 27–48.

— (2006a) "Illness and healer in combat in Middle Kingdom and early New Kingdom medical texts," in *Feinde und Aufrührer: Konzepte von Gegnerschaft in ägyptischen Texten besonders des Mittleren Reiches* (ed., Felber, H.), Leipzig: Sächsischen Akademie der Wissenschaften zu Leipzig: 142–58.

— (2006b) "Women growing older in Deir el-Medina," in *Living and Writing in Deir el-Medine: Socio-Historical Embodiment of Deir el-Medine Texts* (eds., Dorn, A. and Hofman, T.), Basel: Schwabe Verlag: 135–53.

Szpakowska, K. (2003) *Behind Closed Eyes: Dreams and Nightmares in Ancient Egypt*. Swansea: Classical Press of Wales.

— (ed.) (2006) *Through a Glass Darkly: Magic, Dreams, and Prophecy in Ancient Egypt*. Swansea: Classical Press of Wales.

Tanner, J. M. (1978) *Foetus into Man: Physical Growth from Conception to Maturity*. London: Open Books.

# Bibliography

Taylor, J. H. (2001) *Death and the Afterlife in Ancient Egypt*. London: British Museum Press.

Theraulaz, G., E. Bonabeau, S. Nicolis, R. V. Solé, V. Fourcassié, S. Blanco, R. Fournier, J. L. Joly, P. Fernandez, A. Grimal, P. Dalle, and J. L. Deneubourg (2002) "Spatial patterns in ant colonies," *Proceedings of the National Academy of Sciences USA July 11, 2002* 99: 9645–9.

Toivari-Viitala, J. (2001) *Women at Deir el-Medina: A Study of the Status and Roles of the Female Inhabitants in the Workmen's Community during the Ramesside Period*. Leiden: Nederlands Instituut Voor Het Nabije Oosten.

Tooley, A. (1991) "Child's toy or ritual object?" *Göttinger Miszellen* 123: 101–11.

Troy, L. (1989) "Have a nice day! Some reflections on the calendars of good and bad days," in *The Religion of the Ancient Egyptians – Cognitive Structures and Popular Expressions: Proceedings of Symposia in Uppsala and Bergen, 1987 and 1988* (ed., Englund, G.), Uppsala: S. Academiae Ubsaliensis: 127–47.

Uphill, E. P. (1988) *Egyptian Towns and Cities*. Princes Risborough: Shire Publications.

von Beckerath, J. (1992) "Zur Geschichte von Chonsemhab und dem Geist," *Zeitschrift für Ägyptische Sprache und Altertumskunde* 119: 90–107.

von Pilgrim, C. (1996a) *Elephantine XVIII: Untersuchungen in der Stadt des mittleren Reiches und der zweiten Zwischenzeit*. Mainz: Philipp von Zabern.

— (1996b) "Elephantine im Mittleren Reich: Bemerkungen zur Wohnarchitektur in einer 'gewachsenen' Stadt," in *Haus und Palast im Alten Ägypten* (ed., Bietak, M.), Vienna: Verlag der Österreichischen Akademie der Wissenschaften: 253–64.

Wapler, U., E. Crubézy, and M. Schultz (2004) "Is cribra orbitalia synonymous with anemia? Analysis and interpretation of cranial pathology in Sudan," *American Journal of Physical Anthropology* 123: 333–9.

Ward, W. A. (1986) *Essays on Feminine Titles of the Middle Kingdom and Related Subjects*. Beirut: American University of Beirut.

Weeks, K. R. (1995) "Medicine, surgery, and public health in Ancient Egypt," in *Civilizations of the Ancient Near East*. Vol. 3 (ed., Sasson, J. M.), Peabody, MA: Hendrickson: 1787–98.

Wegner, J. (1998) "Excavations at the town of *Enduring-are-the-Places of Khakaure-Maa-Kheru-in-Abydos*: a preliminary report on the 1994 and 1997 seasons," *Journal of the American Research Center in Egypt* 35: 1–44.

— (2002) "A decorated birth-brick from South Abydos," *Egyptian Archaeology* 21: 3–4.

— (2004) "Social and historical implications of sealings of the king's daughter Reniseneb and other women from the town of Wah-Sut," in *Scarabs of the Second Millennium BC from Egypt, Nubia, Crete and the Levant: Chronological and Historical Implication* (eds., Bietak, M. and Czerny, E.), Vienna: Verlag der Österreichischen Akademie der Wissenschaften: 221–40.

— (forthcoming) "A decorated birth-brick from south Abydos: new evidence on childbirth and birth magic in the Middle Kingdom," in *Archaism and Innovation: Studies in the Culture of Middle Kingdom Egypt* (eds., Wegner, J. and Silverman, D.).

Wendrich, W. (2006) "Entangled, connected or protected? The power of knots and knotting in Ancient Egypt," in *Through a Glass Darkly: Magic, Dreams and Prophecy in Ancient Egypt* (ed., Szpakowska, K.), Swansea: Classical Press of Wales: 243–69.

# Bibliography

Wente, E. F. (1975/6) "A misplaced letter to the dead," *Orientalia Lovaniensia Periodica* 6/7: 595–600.

— (1990) *Letters from Ancient Egypt*. Atlanta: Scholars Press.

Werbrouck, M. (1938) *Les Pleureuses dans l'Égypte ancienne*. Brussels: Édition de la fondation égyptologique.

Westendorf, W. (1999) *Handbuch der altägyptischen Medizin*. Leiden, Boston, and Cologne: E. J. Brill.

Whale, S. (1989) *The Family in the Eighteenth Dynasty of Egypt: A Study of the Representation of the Family in the Private Tombs*. Sydney: Australian Centre for Egyptology.

Wildung, D. and S. Schoske (1984) *Nofret, die Schöne: die Frau im Alten Ägypten: Haus der Kunst München, 15. Dezember 1984–10. Februar 1985: Ägyptisches Museum Berlin, 23. März 1985–2. Juni 1985: Roemer- und Pelizaeus-Museum Hildesheim, 15. Juli 1985–4. November 1985: eine Ausstellungstournee der Ägyptischen Altertümerverwaltung Kairo*. Mainz: Phillip von Zabern.

Wileman, J. (2005) *Hide and Seek: The Archaeology of Childhood*. Stroud: Tempus.

Wilfong, T. (1999) "Menstrual synchrony and the 'place of women' in Ancient Egypt. Oriental Institute Hieratic Ostracon 13512," in *Gold of Praise: Studies in honor of Professor Edward F. Wente*. (eds., Teeter, E. and Larson, J. A.), Chicago: University of Chicago Press: 419–34.

Willems, H. (ed.) (2001) *Social Aspects of Funerary Culture in the Egyptian Old and Middle Kingdoms: Proceedings of the International Symposium held at Leiden University, 6–7 June, 1996*. Leuven and Sterling, VA: Uitgeverij Peeters and Department Oosterse Studies.

World Health Organization (2000) "Maternal mortality in 2000: estimates developed by WHO, UNICEF, UNFPA," www.childinfo.org/areas/maternalmortality/maternal_mortality_in_2000.pdf, accessed February 19, 2006.

Zandee, J. (1977) *Death as an Enemy: According to Ancient Egyptian Conceptions*. New York: Arno Press.

Zink, A. R., W. Grabner, U. Reischl, H. Wolf, and A. G. Nerlich (2003a) "Molecular study on human tuberculosis in three geographically distinct and time delineated populations from ancient Egypt," *Epidemiology and Infection* 130: 239–49.

Zink, A. R., C. Sola, U. Reischl, W. Grabner, N. Rastogi, H. Wolf, and A. G. Nerlich (2003b) "Characterization of mycobacterium tuberculosis complex DNAs from Egyptian mummies by spoligotyping," *Journal of Clinical Microbiology* 41: 359–67.

# Index

# Index